ROCK TO RICHES

SELECTED OTHER BOOKS BY THE AUTHORS

Lee Silber:
Chicken Soup for the Beach Lover's Soul (Contributor, HCI, 2007)
Confessions of Shameless Self-Promoters (Contributor, McGraw-Hill, 2005)
Organizing from the Right Side of the Brain (St. Martin's Griffin, 2004)
Money-Management for the Creative Person (Three Rivers Press, 2003)
Self-Promotion for the Creative Person (Three Rivers Press, 2001)
Career-Management for the Creative Person (Three Rivers Press, 1999)
Time-Management for the Creative Person (Three Rivers Press, 1998)

Andrew Chapman:
Power-Up Your GPA: The Proven Way to Great Grades in College
(Capital, 2009)
The Biggest Mistakes in Self-Publishing and How to Avoid Them
(July Publishing, 2009)
The Power of Mentorship for the 21st Century
(Contributor, Real Life Publishing, 2006)
How to Earn Straight A's in College (July Publishing, 2000)
Iron Maiden & Nicko McBrain's Rhythms of the Beast
(Warner Bros. Music, 1990)

ROCK TO RICHES

BUILD YOUR BUSINESS THE ROCK & ROLL WAY

ANDREW CHAPMAN and LEE SILBER

Capital Career & Personal Development Series

CAPITAL
BOOKS, INC.
Sterling, Virginia

Capital Books, Inc.

P.O. Box 605

Herndon, Virginia 20172-0605

ISBN 13: 978-1-933102-65-8

Library of Congress Cataloging-in-Publication Data
Chapman, Andrew, 1966–
  Rock to riches : build your business the rock & roll way / Andrew Chapman & Lee Silber. –1st ed.
      p. cm.
  ISBN 978-1-933102-65-8 (alk. paper)
  1. Entrepreneurship. 2. Success in business. 3. Management. I. Silber, Lee T. II. Title.
  HD62.5.C445 2008
  658–dc22
                              2008027682

Printed in the United States of America on acid-free paper that meets the American National Standards Institute Z39-48 Standard.

First Edition

10 9 8 7 6 5 4 3 2 1

Cover photo: Jenny Kirchner, Richelle Farley, and Brian Pennington
Cover photo concept: Lee Silber
Cover photo composite: Andrew Chapman

I dedicate this book to my hero, my late father. A better businessman you could not find. I miss you, Dad.

–Lee

This book is dedicated to everyone who's looked at the well-worn path of life and instead dared to clear another trail for others to follow.

–Andrew

CONTENTS

LINER NOTES

The following people deserve a standing ovation for all they do, beginning with my wife, Andrea, who has rocked my world for nearly twenty years. I'd like to also acknowledge my family who've been my backing band from the start. Many of my friends deserve backstage passes for their support—you know who you are. I'm very fortunate to have a large and loyal following from my previous books, many of these fans contributed ideas and insights for this project. For my encore I want to thank everyone at Capital for their belief in this project and efforts to make it great. I hope to see you all as I take this book on tour (seminars and signings) throughout the country. Check out www.creativelee.com for dates and times. —*Lee*

First, greatest appreciation goes to my family: my mom, for encouraging my artistic side and buying me my first record album, despite the obvious weirdness of the band KISS; my dad, for encouraging my entrepreneurial side and never thinking any idea was too crazy to talk about; my sister, Debbie, for always believing in me, even though I melted her *Back in Black* album in 1982; and my extended family—Steve, Jade, Alexandra, and Ashley—who are the best I could ask for. Two other people have been like family to me as well: my East Coast best friend, Erin, who's been my unwavering supporter for fourteen years, and my West Coast best friend, Mona, who's put up with my crazy schemes since the turn of the century. I'm also grateful for the many friends who've been there for me in innumerable ways related to the making of this book: Adriane, Heidi, Paulette, Karla, Paolo, Deborah, Len, Joe, Eve, Jeniffer, Chad, Jason, Jeff, Action Jack (for introducing me and Lee many years ago), and the Kuljurgis family. This book also wouldn't be in your hands if not for the great people at Capital Books— Amy (who brought her superb editorial skill to it), Kathleen (for her show of faith in publishing it), and the marketing savvy of Jean and Jane. Massive appreciation goes to Lee for immediately getting and sharing my vision for this book, for contributing all his genius to it, and for all his mentorship and help over the years. Lastly, I can't conclude without thanking all the rockers and entrepreneurs who've been an inspiration to me, and of course, you the reader for investing your time and money in this book. —*Andrew*

INTRODUCTION

Build Your Business the Rock & Roll Way

"I wish I could have taken a class on becoming a rock star. It might
have prepared me for this . . ."
–KURT COBAIN–

SURPRISE! Many rock stars are brilliant business people. Seriously.
Think about it. If they can rise to the top of one of the most competitive
and challenging fields of all–the music business–there's a lot we can
learn from their success.

This book is filled with exactly what you need to know about business, but unlike other books on the subject, we tapped into the unex-
pected entrepreneurial genius of rock idols past and present (because
it's far more interesting to learn about business from Jimmy Buffett than
from Warren Buffett). That's why *Rock to Riches* is written like a cross
between VH1's *Behind the Music* and NBC's *The Apprentice*. It's like two
books in one. You'll be entertained by the fascinating and fun-to-read
facts and behind-the-scenes stories of everyone from AC/DC to ZZ
Top–and gain the knowledge you need to become a better
businessperson. This may be the only business book that's a real page-
turner and possibly the only one you'll ever read from cover to cover–

and use as a reference guide for years to come. And more than that, you will remember the key points because you remember the stories.

As longtime rock music fans, as well as musicians and entrepreneurs ourselves, we immediately saw the potential to put our passions together to write a book for people like us—entrepreneurs who want and need to know how to be better at selling products and services, leading and managing employees; making a profit and cutting costs—but who don't want to read another boring business book. We also felt like we'd been there and done that, and there wasn't anything new out there that gave us the competitive edge we sought for ourselves. That's why rock star examples were the ticket. Let's face it, they lead interesting lives and it's much more enticing to learn about business by going backstage instead of to the boardroom. Chances are, we've included a story (or two) about your favorite band and a tip or technique (or three) that will surprise you and make you say "wow!" We've included hundreds of relevant and often in-depth stories of stars from the beginning of rock and roll to the present. Plus, since rockers are renegades and risk-takers, their lessons are both unique and unorthodox—and they work.

Instead of doing interviews with a handful of rock stars and presenting extensive accounts of their business acumen, we wanted to present tons of stories—from the surprising to the offbeat—from dozens of rockers. So, while our research has taken us through the experiences of literally hundreds of bands and musicians (and 287 are mentioned in just the first three chapters), we couldn't include everyone. (And when it comes to some dates and details, well, you can imagine that some rock stars have fuzzy memories.) However, the good news is, we have a comprehensive companion website for this book—www.RockTo RichesBook.com. And it picks up right where this book leaves off. So, if we did miss any of your favorite rock stars and you have great stories of their business savvy, we'd love to hear them. Regardless, check out the website for more business tips, rock star stories, trivia, interviews, and more.

As for the book you're holding in your hands, well, like a website (or a CD), you can jump around it as you wish. Whether you read it from front to back, or just dive in somewhere and start reading, you'll find plenty to help you build your business. And for those of you who do like skipping around and don't tend to read entire books, we've repeated a number of our favorite stories when they strongly supported more than one business point. In fact, this book is kind of like an album. We have eleven tracks, and they vary in style, length, and tempo—but all rock. So, if you love rock music and want a crash course in business presented in a quick and easy-to-read format (that's also inspirational and informative), this is the book for you. Who knew rock stars could teach us so much about business?

DISCLAIMER

Okay, now that we've said all that, we already know what some of you are going to ask after you've read this book—because we've thought the same thing. For example . . .

Who do you consider a rock star or rock band?

Most everyone in this book is an obvious rocker, but a few individuals aren't—Cher, Madonna, and Kris Kristofferson come to mind. So, we either explained in their story why they were included or we just quickly moved on, hoping you wouldn't notice. Okay, so that last part isn't entirely true. In actuality, we settled on two criteria for the ones on the borderline: (1) they've recorded at least one true rock song and (2) their story was too good to pass up. And remember, what counted as "rock" in the early 1970s, for example, can be very different from what's considered "rock" today.

How come you included [insert your despised rock star's name here]?

We hope our reasoning is self-evident wherever the rocker is mentioned. The goal was to cover broad territory and convey as many business lessons and examples as possible. You're welcome to take a black pen and cross out the examples of rock stars you simply can't stand.

How come you didn't include [insert your beloved band's name here]?

Yeah, yeah, we know. We don't have enough Zepplin in here. So all you Zepplin fans can relax. We love 'em, too. Same goes for Pink Floyd, who aren't represented in this book nearly as much as they are in the grand scheme of rock history. But we didn't correlate the word count for any given rocker with his or her stature in rock stardom. If there is any correlation, it came from how much the rocker has succeeded from a business perspective and how much evidence we could find of this business savvy.

Did you interview these rock stars?

We interviewed exactly one—and we're not telling who it was. We thought about interviewing many more, but this book would've come out in 2020—if ever, and many of you are ready to build your businesses NOW. Instead, our goal was to cover as many great stories, rockers, and examples as possible.

Why do you have more older rock stars than newer ones?

Mostly, it's the test of time. How can we NOT give more credence to Scorpions, for example, who've been rocking successfully for over forty years, than a band that's been successful in the past few years but may be gone soon? It's also true that the longer rockers have been going at it, the more they've experienced and the more lessons we can learn from them.

I think I may have found something that's inaccurate.

Was it the story about Weezer and the iguana? Yeah, we should've known that wasn't true. Actually, we made every effort to be accurate in our stories and details, but in some cases, we uncovered conflicting information. Also, we've found that many rockers have fuzzy memories when it comes to what happened way back when. In fact, some have fuzzy memories about what happened last year. But that's another story. If you read something that you think or know is wrong, let us know, and we'll double-check it and post any corrections on our website.

Some of these guys have engaged in seriously stupid behavior. Aren't you condoning this by making them examples of great successes?

The short answer is "no." In some cases, the rocker is a mixture of bad (behavior) and good (business example). And in other cases (such as Mick Fleetwood's acknowledged $8 million in cocaine usage), we're hoping the stories can teach us what NOT to do.

SETTING THE STAGE

From Dream to Reality—Building Your Business on a Solid Foundation

"There aren't enough people who care about the future. They are too busy worrying about today and what they can do now."
–BERRY GORDY–

Your chances of making it in business are 50/50. Depending on how you look at it, that's either good or bad news. What if we told you there was a way to increase your odds? Interested? Okay, good.

Imagine you are at the biggest rock venue you can think of—a stadium, arena, or giant nightclub. Picture this place filled with people who want to own and operate the same business you do. Weird, we know. So, let's start working our way to the stage by eliminating the competition. Right away, we can ask everyone who doesn't have the same set of talents and training you have to leave. Next, we'll remove all the people unwilling to start small, grow slow, or pay their dues. Anyone who doesn't want to do their homework and put together a basic business plan can head for the exits. Let's eliminate those who don't have a mentor and dislike networking.

Hey, where did everyone go? If you really want to clear the room, ask those who don't know where to get the money needed to start and run a business—and those who don't manage the money they have now very well—to exit stage left. Also, take away the people who don't have the fortitude to make it through the tough times. Lastly, anyone who doesn't believe in themselves and what they are doing 100 percent can take a hike.

Now look around. There are still a few people there, but your odds of making it are greatly improved because you are one of the smart few willing to build your business on a solid foundation. The decisions you make in the beginning stages of a business venture can greatly improve your chances of success and prevent your business from a premature end. No matter what type of business you want to own and operate, you are either moving closer to or further away from stability, profitability, and growth with each decision you make. This chapter is all about making better choices in how you spend your time, energy, and resources in the beginning phases of your venture.

WHERE DO YOU WANT TO GO? (THE DESTINATION)

One thing many rock stars and entrepreneurs have in common is they are in their "right" minds. You know, they favor the right side of the brain. This is the side that makes people want to take risks, try new things, come off as charismatic, and look at the big picture. Notice we didn't mention anything about attention to detail, bottom-line-oriented, or reality-based.

The reasons right-brainers go into business can be many—they don't like to be told what to do, they are idea people and idealistic, and they love to solve problems. Pressure? No problem? Wear a dozen different hats at once? Cool. Write a business plan? Uh . . . That's okay, because all we want to worry about now is the vision for the business. We'll let the left brain handle the "How the heck do we make this happen?" part.

Rick Parfitt, of the band Status Quo, said, "I had desires to be a rock star since the age of nine. I had all these pictures on my bedroom wall and dreamed that one day that would be me." Why do you need to know what you want your business to be like? The same reason rock stars do. It will make it seem more real to you while you are plotting how to leave your dead-end job for the joys of working for yourself.

They say seeing is believing, and being able to picture the look and feel of your business is incredibly empowering. It gets you up in the morning and keeps you going throughout the day. And you are more likely to take action because there is less fear of the unknown. Your brain also works better when it has a clear understanding what the project or problem is (in this case, your business) and will seek solutions once everything comes into focus. Of course, it's a lot easier to get others to rally around you with help and support when you can share your vision with them. Maybe the most important reason of all to be able to describe your business in (at least) broad strokes is—you will be making better decisions knowing what you want and need.

When Zal Yanovsky and John Sebastian started the group the Lovin' Spoonful they had a vision—to create what they called "good time music." That they signed with the Kama Sutra label, had a hit with "Do You Believe in Magic," and put on a great show with some wild antics proves they stayed true to their vision.

A successful business (and band) begins in your head—then plans are scribbled on cocktail napkins over drinks in a dimly lit bar. You begin the planning process with the premise that anything is possible. If you can't describe your business in enough detail to give yourself butterflies (you are so excited about the possibilities) and get others to say "Yeah, man, that is cool, I can totally see it," then we need to spend just a little time focusing on your vision. So, without worrying at all about what's possible or impossible, describe your business without thinking. Just ramble. Jot down any inspiring key words you come across. Next, grab a stack of magazines or use Google's image search and start finding images that show what you want. Then, start to create the vision— what you want your enterprise to look like, feel like, be like—all without worrying about what your left brain is trying to tell you. Now that we have the broad strokes, we can begin to color in our vision with more detail.

CREATING YOUR VISION PLAN

✦ Recording artist Wyclef Jean has worked with some of the top rock stars in music, including Bono, Sublime, Mick Jagger, and Paul Simon. "I used to work at Burger King to save up enough money to get into the studio," says Jean. "I'd say to my boss, 'One day, you'll see—I'm going to be a big star.' And he'd say, 'Listen, give me nine whoppers, six fries, and hold the dream.'" Only a man with a plan could be that confident about his future success while flipping burgers. So the first question is, how big do you want your business to be?

✦ "My goal was riches in the uppermost strata," boasted Harry Nilsson, who did achieve both fame and fortune. How much money do you want to make?

✦ "As a rock star, I have two instincts: I want to have fun and I want to change the world. I have a chance to do both," Bono of U2 once said. Know what? He's done both. Don Henley has made an impact outside of music, too, but he admits the reason he got into rock and roll was to make money and meet girls. What do you want out of your business? Why is it important to you? How do you plan to help others and make a difference?

✦ "The best thing about our success is that it afforded us the lifestyle—I never have to wear a suit. I never have to wear nylons. I can do my hair pink. I can do whatever I want," said super-successful Gwen Stefani when she was in No Doubt. And her solo career has kept her lifestyle going well. What lifestyle is it you want from your business? (Hours, attire, location, people you interact with, how you are treated, the type of work you do, and so on.) Describe an ideal day when you have your business the way you want it.

✦ When U2 first started out, they tried playing covers by the Rolling Stones, the Eagles, and Moody Blues, but found it wasn't their strength. So they (rightly) realized they had to write their own songs—and it was a lot easier. Ideally your business brings out the best in you—you play to your strengths and do what you love to do. So, what brings out the best in you? What do you do well? What comes easy to you? What talents or skills do you have that are your best bet for success?

✦ One act that made a great mark but didn't sell a ton of albums was Graham Parsons, who was revered by the Rolling Stones, Elvis Costello, and the Eagles. If you didn't have to worry about money, what would you try? Don't worry about making money at this point. Even if your business doesn't make money, it may provide you with other perks like status and respect.

✦ Ricky Nelson was a teen idol from his role in the radio show and later television series *The Adventures of Ozzie and Harriet.* When he wanted to make a record (to impress a girl), his famous father, Ozzie Nelson, helped him out musically and got him into Verve Records. Ricky's debut single sold over one million copies before he was old enough to vote. By the time he turned twenty-one he also hit it big with "Hello, Mary Lou."

Rick Nelson (he switched from "Ricky" for a more mature image) also appeared in movies and toured extensively. He had it all. Or did he? During a 1971 performance in Madison Square Garden, Nelson was sick of his old standards and decided to only play his new material—the unappreciative audience booed him off the stage. On the positive side, this event inspired one of his biggest hit songs and another million-seller: "Garden Party." What do YOU really want out of your business? What makes YOU smile? Feel good? What stokes your passion and sense of purpose and ignites your creativity and resourcefulness?

✦ Shannon Hoon, of the '90s' alternative-rock band Blind Melon, said he'd wasted years trying to be what his parents wanted him to be. Are you having a hard time deciding what you want your business to be like? Maybe you want too much too soon. Shrink the parameters by scope or time. And, like Hoon, don't get caught up trying to start or run your business the way someone else may want.

✦ "Don't compromise yourself. You are all you got," said the immortal Janis Joplin. Not sure what you want? Let's focus for a minute on what you *don't* want. What would you *not* do for any amount of money? What are ten things you currently loathe about work? What would *not* be a good fit for you?

Now that we have a clearer picture of your aspirations, let's turn them into something we can use. Here are five ways to get what's in your head out into the world—or at least into a format you can show your family and friends, if you choose.

Vision Summary—This brief *written* document details how you envision your business and the personal and professional goals you want to achieve (i.e., change the world, travel whenever you want, make the cover of *People*, make a hundred million dollars). Do this for your own clarity and for the benefit of others (customers, investors, friends, family). As mentioned above, you can also incorporate inspiring images into it.

Article—Your aspiration can be written in the form of an article, either for intended publication or just your own motivation. Write it in an exciting way that describes what your business and life will be like when you're successful. For bonus motivation, typeset the article to match that of one in a major magazine (e.g., *Time, Fortune, People, Money*) and paste it into an actual copy of the magazine. Take a photo of yourself and use it for the cover.

Prototype—If your business is (or will be) built around an invention or physical creation, design a mock-up to the best of your abilities. It'll give you a tangible item to show others and to help you hold your vision.

Slide Show—Create a short slide show for your business or product. Like the prototype, this can be used to actually show others and promote yourself, or you may simply use it for yourself as a motivator. Using images you grab online, add some music and motivational text and, *voilá*, you have a mini-movie about your business.

Success Room—Sit with a motivational and supportive team (business colleagues, friends, family) and brainstorm how you'll translate your dreams and business vision into a real-world plan. Surround yourself with everything you create, as well as real-life examples of your successes.

PASSION TEST

Homer Simpson said, "I used to rock and roll all night and party every day. Then it was every other day. Now I'm lucky if I can find half an hour a week in which to get funky." Without passion and purpose you might not have what it takes to make it in business. Would you be willing to work fourteen hours a day, sell everything you own, overcome huge obstacles and problems on a daily basis, and maintain your belief in your business when most people tell you it's impossible? Most (sane) people would read that last sentence and say, "You know what? I think I'll just get a job." The best entrepreneurs are those looking for a calling, not just a way to make money.

How do you know if you qualify? You know you are in the right business when you can't wait to get to work in the morning, and sometimes don't even realize it's time to go home in the evening. It consumes you—in a good way. Passion pushes you beyond what you think is possible. Passion provides the courage, stamina, energy, enthusiasm, ingenuity, drive, and determination that will make you a great businessperson.

Guitarist Keb Mo said, "Before I was doing the blues, I was just trying to be a pop songwriter, and the things I wrote didn't have any meaning for me. In hindsight, I see what was missing from them was heart." When you find that perfect product or service to promote, it's almost like you can't help yourself and want to tell and sell everybody. (Granted, this isn't always a good thing when at a party or church, but . . .) The point is, when you truly believe in what you are doing, the excitement is impossible to hide and it's infectious—people are drawn to it (and you) like moths to light. One band that is a good example of this (and there are many) is Rage Against the Machine. Formed in 1991, their debut came out in 1992 and reached triple-platinum status (three million copies sold). The members of the band were not only passionate about their music, they were equally passionate about their politics.

MODEL YOUR BUSINESS AFTER ONE YOU ADMIRE

Most rock stars admit they've modeled some of their music or performance after their heroes. Elvis, the Beatles, and Bob Dylan served as inspiration for some of the biggest names in rock and roll. The same with the Rolling Stones. "I interpret Keith Richards in the same way Keith Richards interpreted Muddy Waters and Chuck Berry," said Rich Robinson of the Black Crowes. Sam Cooke ("You Send Me") influenced a whole host of great artists. And when Rush started out, they sounded a lot like Led Zeppelin, but then they developed their own distinctive sound.

There are businesses that create this kind of fan worship and copycat behavior, too. It wouldn't hurt to emulate your customer service after Nordstrom's or your branding after Starbucks or your approach to innovation and design after Apple. Success leaves clues, and sometimes creating the vision for your business is easier to formulate and articulate when you use another business as a loose reference. Plus, when you study and see how some of the biggest businesses—or just those in your particular area of interest—got off the ground and ended up where they are now, it gives you ideas, insights, and inspiration. It proves it's possible. The outrageousness of KISS and Alice Cooper blazed a path for Marilyn Manson and Slipknot to later follow to fame.

WHAT WOULD JIMMY BUFFETT DO?

Of all the rock stars featured in this book, Jimmy Buffett gets the Grammy for being the best businessperson of the bunch. His success is so far reaching that the proceeds from his music are less than half of his annual income. Jimmy Buffett turned one hit song (1977's "Margaritaville") into a cottage industry. He used the success of that one song to launch his own widely popular chain of restaurants, one of the first Internet radio stations, a record label, his own brand of tequila and margarita mix (and blenders), and a line of clothing and shoes—all bearing the Margaritaville name.

On top of that, he's written four best-selling books, including the tome *Tales from Margaritaville*, and owns a line of shrimp, a recording studio called Shrimpboat Sound, and a second chain of restaurants named after another song, "Cheeseburger in Paradise." Ironically, this success led to a resurgence in his musical career, and "It's Five O'Clock Somewhere" became his biggest hit to date. So if you're looking for ideas about how to build your business, look no further than Jimmy Buffett.

THE DEVIL'S IN THE DETAILS

Okay, we've already allowed our right brains to run amok (it's the wild side of the brain that is always having fun), and now it's time to look at the left-brain side of being in business. There is a time and a place for critical thinking and number crunching—not to mention logic, linear, and small-mindedness—and this is it. Behind every big band there is at least one left-brainer making sure all the pesky (but important) details are being taken care of. It's the same in business. Someone has to take the pie-in-the-sky approach to business planning and someone also has to turn those ideas into pie charts. When starting out, it's usually the same person—you.

The cornerstone of building a business is research. This includes doing your homework when it comes to your location, the industry, the market—and the money. Jimmy Iovine, founder of Interscope Records (Primus, U2, Elton John, Gwen Stefani, and many others), says, "Most people don't know how to get paid. That's an art." Not only do you need to know how to get paid, you need to know when, by whom, and how much.

One of the most eye-opening books about how the music business really works was written by Jacob Slichter, drummer for the band Semisonic ("Closing Time"). *So You Wanna Be a Rock & Roll Star* gives you a behind-the-scenes look at what it takes to make a song a hit. Sometimes ignorance is bliss (we didn't really want to learn some of what's in that book), but in business you need to know this stuff. The same goes for whatever business you are in. Do your due diligence.

You should always hope for the best in business, but it also helps to plan for the worst. And when it comes to the worst-case scenario, the sooner you know what that could be (and can find ways to avoid it), the better. For example, distribution of a product (and all that goes with it) is a big problem for a lot of businesses. Just getting your product out there is a major hurdle, and getting paid in a timely fashion follows soon after.

The Eagles recently signed an exclusive distribution deal with Wal-Mart for their 2007 release of new material, *Long Road Out of Eden*. What are the chances of a progressive rock band like, say, Spock's Beard or Dream Theater getting that same deal? Never heard of them? Exactly. It's better to know going in what the realities are so you can avoid betting the farm on something that won't go anywhere. Another example of how music and business share common ground involves location. In real estate and retail, location is everything. For bands, the choice of venues can make or break a tour. Too big and you lose money. Too small and you lose money. It's got to be just right. So the best tour managers (and business managers) run the numbers and then get the best deal on their venues. The same goes for figuring out how large your market is and how much they'll spend—on your goods and services. Don't guess how many of something you *think* you can sell or what you *think* you can charge. You need to know to the best of your ability.

REALITY CHECK

When the lights go down and the stars steps on stage, it's such a rush—for both the audience and the band. It's what people pay for and it's what the band plays for. If it weren't so rewarding, nobody would show up—on either side of the monitors. What you experience for two hours when you go to a show is the polar opposite to what the band and crew go through the other twenty-two hours. You see, the reality of being a rock star is very different than what you witness on stage. It's the same with owning a business—only without the groupies. There are incredible highs and lows, long hours, incredible isolation, boredom, tedium, hard work, and sacrifice. But it's offset by the potential for rave reviews about your products and service, respect and admiration from your peers, and the potential to become rich. Knowing what to expect from your business is an important part of the planning process.

WORK IN THE BUSINESS FIRST

Before Warren Zevon ("Werewolves of London") released his first solo record, he wrote songs for the Turtles, was the Everly Brothers' piano player, and toured with Manfred Mann. Nine-time Grammy winner Sheryl Crow first recorded jingles for Toyota and McDonald's in the basement studio of producer Jay Oliver and then was a backup singer for Michael Jackson on his *BAD* world tour in the late '80s. As a session musician, Jimmy Page played with the Kinks and Joe Cocker. Sometimes it's not what you earn but what you learn (about the business you want to go into) that's important. Take advantage of any opportunity where you get to shine, no matter how small it seems at the time.

PICK YOUR PATH (THE PLAN)

Flying by the seat of your pants is a romantic notion of what it's like being an entrepreneur. While it's good to be flexible, it's bad to be directionless. The Small Business Administration (SBA) says the lack of a business plan is the number-one reason fledgling businesses fail. Even if you don't use or look at your business plan, the process of creating it is very powerful—and with so much to know and do when starting out, it helps to put things into perspective and organize everything to keep you from being overwhelmed.

Also, if you want a business loan, you'll need to present a business plan. The process of putting a traditional business plan together takes a lot of time—but it's time well spent, especially if you get the loan you need. And it's worthwhile for another reason. Many businesses begin with an idea, but lack the "how will we make money at this?" part. That's where the planning process works wonders. You are forced to run the numbers to not only prove how you will make a profit, but also how you plan to grow your business in the coming months and years. There are a ton of great books on how to write elaborate business plans. But for the purposes of this book, we will just go over the basics for those who don't need a business loan but like the idea of thinking things through.

The Money

It probably won't surprise you to learn that the Beatles are the best-selling group of all time. But it may surprise you to learn that Kelly Clarkson has been one of the top-selling recording artists after winning on *American Idol* and releasing three records. Who would have guessed an unknown singer from Texas, working a series of odd jobs (Subway, Papa John's, and Starbucks), would have become so successful? Someone did, or she wouldn't be where she is.

You will have to forecast your sales: what they'll be now and in the future. In this section of the plan, you also have to estimate what you will need for start-up costs and projected costs for the coming months and years. Keep in mind a common cause of failure in a business is not understanding the true cost of doing business. Most people underestimate how much money is going out in actual expenses and are surprised when they learn they're losing money instead of making a profit—despite strong sales. It seems obvious, but make sure your fees are high enough to cover your costs, or cut your overhead and expenses accordingly.

The Business

Rocker Sammy Hagar claims he "Can't Drive 55" and demands "Mas Tequila" (fortunately not at the same time). Because he's best known as a solo artist *and* the former lead singer for Van Halen, most people probably don't realize he makes just as much money (or more) from his Cabo Wabo Tequila (one of the top imports in the U.S.) and cantinas (Cabo San Lucas and Lake Tahoe). Make sure you understand what your business is all about— what your business is and isn't, what it does best, what makes it unique and special, and who your core customers are. When you examine these aspects of your business, make sure you cover everything from the competition to the buying habits of your customers.

Your Market and Marketing

Wouldn't it be great if your family could promote and manage your band, land you a record deal, and book your tour? Stewart Copeland has his brothers Miles and Ian to thank for their help in launching his band . . . the Police. (Miles went on to start I.R.S. Records, and Ian started a very successful booking agency.) Not many of us have siblings with connections like the Copelands, so we have to figure out for ourselves who our market is, how big our market is, and the best way to reach it. This section can become an entity in and of itself, developed separately as a detailed marketing plan.

Your Competition

You have to know who your competition is, but you don't necessarily have to fear them or try to drive them out of business. The success of the Lollapalooza tour for alternative-rock bands (founded by Jane's Addiction frontman Perry Farrell) and Lilith Fair for female acts (founded by Sarah McLachlan) proves the old saying, "If you can't beat 'em (or don't want to), join 'em."

Band together and refer business back and forth, or join forces in some way. How do you think the two of us, being "competitors" in similar fields, ended up writing this book? No matter what, you need to know who your competition is and figure out what you do better, different, faster, or cheaper—or offer something they don't at all. Study your competition to learn what they are doing that you aren't. Then use that information to decide what you should do.

Your Team

You're probably aware there is nobody named Steely Dan. The "band" is really just two guys, Walter Becker on bass and guitar, and Donald Fagen on vocals and keyboards. Their strength has always been their songwriting skills, and they're renowned for making the most of studio musicians. It's interesting that Donald Fagen was initially reluctant to sing, forcing the band to hire a lead singer. But they quickly realized Fagen's signature sound was better suited to the songs and the rest is history. It's fine to put together a team to help you build your business, but remember, nobody will be as motivated as you are to get it right.

Your Products and/or Services

The Grateful Dead in their heyday created more than music—to "Dead-heads," the band provided something beyond just albums and shows. It was often considered a life-altering experience (and sometimes mind-altering). And if you go to their website today, they still sell more than music. They offer apparel, books, posters, patches, stickers, bags, mugs, tea, and even socks—of course there is music for sale, too. So, describe in detail what you offer and want to offer in your business. Include prototypes, price lists, and plans to make it real. For bands, the demo tape had been the all-important prototype. Today, the demo is an audio download available on the bands' websites or social-networking sites such as MySpace or Facebook, but the premise is the same—show what you do so others will "buy" in.

Your Brand

When you look close enough, you realize a lot of bands have developed a true brand. In addition to their name and sound, this can be their look, logo, and legacy—what they want to be known for. It's important that you decide as well what you want your brand to be. To paraphrase a popular bumper sticker, "Branding happens." Based on a variety of factors, the public will have an impression of your business, favorable or unfavorable or in between. What they expect or don't expect from your business is a big part of your brand, whether you intend it or not. It's better to take control of your brand and make it what you want—before it just happens.

Your Plan

It's hard to imagine a rock star referring to his or her lengthy business plan before agreeing to a booking or buying a piece of equipment. We think this is also true of many business owners. Once you are up and running, you're simply too busy to stop and take the time to review your business plan. Once you hang your shingle (with loan in hand), the business plan is stuffed in a drawer, never to be looked at again. It's hard to find fault with this because every entrepreneur gets busy with the day-to-day operations. But that's why it's best to create a simplified plan for your business, one that you will look at often and use to make decisions about your company's future. The best mini-business-plans are one page—or no pages at all, but instead a slideshow on your computer or iPod featuring images representing what you want your business to be.

YOUR OWN MONEY

When it comes to capital for your business, there is never enough, and even if you could get your hands on more, you may not be better off. Lack of money is not an excuse—it's a mindset. Conversely, too much money—especially easy money—kills motivation and cuts off the creativity to your brain. It takes away the pressure that pushes you beyond what you think is possible. When it's your own money on the line, all of a sudden you become much more frugal, resourceful, committed, and willing to do whatever it takes to make it.

The Internet has been the great equalizer. You can look like a big company on your website without spending a fortune. Plus, you will be able to get going a lot faster and have more freedom when you are self-financed. Translation: There has never been a better time to begin using your creativity and your credit card rather than waiting for a business loan. Not everyone is willing to empty their bank account or max out their credit cards. But bands and businesses are often willing to risk it all because their goals are that important, and they are that confident it will work out.

The lead singer for multi-platinum Linkin Park, Chester Pennington, was working an office job in Arizona when he got the call in early 1999 to audition for the band in Los Angeles. Although the band had no contract and had been rejected by every major record label at that point, once Pennington was asked to join, he quit his reliable job and moved to L.A. to devote himself to Linkin Park full time. Two years later, sales of their first album were nearing five million copies, and Pennington had become a millionaire and successful rock star.

If you trust in yourself and believe in your talent, take matters into your own hands. If banks want you to prove yourself and the profitability of your business, show them you have a following and a track record. You can accomplish this with a working prototype (like the band demo), which—when done right—can generate advance sales, a customer base, and some publicity.

The fun is finding alternative routes to reach your audience/market without spending a fortune. In many fields of business, becoming more independent is on the upswing. Independent music labels now hold a greater share of the market than ever before. Yet people like Frank Zappa chose the independent route even in the late '60s. Zappa was an aspiring musician selling encyclopedias to make a buck when he was paid $1,500 to score the film *Run Home Slow*. He invested his earnings to set up a recording studio, after which, he and the Mothers of Invention released *Freak Out*. He never had to sell encyclopedias again.

Technology is making it easier than ever to produce quality products in small quantities at a low cost, which is the perfect way for an independent-minded and self-motivated person to become an entrepreneur. With a little innovative thinking, you can find new and creative ways (that don't cost an arm and a leg) to produce and sell your stuff. You may have to shift your thinking away from what you once saw as success (such as being in the big stores or playing the best venues) and come to grips with the new reality—bigger isn't always better. Since going the independent route may be the only way to get into business— it is something we may all have to consider at some point in our career. For some it's a last resort. For others it's a lifestyle.

Choose something you love doing so much that you won't mind

using your money to do it all day long, every day. Being independent doesn't mean you will always have to be on your own. It can lead to a contract with a larger company, or you can build your company to flip and sell quickly. Creed's 1997 debut album, *My Own Prison*, was made for $6,000. The band would save up and record, save some more and record, until the thing was done. The CD sold millions of copies and yielded four #1 Rock Radio singles–and their follow-up CD was even bigger. The Indigo Girls also started out doing it all themselves, then chose to find a label to handle a lot of the day-to-day details.

RAISE THE MONEY FOR YOUR TRIP

Do you know why many businesses frame and post that first dollar they earned? It's because making money is what being in (and staying in) business is all about. You need money to make money, and then you need to make more money to stay afloat and eventually thrive.

Maybe your business will change the world for the better, but without the start-up money to get off the ground and extra cash to keep it running, you won't be able to pay the bills–let alone change the world. Money is the biggest obstacle for most entrepreneurs. Many people want to start their own businesses, but few actually do. The excuse heard most often is a lack of funds.

So how do you overcome that obstacle? First off, you don't need much. Bill Bowerman and Phillip Knight founded Nike with $500 each. One of the largest corporations in the medical field, Quest Diagnostics, was started with a few hundred dollars in a dingy New York City apartment. Furthermore, we believe you *should* start small and build your business from the ground up, using sweat equity instead of the equity from your home.

Granted, some ideas take more money to get off the ground. If you want to start a cafe, for example, it will easily cost tens of thousands of dollars. But if others believe in you and want to invest, we say let them. Or, if you are the independent type, build your business using your resources. Since it takes money to make money, the question is, how much do you really need and where can you get your hands on it?

Good news. It's available to you from other people. You know, O.P.M. (other people's money). You can either borrow money (debt), give up part ownership of your venture (equity), or you can get creative with raising capital. (We won't ask, if you don't tell.)

Finding the funds to open—and grow—your business is a lot easier when your idea is so strong and solid that others fall over themselves with checks in hand. So, prepare a strong and solid business plan. Whether the money to start is yours or from others has no effect on your likelihood for success. Paul Orfalea started Kinkos without a penny of his own money. He convinced a bank to lend him $5,000 to open his first outlet (an eighty-square-foot converted hamburger stand smartly located near a college).

OTHER PEOPLE'S MONEY

Sunshine Smith was raising two kids on her own in Key West, Florida, and was about to lose her home to foreclosure when her good friend Jimmy Buffett made her a business partner, and the two opened the first Margaritaville store on Duval Street in 1985. The first day the store opened, they sold out of almost everything, and the business has grown ever since with other locations in Florida and the Caribbean.

"Why should I use my money when I could get other people to finance my dreams?" you may ask. Trust us, this is not a novel thought. Throughout history, creative people have done just that—they've found others to front them the money to create great work. In 1977, Gene Simmons (of KISS) invested in Van Halen the dough to make their first demo tape. Make sure to ask for enough, though, because nothing is worse than having to ask for more. Things always take more time and money than you think they will, so it may be wisest to get a line of credit, if you can.

Most people underestimate what it takes to open and run a business. They'll forget to budget for things like utilities, credit card charges they have to pay out (plus the cost of the card terminal), salaries, or various deposits on equipment. Your goal is to keep everything under budget and on schedule. Know the value of money (even if it's not your own) and spend it wisely. Don't blow money on things that don't generate more money. (Expensive office furniture is a common example.) Do whatever you can to make it last.

In the dot-com boom at the turn of the century, money from venture capitalists flowed as generously as the liquor it was spent on. Instead of building their businesses, too many entrepreneurs spent the money on wild parties, pool tables and Segways for the office, expensive Super Bowl commercials, and other luxuries. Basically, it went into fun instead of building their businesses. We're not saying you shouldn't celebrate key victories in your business or the launching of it—just make sure to prioritize and scrutinize where the money is going. As rocker David Lee Roth put it, "You have to watch where the money goes, and how it comes back."

With that in mind, here are ways you can get the funds you need to start or expand your business, from A to V (since we couldn't think of anything for "Z"):

Ask. Many people enjoy helping entrepreneurs. They feel like they are a part of the business. (A silent part, hopefully.) So let 'em. You deserve help. It's not charity; it can be just what you need to pay the bills while you work on your big break. You just have to be willing to ask and accept. It's not a sign of weakness. It's actually a sign of strength. Buddy Rich launched his own big band with a loan from Frank Sinatra. (If a friend loans you money, still have a written agreement.)

Tell people what you need and see what happens. When a popular Escondido, California, coffee shop (and an excellent venue for local musical talent) was about to go out of business, many of the musicians came to its rescue and raised the $7,000 the owner needed to pay off his debt and keep the doors open.

Bank loans. Banks seem to loan money to people who need it the least. So how do you become the person who gets the gold? Having an impeccable credit record and/or a sterling reputation is invaluable. Get good credit references and prove your credibility. When you have proven yourself worthy and reliable, it's easier to get people to back you. You will also need a business plan.

Barter. You don't have to raise cash. You can also ask for free services, advice, equipment, space, leads, co-op ads, free displays, publicity, and so on in exchange for skills, products, or services you can provide in return.

Borrow. Bob Seger left Capitol Records to sign with Reprise but was dropped. He was broke and had to borrow $1,000 to remix his master tape to get another record deal. Credit is what makes the (business) world go around.

Cut costs. Early on, you have a lot of money going out and not enough coming in. Keep overhead low. Do whatever you have to do—buy your clothes at a thrift shop, drive a clunker, get a roommate, cut back on some of your memberships or subscriptions, or whatever—to keep your expenses down.

Credit cards. It's becoming more and more common for budding entrepreneurs to use "plastic funding." The percentage of small businesses that used credit cards for financing leapt from 16 percent in 1993 to 47 percent in 1998. And following the success of filmmaker Robert Rodriguez's super-low-budget *El Mariachi*, countless aspiring filmmakers started to use their stacks of credit cards to fund projects. (Rodriguez, however, reportedly funded most of his $7,000 budget by volunteering for medical research studies.) Just remember to pay close attention to the terms of your cards, especially now that the card issuers don't have the same restrictions on fees and interest rates they had before.

Get a day job or sell your skills. Berry Gordy was a boxer who used his winnings to open a jazz record store. Although this was his dream job, it failed. He then went to work for Ford Motor Company during the day and spent his nights making music. He also used his salary to fund trips to New York where he did have some success selling songs (such as "Lonely Teardrops")—but he quickly realized the real money was to be made by *owning* the record label, rather than working for it (or working for Ford). So with the encouragement of his friend Smokey Robinson, Berry borrowed $7,000 from his sister and used $700 of his own money to set up a makeshift recording studio, which he appropriately dubbed Hitsville USA, and formed his own company, called Motown Records.

Deposits. If you can manage to get those first few clients (if you have a service-oriented business), ask for deposits to start the work. In many industries, such as design and printing, this is customary. Depending on the work you offer, you may be able to get up to 50 percent of your money up front. And if you need certain equipment or supplies, this could be enough to get going.

Family money. Countless would-be entrepreneurs have turned to family for funds. Rap-rocker Kid Rock broke through to success, in part, because his dad loaned him $5,000 to record an album. And that was after Rock had run away from home.

Fundraising. Chances are, you get gifts every year for your birthday, Hanukkha, Christmas, or anniversary. Why not ask for some of these to be cash or items you can use for your business?

Gamble. The most amazing story of raising money is Fred Smith, the founder of FedEx. When he was unable to cover the payroll, he took what was left of the company's cash and flew to Las Vegas and won enough on the craps tables to keep the company afloat. What if he had lost?

Garage sale. Sell some of your old things that are just sitting around doing nothing. Clean up the garage and collect some much-needed cash in the process. For bigger money, you can sell your car, home, or jewelry—or use them as collateral for a loan to build your business.

Grants. Performance artist Laurie Anderson is an art-world superstar who blends music and social commentary with intriguing imagery to showcase her diverse and immense talent. Early in her career, she supported herself as a freelance art critic and interviewer, as well as by teaching poetry at Rikers Island prison. But it was after she started to attract grants from the National Endowment for the Arts that she was able to devote all of her attention to her art—and her career began to take off.

One of those grants was an artist-in-residence that led to the creation of one of her most well-known pieces, "Handphone Table (When You Were Here)." But her most commercial music success was her song "O Superman," a single she released in 1981 that went to #2 on the U.K. chart and sold 800,000 copies (which she self-published and sold via mail order before signing with Warner Bros). Following that, her 1984 album, *Mister Heartbreak*, reached #60 on the U.S. Billboard Chart.

Inheritance. People are living longer than ever. So what, you say. Yeah, well, that inheritance you are counting on could be a long time in coming. Ever see those bumper stickers that say, "We're spending our kids inheritance." Scary, isn't it? They may spend it all before you get it. Sixty-two percent of people between the ages of thirty-five and forty-five expect an inheritance. So, what's so wrong with asking for it early? That way they can see you enjoy it. And there may be some tax breaks for them to lower their net worth.

Pay for referrals. When you're just starting out, it's common to have a lack of revenue and customers. Make sure to let everyone around you know that you'll be happy to pay a percentage to those who refer business to you. In the rock music business, almost everything is built on sharing pieces of the pie.

Pool resources. Maybe you can get others to pitch in and share equipment, office space, ads, and whatever you need. In best-selling author Po Bronson's 2002 book, *What Should I Do with My Life?*, he writes about a group of artists (writers, painters, musicians) who joined together to rent, share, and run a large space in San Francisco.

Pre-sell. Get customers to pay you up front by offering a special price or incentives. Most concert tickets are sold well before the date of the event.

Private investors. KISS helped launch (in the U.S.) Cheap Trick, AC/DC, Scorpions, and Judas Priest by funding part of their tours. Can you get someone to underwrite any of your expenses?

Rent out your gear. Whatever you might have in the way of equipment could be converted to money when you're not using it. David Lee Roth rented his P.A. system to Van Halen (when they went by the name Mammoth) before he became their singer. (They eventually realized it would be cheaper to make him the singer and get access to the equipment for free.)

Sell off part of your business to the competition or a complementary business. This could include part of your fixed assets (like furniture) or inventory. It could also include intellectual property—you might have an invention or product idea you can't develop that can be sold for cash. You can sell your receivables; there are companies who will pay you a percentage of what you are owed, and then they keep whatever they collect.

Spec work. Get people to work with you on spec (speculation). If you want to buy a business, for example, perhaps the previous owner could give you terms. Could you make your employer your partner? That's how Candice Carpenter, a single working mom started iVillage.com, a one-stop shop for information and ideas for women. (She didn't even own a computer at the time.) She was working as a consultant at AOL to help figure out how to create content for its customers. After she made her recommendations, they suggested she start her own company and create the sites herself, with AOL backing her. That became iVillage. She also raised money from investors and formed a strategic partnership with NBC, then landed sponsorship from advertisers that tied in with her audience—women. These advertisers provided iVillage with most of its revenue.

Sponsor. Bands that allow their music to be licensed for soundtracks and commercials also have another way to get paid and promote themselves. It's not selling out; it's called survival.

Teach what you know. Bryan Ferry of Roxy Music taught an art class part-time to keep money coming in while he pursued music. Sheryl Crow taught music during her pre-fame years. If you have expertise and the ability to teach, chances are, there is an avenue for you to earn an income on the side while you get your main business going.

Terms of endearment. Ask your suppliers to give you terms whereby you pay at some point in the future (usually within 30-90 days). Get advance orders, then take those orders to manufacturers who agree to accept payment directly from retailers to finance your venture without a loan. Or do drop-shipping—you contract with a supplier or wholesaler, you run ads for sales and collect the money, and they ship directly to the customer.

Venture capital. ("Vulture capital" as it is often called) comes from investors who will finance your start-up in exchange for equity in your company. Venture capitalists are looking for companies with the potential for explosive growth. If you really want venture capital you need to network. Make it a point to publicize your success. You need a concise but thorough business plan with lots of numbers. It may be a lot of work–but it's worth it for many people. There are also what are called "angel" investors who will loan you money from their personal wealth to help you get started. They want a return on their investment, of course, but it isn't quite as costly as venture financing, nor as complicated.

Soulcracker was one of four bands chosen to take part in VH-1's reality-based show *Bands on the Run.* The band's popularity shot through the roof within seventeen hours of performances, running around, and wild rock antics airing over a three-month time period on VH-1.

"We have a lot of luxuries now," Sutton says. "We have a booking agent, we can play shows and get all-age gigs. We're very lucky."

Though, like any other indie band, things didn't always come easy for Soulcracker. They had to hit the pavement, touring constantly, playing over 200 shows a year for five years straight before they got their big break. And their first big break turned out to be nothing more than a false start when the label that signed them closed shop. To make matters worse, the band had racked up a recording bill of $30,000 and were left holding the tab when the label went under–forcing them to get a loan from a venture capitalist who only paid part of the bill. After this defeat, Soulcracker went back to doing what they've always done, releasing their CDs on their own label, Large Marge Records, and touring nonstop until the VH-1 show came about.

GO SLOW STARTING OUT

According to New England Business Services, Inc., most small businesses are profitable within the first two years, contrary to what you read and hear. But that still means you have two years where you have to scrape by. The goal is to get your foot in the door and that sometimes means that you start small.

Start out with small manageable dreams because small things can be achieved–and once you achieve a small dream and realize a small success, it gives you confidence to go to the next step. This goes against the mentality of many of today's entrepreneurs who think too big. It doesn't matter where and how you begin, it's where you are going and how far you get that counts. The problem is, many people aren't willing to pay their dues and don't feel as if they should have to do the hard work that almost always precedes success. It's okay to want it all, it's just not healthy to want it all for free—right now. When things are handed to you, there isn't the appreciation (and feeling of self-worth) that comes from earning it. Here is a list of benefits that come with starting out small and slowly:

Get up and running easier. Singer-songwriter-guitarist David Gray was dropped by two major labels, which left him broke. But instead of sulking, he got busy. He couldn't afford studio time, so in 1998 he quickly recorded two demos in his London apartment (you can hear traffic and his neighbor's vacuum in the background). Using cheap mics, simple drum machines, loops, samples, and a synthesizer, these demos became his fourth album, *White Ladder*, which contained the hit song "Babylon."

Get a sale under your belt. No matter how small, every sale helps in the beginning. Even if you feel you are destined for big things, it's smart to start small scale. The band They Might Be Giants began their career by recording their live performances and offering their songs on a dial-a-song service.

Do it with less debt. You don't want to get into debt before you begin to see some success. It makes more sense to keep your overhead expenses low at first and build as you go. Use the revenue you generate toward things that build your business and augment that with sweat equity. Find free ways to do things you can't really afford, just yet.

Containing costs is an ongoing and very important thing for any business. Differentiate between what is a necessity and what is a nicety. Don't buy a bunch of equipment and incur a ton of upfront costs. Buy as you go and as you need. Borrow before you buy—if you ever really do need to buy—or wait until you get a big customer. What do you really need to begin? What can you afford? Make a list and rank each thing by importance. Add up the price of each. Start eliminating and only go with what you truly need. Beck's first professional recording was done on a portable eight-track recorder with a keyboard, guitar, and drum machine. Less overhead can mean more profit.

Prove yourself. Self-produce so you can prove there is a market out there. Rush self-produced their first album, as have quite a few successful bands before and since. Sometimes it's hard to get people behind your ideas until you show them.

Test and tweak. Starting small allows you to test a new idea before rolling it out in full force. You can find the faults, tweak the plan, and proceed with caution—and thus save a lot of money in the process.

Have it your way. "I'm a small vineyard. And I'm not willing to sacrifice the way I make wine to get into Safeway. There is always room for uniqueness," said Tori Amos.

Build confidence. Bryan Adams wrote songs for BTO and KISS before going solo. And KISS guitarist Vinnie Vincent was a staff musician on the 1970s hit TV show *Happy Days* years before hitting the big stage. There is nothing like building a strong following and experience before making the leap to the national (or international) level. Having people give you positive feedback (even if they are family and friends) is the kind of boost our fragile egos need before we face the not-so-friendly crowds (and critics) of a bigger arena. Experience makes us more confident and lets others know you can do it. It's certainly easier to sell yourself when you've had some success, no matter how small.

Make more. Bigger isn't always better. Don't forget that the bigger label or company doesn't always mean more money. A number of bands, due to poor contracts, never earned enough to sustain themselves even when they had hit records. A huge client may look good on paper, but if they don't pay on time, are difficult to deal with, or eat up your energy and resources, you could be worse off than before.

Less pressure. Remember, things always take twice as long as you expect them to. So relax and enjoy the ride, because when things get going, you will look back fondly at this time as the calm before the storm. Take a load off and stop worrying that you should have made it by now, and stop comparing yourself to others who have the success you seek. Find small things you can do right now, today, that move you forward and start to build momentum. You don't have to downsize your dreams, but you can look for ways to simplify to a smaller scale.

Don't have to quit your day job. Read Chapter Two, "From Garage to Arenas," to learn about the day jobs many successful rock stars used to fund their paths to success. By starting small and slowly, you can leverage your day job into a source of benefits (health insurance, access to equipment, contacts, etc.) and financial stability. Ideally, instead of viewing your day job as a frustration and hindrance to your goals, you'll see it as a path to them.

Get in the game now. And get in the game any way you can. Roy Orbison didn't look the part of a rock star, but he had the voice—and he could write rock songs that sold, although his early recordings with Sun Records weren't hits at the time. ("Ooby Dooby" was a later hit for Creedence Clearwater, however.) Once he was dropped from his label, he went on to write songs for other artists. This got him back in the studio to record his own songs, including "Uptown," "Only the Lonely," and "Pretty Woman."

Grassroots. Build a base of hardcore fans or loyal clients. This grassroots approach begins a groundswell that can help your business get as big as you want it to be. Iron Maiden continued to work hard to build a following through relentless promotion, even while they couldn't get any radio play. But, it was those early hard-won fans who formed the base for the band's eventual stardom. And you don't need a number-one record or a million-dollar business to be a success. As long as you love your life, that's what success is. Don't be seduced into thinking that you have to have it all. It's okay to start small or, if you choose, to stay small.

Dominate your niche. Be a big fish in a small pond. Sometimes the big companies overlook a small niche that isn't worth their while. This can be just the edge and opportunity you need.

More opportunities. It's sometimes easier to get a break when you start small. The Dave Matthews Band was able to sell a half-million copies of their early releases on their own label, Bama Rags, as well as tons of T-shirts and other memorabilia through mail order and at live shows.

Build your band. Jewel built a local buzz playing cafes in San Diego and by being a persistent and personable performer. The locals were rooting for her, which led to a cover story in the paper, which led to a record executive coming to see her play. (He signed her to his label.)

So, it may mean a shift in your thinking and immediate goals. In the early stages of your business, you may be looking to build your mailing list rather than your bank account. This means getting the word out. If you've created a product, you may have to place it in less-prestigious stores to start. But that's a great way to build your brand. If you're a musician, of course you want to perform at the place where the stars play—but playing small venues is better than playing for yourself in your bedroom.

We have seen bands in some really strange places, but it works. One band played on the roof of a boat during spring break with a big banner revealing the band's name. Local media covering the attraction interviewed the band, and a local radio station broadcast their second set. No matter where you are, you're at the center of your world. Begin with local notoriety, which can lead to bigger and better opportunities. Focus on your hometown first and then nearby towns where you know people. The proximity allows you to hit hard, stay in contact on a consistent basis, and build a strong fan base. (They tell their friends who tell their friends, and so on.) It also simplifies your marketing efforts and streamlines your thinking. Your target is more geographic than demographic, which eliminates wasted effort and expense.

Less overhead. Keyboardist Rob Mullins has an impressive resume, including a Grammy nomination. And it can all be traced back to his self-penned, self-produced, and self-marketed *Soulscape* album—when he ran his own record label from his basement before he became an in-demand performer.

You can do it yourself. Jimmy Buffett was his own agent, accountant, manager, and roadie for his first tour, headlining at Steak & Ale restaurants all across the Midwest for $500 a week. By handling all the aspects of his business himself, he was able to afford to keep it going long enough to generate the profits needed to hire others later on.

More likely to succeed. If you want too much too fast, your unrealistic expectations can be setting you up for a fall. And if you anticipate hitting it big right away, you'll fail to appreciate the small series of successes you are racking up along the way. One of the authors of this book recalls working at a radio station in the late 1980s and being urged by a DJ to go see a band. Despite virtually no one being there (the parking lot was empty), that band–R.E.M.–did indeed put on a show worthy of telling people about.

NETWORKING

In the music industry (and business in general), it truly is who you know. So get to know as many key people as possible. Doug Fieger was in high school when he wrote a letter to Jimmy Miller, asking if the prolific producer (Blind Faith, the Rolling Stones) would sign his band, the Sky. Amazingly, Miller came to Detroit and listened to a few songs in Fieger's basement. The band was signed, and Miller produced their record.

Unfortunately, the album didn't generate as much fanfare. But all was not lost. This led Fieger to co-found another band in 1978–the Knack. Their Beatles-like sound (in the disco era) was very well received and applauded by the likes of Tom Petty and Bruce Springsteen. In 1979, their signature song ("My Sharona") was Capitol Records' fastest-selling single *since* the Beatles.

There are many stories of networking and connections getting rock stars to their goals in fascinating ways, but one of our favorites is the story of Brad Delson. Delson, lead guitarist and co-founder of Linkin Park, was splitting his time between classes at UCLA and an internship at Zomba Music in the late 1990s, while his band was struggling to get a record deal. Delson's boss at Zomba was Jeff Blue, and Delson impressed him with his work ethic. Fast-forward to late 1999. Blue had become a vice president at Warner Bros. Linkin Park was trying for a record deal with them. (They'd been turned down three times by Warner, and over forty times by other labels.) Guess what happened? Yep, with Blue there, they got the deal. And two years later, Delson was a millionaire, Grammy-winning, platinum-album rock star. You simply never know how things are going to turn out. And you never know how a contact you've made in the past will come back to benefit you. So make and cultivate those contacts; they are truly worth gold.

LAWYERS, GUNS, AND MONEY

Rockers who became lawyers include Barry "the Fish" Melton (Country Joe and the Fish), Jackie Fuchs (the Runaways), Elliot Cahn (Sha Na Na), and Manny Caiati (ex-bassist for Joan Jett).

NOW GET GOING

As musicians ourselves, we are big fans of the progressive rock from the 1970s (Yes, ELP, Pink Floyd, King Crimson, and others). The music showcased accomplished musicians and their instrumental prowess—many of us sat at home trying to replicate this music on our own, and it was darn near impossible. Then along comes punk. Suddenly, a person (not necessarily a "musician") could learn three chords and be performing within a week. There's something cool about that kind of simplicity. There are so many excuses why people don't go after their dreams of being in business for themselves. Most say, "I'll start as soon as . . . "

But there will *never* be a perfect time, and your ducks will *never* all be in a row. Start small, start now, and just do it. Here are some words of wisdom and stories of inspiration to close this chapter and help you along the way.

+ "Free your mind and your ass will follow," advises George Clinton, a.k.a. Dr. Funkenstein, inspiration to Red Hot Chili Peppers and other funk-rock bands.

+ Neneh Cherry says, "You don't have to be a great musician to make great records. You just have to have a lot of good ideas." Find out what you are good at, what you really like to do, and turn it into a business for yourself.

+ "I may have been the only person in my high school class who didn't go to college—but I am also the one who's sold 8 million records," said Carnie Wilson. You don't need a degree to start a business. Use your creativity and genius to make yourself a millionaire.

✦ Dan Aykroyd had *no* professional musical training when he joined John Belushi to form the Blues Brothers. Nevertheless, he taught himself how to sing and play harmonica, and their first album, *Briefcase Full of Blues*, went on to sell nearly three million copies. (Aykroyd is also a successful entrepreneur with the House of Blues nightclubs and restaurants.)

✦ At a show in San Francisco in 1973, Keith Moon, the Who's drummer, took animal tranquilizers (on top of his usual legendary alcohol consumption) and couldn't finish the set. Scott Halpin, a drummer who happened to be attending, was pulled from the audience and played with the band for the four remaining songs. (One of which had been unreleased.) So what if you are a last-minute replacement? It's your time to shine, so make the best of it.

✦ Lisa Loeb had a #1 hit single in 1994 ("Stay") *before* she signed with a record label. She may be the first artist ever to have done so.

FROM GARAGE TO ARENAS

Getting Your Business Off the Ground

"So many women have said the very same things I'm saying, just in
different ways. I hit a chord and suddenly people heard it."

–LIZ PHAIR–

Sometimes you have to start small. In fact, almost all the time, a new
business has to start small. For each mega-funded, venture-capitalized
technology start-up, there are thousands of individuals struggling to
make a go of their enterprises on a shoestring budget. And for some,
they only have the budget of the little thing at the end of a shoestring.

Fortunately, many businesses—now huge businesses—such as Apple,
Ben & Jerry's Ice Cream, Hewlett-Packard, and Quest Diagnosics, started
with very humble beginnings. Likewise, nearly all huge rock stars and
bands were launched on a wing and a prayer, doing anything and everything they could to spend as little of their meager resources as possible. All entrepreneurs can do the same.

Judging by the way many of the start-ups in the dot-com boom blew
through the millions of dollars that were handed to them, massive funding isn't at all a predictor of success. And it's quite likely many rock

stars would've quickly crashed and burned had they started out with a fat bank account.

Instead, they scraped and clawed their ways to the top, staring adversity down and marching forward despite the odds. And start-up entrepreneurs need to as well.

The lesson to be learned in this chapter is: start small, live lean, and focus on what matters most.

DON'T QUIT YOUR DAY JOB

This advice doesn't fit the fantasy of chucking it all and starting your own business, but for many entrepreneurs and rock stars, the wisest thing they did was to keep their day jobs in the beginning.

Okay, for fun and to make the point, see if you can match the following rock stars with the day jobs they held in their early years as aspiring artists:

John Bonham (Led Zepplin)	Cab driver
Nicko McBrain (Iron Maiden)	Guitar Center employee
Eddie Vedder (Pearl Jam)	Construction worker
Slash (Guns N' Roses)	Machinist
Tom Sholtz (Boston)	Roadie
Rod Stewart	Plumber
Jimmy Buffett	Stripper
Henry Rollins	Bartender
Dave Matthews	Grave digger
Peter Gabriel	*Billboard Music* magazine employee
Belinda Carlisle (The Go-Gos)	Bank teller
Joe Cocker	Gas-station attendant
Vince Neil (Motley Crue)	Travel agent
Pat Benatar	Electrician
Courtney Love (Hole)	Ice cream shop manager
Paul Stanley (KISS)	Bob's Big Boy hostess
Stevie Nicks	Information technology worker

You'll have to go to the end of this chapter to see the answers. But it's clear from this list that the road to the top is not always full of glamour. In fact, as you'll read elsewhere in this book, Paul Stanley kept his day job until KISS's *fourth* album. Def Leppard started out selling their own albums by mail order out of one of their parents' houses. Bryan Ferry of Roxy Music fame worked various full-time manual labor jobs to survive but felt he was going nowhere. Finally, he decided to take a part-time job as an art teacher, which left him enough free days to write songs and take demo tapes to record companies.

For bands that never break past being an opening act, even at the highest level, their members' day jobs are a fact of life when not on the road. Victor Agnello was the drummer for the metal band Lääz Rockit, which opened for many A-list bands in the 1980s. He says, "We'd make enough money while we were on the road to live and have a great time. We would tour the U.S., Europe, or Japan, living like rock stars, and then come home and have to return to our 'regular' jobs. I was a construction worker." Interestingly, Agnello is now an enterpreneur–a medical doctor in private practice, making far more money than he ever did with Lääz Rockit in the '80s.

If you have to work for extra money, it's a good idea to aim for something in the same area or field as your business. There's nothing like gaining valuable inside knowledge and experience working somewhere, anywhere, in the industry you want to start a business in. Work in the business you want to own. Although *Vogue* magazine isn't connected to the music business, working there gave a young Gene Simmons valuable exposure to how marketing and advertising works (not to mention access to a photocopier to reproduce early concert flyers). Regardless of what type of work you're in, if not already running your own business full-time, pay attention to your work and what's around you for clues, short cuts, trends, and connections that can benefit you in your venture.

THE FRUGAL START-UP

Whether you've quit your day job or not, the wise entrepreneur knows that every dollar spent is not a dollar kept. And those kept dollars are often needed to fuel the business in slow times (or just pay those overdue bills).

Countless bands have toured in their early years in old station wagons, vans, trucks, and whatever they could get their hands on cheaply. Often, these vehicles would also serve as their mobile motels. And when not touring, many bands in their beginning days, such as Metallica, used their rehearsal spaces as living spaces.

Think to yourself–are there places in your business where you are double-spending? Sure, you may already be running your business out of a spare bedroom in your home. But are there ways you can make free use of things you already have access to or are paying for? For example, maybe you can use an existing website (a friend's, colleague's, or your personal one) instead of paying for another one? Better yet, consider creating a blog for free at blogger.com or wordspace.com instead of having a website to start–you can do a lot with a blog to get going. How about using your cell phone as your business number? Instead of investing valuable start-up funds in a bank merchant account (which often costs $50 to $75 a month, even if you're making no sales), consider using PayPal (a lesser-priced way of accepting credit card transactions than a bank merchant account).

Using what other people have is also a great way to save funds for other purposes (such as Gene Simmons using the photocopier at his *Vogue* job). We're not suggesting you should pilfer or misappropriate things from your day job. And we're certainly not saying you should use your neighbor's open wireless network for your Internet connection. But there are many ways to make use of what others have, either through bartering, partnering, or paying.

Van Halen, when it was originally known as Mammoth, rented sound equipment from David Lee Roth for $50 a show–until they realized they could have it for free by including him in the band. Semisonic (late-'90s' hit "Closing Time") rented their tour bus from another band. And KISS's first costumes were tailored by co-founder Paul Stanley's mother.

The bottom line (pun intended) is that every dollar you spend on things that don't relate to your dream will slow your progress. Cut back on expenses (sacrifice) so you can make your business go. You can't party like a rock star until you *are* a rock star.

PARTNER AND PROSPER

The typical entrepreneur is a do-it-yourself kind of person. She or he is often multitalented, and as a result, it can be too tempting to do (or try to do) everything instead of finding others to do it. And when it comes to vision, frequently they have a hard time sharing it—not in telling people, but in partnering with others to share the load.

But the experienced entrepreneurs have learned, at some point you can't do it all alone. Ben had Jerry. Hewlett had Packard. Smith had Barney. The point is, it takes two notes to make a chord.

Great rock partnerships date back to Elvis Presley and Colonel Tom Parker. Elvis might have been successful without the Colonel, but he wouldn't have been *Elvis*. The Colonel knew exactly how to promote the man he dubbed "The King." And most likely, John Lennon and Paul McCartney wouldn't have made the history they did if they hadn't teamed up.

Partnerships, if done right, open up avenues that otherwise wouldn't exist, as well as offer complementing strengths to each partner. The Eagles were a decently successful band in the early 1970s with a distinctly country feel and hits such as "Desperado" and "Peaceful Easy Feeling." But the addition of guitarist Joe Walsh in 1976, who'd had a number of hits himself, added an edge to the band that hadn't existed—and their next album, *Hotel California*, shot the band to unprecendented critical and commercial success and prominence. It wasn't that Walsh did it himself, but the change in energy and synergy that came about after he joined the band made a difference.

Many studio musicians have become big by joining with others. Andy Summers had a long and successful career as a sideman before becoming the Police's guitarist. (Sting was a school teacher before starting the Police.) And John Paul Jones was an in-demand studio musician and producer living very comfortably before deciding to join an upstart band called Led Zepplin.

Sometimes collaborations allow you to break into new territory. The multitalented and mercurial Kid Rock had been a huge success in both the rap and rock arenas, but when he teamed up with fellow rocker Sheryl Crow, they were both able to break into the country music charts. Metallica teamed up with producer Bob Rock to create their self-titled album in 1991 (also called *The Black Album*). Rock's more polished style and ear for radio-friendly songs did not endear him to many fans of the band's more raw thrash sound, but it earned Metallica their first Billboard hit songs and their first platinum album. And the resulting play on mainstream radio and MTV opened the band up to a whole new range of fans. A few years later, Metallica broke further into new territory by teaming up with the San Francisco Symphony Orchestra and conductor Michael Kamen for a two-night concert that was recorded to become the *S&M* album. Metallica and Kamen ended up winning a Grammy for their collaboration and inspired many other rock bands to do symphony albums and shows.

Producer-artist and songwriter-singer collaborations can prove to be invaluable to chart-topping success, resulting in long-term lucrative partnerships. Songwriter Bernie Taupin and Elton John credit each other immensely for their mutual accomplishments, and producer Mutt Lange and Def Leppard together created the majority of the band's most-popular albums.

Too often entrepreneurs become proprietary about their efforts, especially at the early stages. We know—both of us were the same way (and have to fight the urge to fall back in that mode). But our recent prized accomplishments have come through collaboration, either together or with others. Keep your mind open to ways you can partner with others for your mutual benefit. Are there product developments you can join forces on? Are there specific entrepreneurs in your circle whom you think could help you and vice versa? What areas of your business are slow in maturing? How could you connect with another company or individual to speed things up? When you have a fledgling business, sometimes teaming up with another one can help you move more quickly from the garage to the arenas.

Collaborations can come in many forms and sometimes will be temporary or even one-timers. The Monkees had Jimi Hendrix open for them—*the Monkees*—so they could promote themselves to each other's fan base (though we doubt many people ended up with Monkees and Hendrix albums in their collections). Likewise, Herman's Hermits helped the Who get exposure in their early days. And a few years later, both beneficiaries, Jimi Hendrix and the Who, ended up sharing the bill for a show. Unable to decide who would go first, since neither wanted to open for the other, the story goes that they tossed a coin and the Who won. Not to be outdone, however, Hendrix lit his guitar on fire. This wasn't new, though. A decade earlier, the same thing happened with Jerry Lee Lewis and Chuck Berry. Lewis lost and had to go out before Berry–but set his piano on fire and reportedly said to Berry as he left the stage, "Follow that!"

The point is–friendly competition can go a long way. Many industries, such as music, don't have exclusive competition. In other words, just because someone has a CD or download by 3 Doors Down doesn't mean they won't buy one by Staind. It's true that some products are basically exclusive in competition–few people have more than one vacuum cleaner in their home, and there's not much need for two toasters in the kitchen. But if you're not in this situation with your business or product, consider your competition friendly and having potential for collaboration. The results can do a lot for getting your business off the ground and to the next level.

GETTING OUT OF THE GARAGE

Here are some miscellaneous additional tips and lessons for getting your business off the ground:

There's no such thing as an overnight success. As someone once said, "Your big break is really a series of small cracks." Another adage comes to mind: "It's not a sprint but a marathon." In getting your business going you need to be prepared for the long haul. The problem is, we see the success of others as seemingly immediate or quick; we don't appreciate all the small steps (and struggles) that preceded it.

The unique Internet radio site Pandora.com has gotten very popular in the past couple years (six million subscribers)–but it actually started in 2000 and ran out of money for two years before getting more funding in

2005. Carlos Santana started his musical career playing in a strip club in Tijuana, Mexico. And early on, the Red Hot Chili Peppers also played at one in Hollywood (the Kit Kat Club), which is where they came up with the idea to perform nude except for socks worn over their "peppers." In fact, Wendy O. Williams of the Plasmatics *was* a stripper, and Dale Bozzio, lead singer of Missing Persons, posed for *Hustler* magazine.

Okay, so we're not saying you should pose nude (or that anyone wants you to), but keep in mind that success is a long road, and you often have to do whatever it takes to keep going. Next time you're feeling dejected that success is taking too long, remember Judas Priest. Early in the band's history, they ran out of money while on tour in Europe and had to brush their teeth with snow.

Find sponsors. There's Liz Phair and Calvin Klein, Lenny Kravitz and Tommy Hilfiger, and Filter and Miller Genuine Draft beer. Almost thirty years ago, Judas Priest had a deal with Harley-Davidson. All the big festivals, like Lilith Fair and Ozzfest, have been sponsored. And Moby has made much of his music "sponsor friendly" by thinking about its potential in commercials and other uses as he writes it. He's one of the leading musicians in licensing. Bands who allow their music to be licensed for soundtracks and commercials also have another way to get paid and promote. Look for ways you can leverage exposure for your business or product through sponsorship. Sure, you may not land Calvin Klein (at least not right away), but you can develop decent income streams that may be the difference between being in business for yourself and finding a "real job."

Tend to the boring stuff and understand money matters. While some bands are known for destroying their hotel rooms, Jimmy Buffett would lock himself in his to organize receipts and invoices. He understood that being a successful businessperson means having a *day-to-day* awareness of how much money you're bringing in and how much you're paying out. As the successful entrepreneur K.C. Truby says, "Most people will check the weather every morning but not bother to check their bank account."

Know that every problem has a solution. Cher once said, "If you really want something, you can figure out a way to make it happen."

And man, did she. A child of divorced parents, living in a foster home, and dropping out of school at sixteen due to (undiagnosed) severe dyslexia, Cher didn't let any of that stop her and teamed up with Sonny Bono to have a hit song ("I've Got You, Babe") when she was only nineteen. She's since gone on to achieve unparalleled success and acclaim in not only music, but also television, film, and theater. If she can do it, so can you. Figure out how to make it happen.

Success comes in many forms, so don't think you only have one path. In the 1960s, Van Morrison was in the band Them, but things weren't going so well. He was, however, writing songs for other bands, and one of those ("Gloria"), which he wrote for an Irish band, reached #71. Then, the same song was recorded by the Shadows of Knight and reached #10 (after it was "cleaned up" for teenage radio). Following these two accomplishments, Morrison went on to a successful solo career featuring the hit "Brown-Eyed Girl."

We entrepreneurs can be a stubborn bunch. And it serves a purpose—it helps us to prove naysayers wrong and to have the will to forge ahead, as Cher did in the story above. However, sometimes it can blind us to a better path, one more true to who we are and what we want to achieve. So, be stubborn, but don't wear blinders.

Immerse yourself in the world you want to live and play in. Rocker Sebastian Bach (singer for '80s' glam band Poison) has always been a huge KISS fan, with a massive memorabilia collection to prove it. And countless musicians cite KISS as the prime motivator for their chosen professions—having been to many shows, owned all their albums, dressed in their makeup and outfits for Halloween, belonged to The KISS Army (fan club), and learned their songs as kids. Of course, other bands have spawned many a budding musician, but the point is—whatever you see yourself doing—throw yourself into that industry or field as best you can. Subscribe to trade magazines, attend conventions and trade shows, join the associations and groups you can afford to, interview key entrepreneurs and executives, and read the "About" pages on related company websites.

Work in the field to test the waters and learn the ropes. One great way to act on the advice in the previous tip is to work for a company in your field of interest. Sylvester "Sly" Stone was a San Francisco deejay and record producer before founding Sly and the Family Stone, with hits such as "Everyday People." Apprenticeships were a common path at one time, but no longer—do the equivalent and learn all you can. Who is more likely to start and run a prosperous restaurant, someone who's worked in one or someone who hasn't?

It's always darkest before dawn. Imagine coming all the way from England to the U.S. to do a tour and hardly anyone shows up at your concerts. Then, to make matters worse, your opening act at a show in San Bernardino, California, is a group of performing seals. If you're like 99.9 percent of the population, you probably would've given up right then and there and gone back to England to become, say, an optician. But the Rolling Stones weren't ready to give up. After that disappointing tour in 1964 (they didn't get any satisfaction), they soon became massively popular. There really is a "tipping point" (as the book of the same title explains), and it can happen at any time.

In late 1956, Elvis was a huge hit after his appearance on *The Ed Sullivan Show*. But at the beginning of that year, he performed for a hundred people as an almost-unknown singer on a dinner cruise boat on the Potomac River in Washington, D.C. Remember, success is always around the corner—you've just got to keep going around the corners until you find it.

Network, meet people, and make contacts. Harry Nilsson worked at a Los Angeles bank during the day and wrote songs for others at night. He wrote "Cuddly Toy" for the Monkees, wrote and recorded the theme song for the TV show *The Courtship Of Eddie's Father*, and his song "Paradise" was recorded by the Ronettes and produced by Phil Spector. Then in 1967, Nilsson recorded *The Pandemonium Shadow Show* for RCA, which found an audience with the Beatles, especially John Lennon and Ringo Starr. Although Nilsson's initial album was not a big seller, he did have later hits with "Everybody's Talkin'" (#6 in 1969) and "Without You" (#1 in 1972).

He's perhaps most known for his song "Coconut" ("put the lime in the coconut"), which made it to #8 in 1972. In the mid-1970s, Nilsson and John Lennon often hung out together in Los Angeles, causing trouble at the Troubadour and making the papers as party animals. And it was during this time that Nilsson's recording contract was up for renewal at RCA Records. Thanks to Lennon's influence, he got a deal reportedly for $1 million per album, even though his albums had not been huge sellers (despite his hit songs). The old saying, "It's not what you know, but who you know," is as true as ever. In fact, it may be more true today than ever. Once upon a time, you could put out a superior product or offer a superior service and expect to have at least decent success. Due to the insane competition nowadays, however, the connections we foster with others coupled with a passion for our work and goals are far more likely to contribute to our success than what it is we offer in terms of a specific product.

Get out there and show what you can do. Janis Joplin blew people away at the 1967 Monterey Pop Festival with her passionate performance—and it pushed her into the limelight. In 1968 with Big Brother and the Holding Company, she recorded "Cheap Thrills," which sold over a million copies. Then, in 1969 and 1970, she went out on her own to acheive the hits "I Got Dem Ol' Kozmic Blues Again, Mama!" and "Pearl."

Rock stars find all sorts of creative ways to offer samples of their product (radio airplay, benefit concerts, free downloads, soundtracks for films)—what can you offer? Maybe it can be a sample of your knowledge through public speaking. Some savvy knowledge-oriented professionals (accountants, consultants, attorneys, etc.) offer "Lunch & Learns" where they invite potential and existing customers to their office for a small group seminar over lunch.

Details, details. Van Halen was famous for including a clause in their contract with venues that there be no brown M&Ms in their dressing room. Seemingly a snobby rock-star thing to do, it was actually a savvy move—to monitor how closely the venues adhered to the contract. Brown M&Ms in the dressing room meant other problems may be hiding. Moving up with your business means starting to pay more attention to details.

It's one thing to start a venture at your kitchen table or on your laptop computer at a cafe, but if it's successful enough, you'll need to formalize a few things. Generally speaking, the one thing you'll most likely need is a business license. You can get off the ground doing double duty with your cell phone, Internet access, and other things for both personal and business usage—but it's hard to get too far without a business license.

Every jurisdiction is different, so check with yours for the requirements; typically, there's a listing in your local phone book or on the front page of your area's government website for "business licenses." If you're using your home phone for your business line, make sure it's not a listed number—phone numbers are easy to search online for an address, and you could find a customer at your front door surprising you in your pajamas (or worse) one day. So, keep an unlisted number or use your cell phone for your business number. Lastly, depending on your type of business, an attorney may be necessary at an early stage. You may need to incorporate or form a limited-liability partnership or some other legal entity. Regardless, consider seeking an initial consultation with an attorney to discuss this.

You can also find good advice on business structuring from your nearest SCORE (Service Corp of Retired Executives) office or its website (www.score.org). And one day, when success has arrived, you'll *definitely* need an attorney. Stevie Wonder's 1976 contract with Motown was reportedly worth $13 million and was 120 pages long. Like Steve Wonder, you'll eventually be better off having an expert read legal documents and decipher them for you. As Tony Iommi of Black Sabbath advises, "Learn to play two chords, and then get yourself a lawyer before learning to play the third."

SUMMING IT UP

Nearly every rock star began with a meager and humble start. How you start and what you start with are not nearly as important as simply starting—and having the right mindset. But achieving your goals will be far more likely if you start small, be modest, and focus on what matters most.

How bad do you want it? Live on less now so you'll have more later. Even if you achieve sudden success and start earning a decent income, be prudent. The glam-metal band Warrant had record sales in the millions of units in the late 1980s—but due to unbridaled optimism and the resulting excessive spending, most of the band members had to declare bankruptcy in the early 1990s when their record label dropped them.

Going from the garage to arenas means taking the "garage approach"—keeping your business stripped down and lean, and using as much of what you have on hand as you can. Do this and you'll dramatically increase your chances of playing at the arena level. As Marty Balin of Jefferson Starship said, "Think big, plan big, but act small."

DAY JOB QUIZ ANSWERS

John Bonham (Led Zepplin)	Construction worker
Nicko McBrain (Iron Maiden)	Machinist
Eddie Vedder (Pearl Jam)	Roadie
Slash (Guns N' Roses)	Guitar Center employee
Tom Sholtz (Boston)	Information technology worker
Jimmy Buffett	*Billboard Magazine* employee
Henry Rollins	Ice cream shop manager
Dave Matthews	Bartender
Peter Gabriel	Travel agent
Belinda Carlisle (Go Gos)	Gas-station attendant
Joe Cocker	Plumber
Vince Neil (Motley Crue)	Electrician
Pat Benatar	Bank teller
Courtney Love (Hole)	Stripper
Paul Stanley (KISS)	Cab driver
Stevie Nicks	Bob's Big Boy hostess
Rod Stewart	Grave digger

THE "IT" FACTOR

Creating the Uniqueness and Focus of Your Business

"The Who myth is difficult to live up to."

–PETE TOWNSHEND (THE WHO)–

The best rock-and-roll brands (and business brands) make people say, "I gotta have that!" They also answer the question, "Why should I buy from you?" But how do the big names do it? The answer is: branding.

A solid brand is memorable, attractive, and delivers. Two of the main components of a solid brand are uniqueness and focus, and they help to make a brand memorable and attractive. Following on this is a brand promise, either explicit or implicit. And this is what the brand must deliver. All of this is, of course, easier to discuss than to do–but an effort must be made to create a solid brand based on these principles or your business risks going under or wallowing in mediocrity.

Fortunately, the rock music industry is full of successful and exemplary brands. By taking a page from their brand book, we can all improve our brands, if not create one that really rocks.

UNIQUENESS

Uniqueness is crucial if you want to be remembered. And what brand (or band) will be successful without being memorable? If you saw a woman walking down the street in a bright green suit with an orange top hat, you'd probably remember her for quite some time. She was unique. And a brand needs to stand out as well. Keep in mind, your brand doesn't have to be garish or absurd to stand out. Standing out is relative.

When Apple started creating computers three decades ago, they didn't have to raise the bar that high to get noticed. In a world of geeky computers that were more programmer-friendly than user-friendly, they just needed to make theirs geared more toward the average person. The first step in that accomplishment was the graphic user interface, which we all take for granted today. "Why should people have to deal with c-prompts and commands?" they thought. "Let's make it so they can really *see* what's going on and choose what they want to do visually." And along with the graphic user interface, the mouse was born. And later, Apple kept ahead of the curve by taking their Macs out of the same ol' boring beige box and releasing the colorful and shapely iMac.

Likewise, in the world of rock, the biggest and most-successful brands dared to be unique. Not run-of-the-mill rock-and-roll unique, but over-the-top unique. In the 1950s' rock standard of doo-wop and be-bop, Elvis threw in raw sexual energy. In the early 1960s' standard of clean-cut rock idols, the Beatles shocked the world with hair that hung *over their ears*. In the late 1960s, acts such as Jimi Hendrix, Led Zepplin, the Who, and Black Sabbath took on a harder and psychadelic edge, moving completely away from the pop tone earlier in the decade.

Then, in the 1970s, uniqueness came in the form of many types of rock—Pink Floyd and Yes with progressive rock, Alice Cooper and Kiss with theatrical rock, the Allman Brothers and the Eagles with country rock, the Sex Pistols and the Ramones with punk rock, and numerous others. As you can see from this very cursory look at the roots of rock's geneology, it's easier to be different in the beginning than once an industry has taken hold. If your industry or business is saturated with many competitors attempting to outdo each other, you may want to think about redefining what you do–create a new category in which your business can stand out.

CREATING AND CULTIVATING AN IMAGE

Rock stars have many ways to establish their uniqueness, but perhaps the most "rockish" way is through image. Rock music is only partially about the music; a big part of it is image. So, establishing a legendary brand in rock music requires a revolutionary image.

One of the first clearly designed images was that of the Beatles. In 1961, Brian Epstein saw the band play and offered to take them on as manager. When they agreed, Epstein knew something had to be done to emphasize how special the band was–and it was his idea to have the band adopt matching mop-top haircuts and dress in suits. (Their previous look was more of the James Dean kind, with leather jackets, ducktail haircuts, and blue jeans.) The mop-top look reportedly helped secure them a record deal, and their meteoric path to fame had begun.

Other artists who developed strong trademark images include Elton John (big glasses and extravagant hats), Talking Heads (David Byrne in his extra-large suit), Jimmy Buffett (his pirate/party persona), and of course KISS with their makeup and costumes.

In the past twenty years, arguably the most revolutionary shift in rock music came with Nirvana and the grunge movement. For the record, Nirvana didn't start it–other bands in the Seattle area, such as Mudhoney, pre-dated Nirvana with that flavor. (A Seattle grunge band called Green River disbanded in 1987 and its members went on to start Mudhoney, Soundgarden, and Mother Love Bone.) But it was Nirvana that captured the sound, angst, and image of the grunge sound and delivered it in a way that grabbed America like no band had in a long time. Chances are, if you're between thirty and fifty, you probably remember first hearing "Smells Like Teen Spirit" and thinking, *Who is that?*

To put Nirvana's image into perspective, let's rewind to 1988 and flip on MTV. What we see is a lot of glam-rock bands, such as Warrant, Firehouse, Poison, Ratt, L.A. Guns, and Skid Row. The look was massive hair, spandex, massive makeup, high-top sneakers, headbands and hats, and colorful scraps of cloth strewn about their outfits making some of them look like human pinatas. And even bands that didn't fit the glam-rock sound in the late '80s, such as Bon Jovi, Guns N' Roses, Aerosmith, and Living Colour, were right in step with the look (though to a lesser degree). The rock world was ripe for change.

And sometimes when change needs to occur, the establishment needs to be blown out of the water. That's exactly what grunge did, with a 180-degree shift in image (and to some extent, music). Suddenly, in 1991, the look was hair that hadn't even been combed (forget teased and sprayed), clothes that look like they'd been slept in or thrown on from the "maybe clean" pile, and lots of scraggly unshaven faces. Kurt Cobain, reluctant icon of the genre, often wore a *cardigan sweater*, a la Mr. Rogers, as a giant "screw you" to the prevailing fashionistas and their carefully chosen wardrobes.

This isn't to say images are always contrived (or that Cobain's was). But they are a reflection of who you are and what your brand is trying to communicate—and thus the audience you're connecting with. Could John Cougar Mellencamp have earned the trust of and resonated with blue-collar, middle America had he looked like one of the guys from Devo? (Hint: no.) Mellencamp's look was true to who he was, and it had to be for his fans; Devo, on the other hand, was completely con-trived, looked weird, and fit in with fans who thought "weird" was cool.

The key is alignment. If your business doesn't seem to be attracting the customers you want (or enough of them), take a look at how you're presenting yourself, whether as a company or an individual. While dress-ing up very nicely and presenting a look of wealth might be the way to attract high-paying clients, perhaps what you truly want are ones who are low-maintenance. A young, new real estate agent near Washington, D.C., wanted lighthearted and fun buyers and sellers. "Why not enjoy what I'm doing?" he said to himself, and he did something unthinkable to most agents. He sent out a refrigerator magnet featuring a photo of his smiling face—wearing a set of ugly, joke teeth. Done in such a way as to obviously be poking fun at overly self-important real estate agents, it was a gamble but it worked. And that agent went on to become one of the most successful new agents of that year in the area.

Quiz: What do Bryan Adams, Phil Collins, Bon Jovi, and Ringo Starr all have in common? They all have a "good guy" image in an industry known for rampant sex, drugs, and trashed hotel rooms. At no risk of becoming a rock-and-roll cliché, these guys have carved out a good niche and earned themselves financial independence in the process.

But it's no surprise that many rock stars prefer the classic bad-boy image (even if they aren't boys, such as Janis Joplin and Lita Ford)–the Who, Guns N' Roses, Limp Bizkit, Godsmack, and Van Halen, just to name a few. For them, they like the lifestyle that comes with it, or they know their audience wants that image, or both. It's true that some rock stars are just living their image, without any thought as to their brand, but there are also some who perpetuate the image of badness when it's not who they are or when they've personally outgrown that lifestyle.

And then there's neither bad nor good, but just strange. Rock has certainly had its share of this as well. Perhaps the earliest was Screamin' Jay Hawkins, best know for his 1956 hit "I Put a Spell on You." Hawkins was famous for his extravagant wardrobe, as well as having a bone through his nose, carrying a stick with a skull on it, and traveling in a zebra-skin-covered station wagon followed by a hearse. Some consider him to be the first shock-rocker, preceding Alice Cooper. Then, following Hawkins, many rock stars carried the concept of strange to new levels, from the Crazy World of Arthur Brown in the 1960s to Ziggy Stardust (David Bowie) in the 1970s to GWAR in the 1980s to Marilyn Manson in the 1990s to Slipknot today. While all of these acts are accomplished in their music, their image is equal to their music in connecting with fans.

Whatever image you create for your business and cultivate, when it's successful, make sure you protect it. Because your image is an intregal part of your brand, if you don't protect it, you're risking your brand. Fleetwood Mac's original lineup as a blues-rock band included Peter Green, Jeremy Spencer, Bob Weston, and Mick Fleetwood. At one point, Green left the band so abruptly they called the police and private detectives to find him and had to cancel a gig at the famed Whisky a Go Go in Los Angeles. Then, guitarist Jeremy Spencer left the band in the middle of a 1971 tour to join a religious street group called Children of God. And finally, at the end of their 1973 tour, Mick Fleetwood fired guitarist/vocalist Bob Weston for having an affair with his wife. During this time, the band took a hiatus and manager Clifford Davis sent out a replacement band as Fleetwood Mac. Promoters and audiences weren't thrilled, and they were wary about getting a phony group in the future. Fortunately, over the next few years, Fleetwood Mac's damaged reputation recovered with the addition of members Lindsey Buckingham, Stevie Nicks, and John and Christine McVie, and they enjoyed the mega-success of 1977's Grammy-winning *Rumours* album.

Rock stars have also had to engage in litigation from time to time to protect what they've earned. Peter Frampton sued surfwear manufacturer Billabong for using his likeness and lyrics on T-shirts and bikini bottoms without his permission. (Billabong had used a slight variation of his 1975 song "Baby, I Love Your Way"–"Baby, I love your waves"). The suit was settled out of court.

Singer-songwriter Tom Waits is well known for his gravelly voice and sued a potato-chip company that had used a soundalike in their ads. The multi-million-dollar judgment in his favor prompted Waits to say, "Now by law, I have what I always felt I had—a distinctive voice." And most recently, drummer Travis Barker of Blink 182 is reportedly considering legal action against Rockstar Energy Drinks for using his likeness without his permission.

To avoid future problems (and ensure future revenues), KISS co-founder Gene Simmons (and to some extent, Paul Stanley) was savvy in protecting the band's valuable image at an early stage. They trademarked their iconic makeup designs and the band's logo. As a result of this move, they are the beneficiary of over 2,500 KISS licensing and merchandising deals (more than even the Beatles). And when guitarist Ace Frehley and drummer Peter Criss left the band a second time in 2004 (the first was in the early 1980s), Simmons and Stanley were able to continue the band's tour with other musicians in Frehley's and Criss's makeup and costumes—because they owned the rights. (While a smart move on one hand, it did result in derision from some longtime fans.) Similarly, Mick Jagger registered his name as a trademark and has licensed it to more than twenty items, including a lip balm. Now, *that's* branding.

CREATING AND CULTIVATING A SOUND

While image is a strong part of a successful brand, the product certainly is as well. It's a major part of the brand promise that your followers expect you to deliver. And due to the subjective nature of music, rock stars have it difficult in this area. They have to continue creating music that's different enough to keep their fans interested, but not so different as to alienate them.

For four decades, AC/DC has stayed true to their sound. While other bands succumbed to disco, glam-rock, grunge, rap-rock, or other trends, AC/DC has continued to crank out their trademark three-chord, adolescent-appeal, blues-based sound. There are no insightful songs with sociopolitical themes, there are no eight-minute epics to display their composition skills, and there are no keyboards or horn sections to express any jazz leanings. Just simple rock songs performed with earnest that you can't help but move to. As guitarist and co-founder Malcolm Young said, "We put out the same album every year with a different cover! But the kids still like it." His brother, guitarist, and co-founder Angus Young, puts it this way: "Some people say we have thirteen albums that all sound the same. That isn't true. We have fourteen albums that all sound the same." This stay-true-to-their-sound approach has placed them near the top of the all-time best-selling charts, and the estimated best-selling album worldwide (*Back in Black* at forty-two million copies).

As we're writing this, U2 is playing on the radio. What a perfect example of delivering a brand promise—both in image and sound. Perhaps the exact opposite of AC/DC, U2 has always sought to be important in their message. Their sound is unique, from the minute you first heard "Sunday, Bloody Sunday" to the minute you first heard "Beautiful Day." And their image is certainly unique—perhaps no other band has thrown itself so far into the socio-political arena, leading its singer to meet with dignitaries of all continents to try to solve some of our world's biggest ills. It's a perfect example of how "image" can be in alignment with reality. Like AC/DC, though not as long, U2 has reigned for decades with no let-up in sight.

Sometimes a rock band develops a signature sound in a specific way. In the 1970s, Chicago was famous for their horn section, Jethro Tull became known for incorporating the flute, and Kansas became known for their use of violins, especially on the track "Dust in the Wind." Yes, Rush, and Triumph (the latter two both from Canada) all had distinctively high-pitched singers, and Rob Halford of Judas Priest started the heavy-metal trend of operatic singing with his wide vocal range, popularized also by Bruce Dickinson of Iron Maiden.

Other very distinctive (and occasionally trend-setting) vocal styles include those of Oasis, Korn, Crash Test Dummies, Nirvana, Offspring, the Beastie Boys, and Led Zepplin. One band with a trademark sound, both vocally and musically, is Talking Heads. Singer and creative force David Byrne said of their approach: "We decided we wouldn't do guitar solos or drum solos, we wouldn't make any grand gestures. We'd try and be very to the point." Despite their eclectic style, they managed commercial success with a number of hits in the late '70s and mid '80s, and due to their eclectic style, they influenced a wide spectrum of artists including Bonnie Raitt, Living Colour, U2, Ice-T, and Radiohead (whose name was taken from the 1986 Talking Heads song "Radio Head").

As we discuss the intention behind a successful brand, it's also important to keep in mind that a brand (or some aspect of it) can happen by accident. But it's the savvy entrepreneur (or rock star) who knows how to capitalize on it. Black Sabbath guitarist Tony Iommi was injured at an early age working in an industrial plant in England. The accident left his right hand lacking parts of some fingers, and being a left-handed guitarist, this meant his disfigured hand was the one fingering the fretboard. Not willing to give up guitaring, Iommi figured out how to tune his guitar differently to allow him to play certain chords with his injured hand. The result was effectively a down-tuning, which resulted in a deeper, darker sound that fit precisely with the developing Black Sabbath image, stylistically underscoring the macabre lyrics that bassist Geezer Butler was penning.

In another accident turned into an advantage, AC/DC (which was code for "gay" in the 1970s) took advantage of misunderstandings about their name to land gay-themed gigs in their early years. (They picked the name not for its gay meaning but because it was easy to spell and remember, a smart move as we'll see in the next section.)

Things happen in business all the time that seem to run counter to our entrepreneurial goals. The wise entrepreneur looks at every apparent setback as potential guidance toward a better brand, service, product, or path. Another rock-related example is the Sony Walkman. It was a "failed" attempt at another product (a pocket tape recorder) until a wise executive at Sony recognized its potential and revolutionized how we listened to music in the early 1980s. The adage is that failure is opportunity in disguise. Keep that in mind, because many of the best advances and innovations in products, services, and systems have come from "turning lemons into lemonade."

WHAT'S IN A NAME?

Perhaps nothing needs to be as unique to any band or business as its name. And the name must be memorable. While having a longer name doesn't necessarily mean people will forget it, nearly every successful band has been wise enough to choose names of only one or two words (and we'd be wise to learn from that).

Spelling helps, too, whether intentionally misspelled (Led Zepplin, Def Leppard, Linkin Park) or simple to spell (Rush, Yes, Kid Rock, 311, U2) . "I like our name because it's easy to spell," said Ric Ocasek of the Cars. Likewise, guitarist-vocalist Paul Stanley is credited with coming up with the KISS name because it was easy to remember and spell. (And to make it more prominent in text, in the era of the typewriter, they spelled it in all caps.) And to quote the 1995 rap-metal collaboration "Judgment Night" by Biohazard and Onyx, "Say whatever the f— you want, just spell my name right." After all, if your name isn't easy to remember and communicate, how will it be easy to spread the word?

Jon Anderson knew the value of this in deciding on the Yes name: "We wanted a name that was very quick and precise. We wanted a strong conviction in what we were doing. We had a strong and straight title for the band."

In fact, more-complicated names will often evolve to shorter ones as people naturally seek to make them easier to remember, such as FedEx (once Federal Express), IBM (once International Business Machines), and Nabisco (once National Biscuit Company). Fans often refer to Led Zepplin as simply Zepplin, Black Sabbath as Sabbath, and Iron Maiden as Maiden. As with IBM, popular, long band names often became acroynms—Electric Light Orchestra (ELO), Bachman-Turner Overdrive (BTO), and Emerson, Lake, and Palmer (ELP). More often, however, bands with long names simply don't last.

Individual rockers also change their personal names to become more rock-star worthy or easier for others to communicate. Rush's Geddy Lee was born Gary Lee Weinrib, Bob Dylan's original name was Robert Zimmerman, Gene Simmons was born Chiam Witz (in Israel), and Marvin Aday used his childhood nickname to become known as Meat Loaf. David Bowie was born David Jones, but went with Bowie (from the popular hunting knife brand) to avoid confusion with Davy Jones of the Monkees. In some cases, there's no way the rocker could've been taken seriously in his genre with his given name—which conveys horror metal better, Rob Zombie or Robert Cummings? Or in the case of Guns N' Roses, it's more bad-ass to be Axl Rose, Izzy Stradlin, Duff McKagan, and Slash instead of, respectively, William Rose, Jeffrey Isbell, Michael McKagan, and Saul Hudson.

Sometimes, it's hard to come up with a name, though. And with the dominance of the Web making a good URL important to your brand effort, you need a name that's truly unique in order to find a dot-com name that's not taken. Look all around you for inspiration. Names often come from the most unlikely sources, but if you don't keep your eyes open, you won't see it even if it's right in front of you. Here are some sample rock band names and their inspirations:

✦ Lynyrd Skynyrd—Based on a high school teacher named Leonard Skinner.

✦ Spandau Ballet–Graffiti on a bathroom wall.

✦ Grateful Dead–Jerry Garcia saw the two words next to each other on a page and they jumped out at him.

✦ Blood, Sweat and Tears–Organist Al Kooper thought of the name after seeing his keyboard covered in blood and sweat after he'd cut his finger during a jam session.

✦ Pink Floyd–Despite rumors that it's a phallic euphemism, the name actually came from two blues musicians: "Pink" Anderson and Floyd Council. Interestingly, Pink Floyd originally went by the name Meggadeth, almost twenty years before the metal band Megadeth.

✦ Fleetwood Mac–In 1967, guitarist Peter Green and drummer Mick Fleetwood decided to start a band in place of the one they were in and wanted their bassist, John McVie, to join them. McVie wanted to remain in their existing band, however, so they successfully enticed him by naming the new band "Fleetwood Mac."

✦ Seven Mary Three–It's been misinterpreted as having a Biblical meaning, but it actually came from the 1970s' hit TV cop show *CHiPs*. Officer Jon Baker's unit number was 7M3, called on the police radio as "7 Mary 3."

✦ Dire Straits–Named for the financial status of the band at the time.

✦ Hootie and the Blowfish–Singer Darius Rucker had two college friends, one nicknamed "Hootie" and the other "the Blowfish." Neither is in the band, and Rucker is not "Hootie" as many people mistakenly believe.

✦ Marilyn Manson–A combination of famous and infamous: Marilyn Monroe and Charles Manson.

Be careful your inspiration isn't unattractive, difficult to remember or say, or already taken:

✦ In the film *That Thing You Do*, the Oneders had to change their name to the Wonders because their manager (played by Tom

Hanks) was finding that people didn't know how to pronounce it.

✦ The Doobie Brothers were originally named Pud.

✦ Audioslave found out their name was already being used by another band in England, so they paid the English band $30,000 to use it. Ironically, they were later panned by critics for having an "assinine" name that was "one of the dumbest" in recent history.

✦ Chances are, Sex Maggots wouldn't have become a multi-platinum band if they hadn't changed their name to Goo Goo Dolls.

✦ And grunge may not have taken the rock music scene by storm in the early '90s if the bands Mookie Blaycock and Pen Cap Chew hadn't renamed themselves Pearl Jam and Nirvana, respectively.

Lastly, as evidence that the right name can make all the difference, we present the Mob. Most likely, you've never heard of them. In 1981, they managed to scrape together enough money to buy studio time to record four demo songs. The resulting tape was then shopped around to numerous labels. None were interested and rejected the Mob outright.

The band took on a new manager, and he suggested they change their name to Queensrÿche (from their demo song "Queens of the Reich"). Furthermore, he suggested putting an *umlaut* over the "y" in the fashion of two other heavy-metal-band names of the time–Blue Öyster Cult and Motörhead. (This trend would be soon seen in many other hard rock and metal band names throughout the 1980s, such as Mötley Crüe.) The demo tape – containing the *exact same* four songs– was then distributed throughout the industry and received much attention (and acclaim from the rock mag *Kerrang!*).

Based on this newfound buzz, Queensrÿche released the demo as an EP on their own record label, and then landed a deal with EMI Records, which re-released the EP on a national level to moderate success. Seven years and three albums later, Queensrÿche released the critically acclaimed *Operation: Mindcrime* to significant sales, and in 1990, they hit the peak of their commercial success with the triple-platinum album *Empire*, which hit #7 on the charts. What's in a name? Sometimes everything.

LOGOS AND ALBUM COVERS

Along with a band's name, a logo is one of the best ways to create an immediate memorable impression. The rise of bands through the 1970s and 1980s using official logos is indicative of the connection logos have with fans and the public. As teens in the late '70s and early '80s, we recall how many of the guys (and girls) had well-rendered band logos drawn on their school notebooks. Think of this as a form of word-of-mouth marketing, since the better drawn logos always generated conversation. And of course, the exposure of these logos being seen (sometimes on bathroom walls as well) was a bonus for bands.

Cool logos also found their way onto denim jackets and jeans in the form of patches (and sometimes in marker drawings). Would any of this have happened if those bands didn't have logos? Not likely. And in fact, the trend in band "logo wear" has returned with logos of Korn and Slipknot joining logos of Metallica and Def Leppard on jackets, jeans, and clothing. So don't underestimate the value of a logo, especially if your business needs to be visually prominent in advertising or the public.

Some of the more famous logos include those of the Beatles, the Who, the Rolling Stones, Grateful Dead, KISS, Yes, AC/DC, Sex Pistols, Scorpions, Iron Maiden, Metallica, and Korn. One of the first bands to use a consistent and official logo, KISS, in their earlier days, refused to play at venues that wouldn't allow them to hang their lighted logo sign behind the drum riser. Reportedly, in one show, a compromise was reached when the logo sign was placed upright on the left side of the stage because the ceiling was too low to hang it.

Most any rock fan born in the 1960s and 1970s would probably agree that album covers have become a dying (or dead) art. However, from a branding perspective, they were huge in the era of vinyl when the packaging was 12-by-12 inches. Some of the most famous artists of the vinyl era, such as Andy Warhol, were commissioned to do cover art for rock albums. And their creations were an important part of the band's brand.

"Finding an Iron Maiden album in record store," writes David Konow in his book, *Bang Your Head: The Rise and Fall of Heavy Metal,* "a crusty ghoul with a knife in his hands, stalking the streets of a dreary old gas-lit

England on the cover, you knew the band didn't sound like Captain and Tennille." And many fans bought albums just on the coolness of the cover. There was a certain expectation—usually met—that you had as a result of the cover art. This is part of the "brand promise."

Is your logo and packaging reinforcing your brand promise or detracting from it? If you're not sure, perhaps it's time to do focus group research—whether it's informal or done through a marketing agency. Or ask your existing and prospective customers. The key is to find out what people *feel* about your packaging, not necessarily what they think, because people react emotionally to packaging and emotional response is usually the strongest factor in buying or not buying something.

Lastly, packaging can be a way to attract attention to generate word of mouth. It's not always right for every situation, but when it is, it can be very effective.

But perhaps you need something controversial. While there has been controversial packaging throughout rock history, perhaps none elicited the reaction the Beatles' eighth album did in the summer of 1966. The original cover for *Yesterday and Tomorrow* featured the group in butchers smocks covered with cuts of meat and parts of baby dolls. This cover would've generated controversy in 1996, so you can imagine (or perhaps you remember) the backlash that occurred in 1966. The net result was the album was pulled from record stores, radio stations banned their songs, and various protests ensued until the cover was replaced with a more public-friendly one. (Originals now fetch over $10,000 in online auctions when they pop up.) But of course, all that discussion and discourse resulted in *a lot* of attention for the Beatles and sales for their records. And it was just one of the many episodes in the Beatles' relatively short tenure in which they astutely capitalized on publicity, even when it was negative.

FOCUS, FOCUS . . . WHAT WERE WE SAYING?

Oh yeah, focus. As mentioned at the start of this chapter, the two pillars of a solid brand are uniqueness and focus. By focus, we mean you should have a thorough understanding of your strengths, capabilities, and business goals. Uniqueness without focus is something cool but undefineable; focus without uniqueness is better than nothing but it's not special. Together, however, you have something people are attracted to and inclined to tell others about.

Entrepreneurs, like creative types, are idea people to the core. And when idea people get going, they can be all over the place. Just ask us; we'll tell you—and tell you about our latest idea at the same time. So, achieving uniqueness is not always the challenge for entrepreneurs that focus is.

We mentioned AC/DC as having a unique sound that they've stuck with for decades. Not only did that give them a trademark sound, but it also was a perfect example of focus. Going from A to Z, another band with a similar blues-based sound is ZZ Top. Although they incorporated synthesizers into most of their 1980s' songs, especially their hits, beneath it all was a clear and focused kind of music that was distinctly theirs—and it's been that way for almost forty years.

"You certainly can do a lot with three chords," said guitarist Billy Gibbons, "and that's all we've needed. It's certainly all we know." Sometimes it's not about knowing more, but being really good at what you know and sticking to it. But again, that's the challenge. Focus. Frequently, when bands break up it's because they've lost focus, and certain members want to go in a stylistically different direction. In the best-case scenario, these members can engage in side projects to express this developing side of their musical interest, such as Phil Collins in Brand X. But most often, they just need to go their own way as did David Lee Roth from Van Halen and Bruce Dickinson from Iron Maiden, to name a couple. (Ironically, both have since returned . . . for now.)

The hard part about focus is resisting temptation and sacrificing. In any business, opportunities and ideas come your way on a regular basis. Some are obviously not a good fit, some are obviously worth moving on, but most are in the middle—*should we do this or not?* The answer isn't clear. What to do?

Part of the solution is in having a statement of focus. Similar to a mission statement (and perhaps the same thing, if it works for you), your focus statement is (a) very thought through, (b) clear, and (c) in writing. This statement should be posted wherever you spend a lot of time in your business. For some of you, that'll be on or near your computer monitor. For some of you, that'll be near the phone. For some of you, that'll be in your car. Whatever the case, it's there to constantly remind you what the focus of your business is. Eventually, this statement will be embued in your subconsciousness and help govern decisions in your business to prevent loss of focus.

To develop this statement, you need a clear understanding of yourself and your audience. Regarding yourself, this should be a thorough and detailed assessment of your strengths, capabilities, and business goals. There's no use focusing your business in an area where you don't have strengths, are not capable, or where it doesn't match your business goals. That's rather obvious, but short of the obvious is a very gray area where entrepreneurs can get trapped–thinking you know yourself better than you do and investing your time, energy, and money in a business pursuit that's just not right for you.

A lot of people are attracted to sales jobs every year for this reason. They want money, they want to be outside, they want autonomy, they want to meet people, whatever–but they forget that sales is about producing, it's a numbers game, and it can involve long hours. Soon, the attraction of the work, whatever it was, wears off and discontent sets in. A thorough self-assessment could've revealed this to begin with, and instead of focusing on sales, the focus could've been properly placed elsewhere.

Here's another example. As your business is developing (either in actuality or in your mind), you see that it can offer products and services. Without a good understanding of yourself, you may be tempted to offer both or offer the wrong thing. We know of an entrepreneur who invests in real estate and has been struggling for some time. Not struggling financially, but rather emotionally because she's not happy with what she's doing. Like many entrepreneurs, she went down a path, experienced enough success to keep going, but feels empty and unfulfilled. She's an introvert, so you'd wonder why she would become a real estate investor–it's a highly personal and networking field–but that's what happened. After taking our suggestion to create her own focus statement, she discovered that she'd be better off transferring her in-depth knowledge into creating a product she could sell online, such as an audio program, home-study kit, or book. By focusing on this instead of the investing she's been doing, she can create a business for herself that's more in alignment with who she truly is.

The other side of creating your focus statement, as mentioned before, is having a clear understanding of your target audience—your potential or existing fans. The more you understand them and their complete demographics, the better you can create a statement of focus for how you will reach, serve, and satisfy that group of people. And as a result, if you review this focus statement regularly, you won't be tempted to branch out into areas that won't benefit your target market.

DELIVER ON BRAND PROMISE

Once you've developed a clear uniqueness and focus for your business, you then create a brand statement. This statement carries with it a brand promise, either explicit or implicit. Put this statement in writing and keep it with you as a reminder to yourself of your brand promise. Make no doubt about it, your customers and potential customers will have an expectation based on what they know of your business—either good, bad, or in between. So, the key is to take control of this expectation as best you can and create the expectation that fits with what you can deliver. This is your brand promise.

We mentioned earlier in this chapter U2 delivering on their brand promise. This certainly wouldn't be the case if they suddenly started playing head-banging music with a Satanic backdrop behind the stage. Conversely, Ozzy Osbourne wouldn't have done so well with fans if he'd interrupted his show with a monologue about politics and poverty in third-world countries. Other rockers who've made strong political statements in their music and performances include Rage Against the Machine, Ted Nugent, Bob Geldof, and Coldplay. Meanwhile, other rockers who've stayed very apolitical have been booed in concert when they started to share their opinions.

While the previous examples reflect brand promise in the way of image, it's important to remember your brand's promise in the way of product or service. What are you providing your customers exactly? Once you've perfected (or nearly perfected) what you offer, keep it fresh by changing it only slowly. Think evolution. Most people prefer stability by nature and resist change. So, once you're delivering your brand promise through your product or service, and your customers are mostly or completely satisfied, don't change your recipe too much too quickly. Just evolve it slowly over time to stay in touch with your clientele.

Because brand shifts usually take time, this also means shifts for the better won't happen overnight. Sheryl Crow came from a musical family, has a degree in music, and taught music. But because she was a back-up singer for so many years (including with Michael Jackson in the late '80s), it took her a long time to rise to stardom as a solo act. "I had the terrible stigma of being a backup singer," she once said. "It took years for anyone to take me seriously." But those years finally paid off when her 1994 release of *Tuesday Night Music Club* earned her three Grammys and sales of over seven million copies in the 1990s. Her follow-up self-titled album in 1996 achieved similar acclaim and popularity.

Conversely and unfortunately, negative brand shifts can happen almost immediately. One of the biggest brand-promise disasters in rock history came from Billy Squire. Squire hit superstardom with *Don't Say No* and *Emotions in Motion* at the beginning of the 1980s, with both albums topping the charts on sales of several million copies and spawning nine hit singles. His next album, 1984's *Signs of Life*, was released with an immediate hit–"Rock Me Tonite" (#1 on the Album Rock Tracks chart)–and Squire seemed ready to ride a wave of success for years to come. Unfortunately, the video for "Rock Me Tonite" came out before that could happen. The video–featuring Squire dancing around in a decidedly feminine way, writhing around in a bed of satin sheets, and wearing a pink tank-top and playing a pink guitar–freaked out his following who had viewed him as a true rock guitar hero. There was some debate that it was a spoof of Jennifer Beals' dance in *Flashdance*, but it didn't matter. Squire lost his fan base, and his two later albums in the '80s barely sold over a half million copies collectively while Squire went from headlining arenas to playing small theaters (though he did have some hits into the early '90s.).

The lesson here is, choose your brand promise very carefully—once you've committed to that path, it can be difficult to turn around and very easy to take a wrong step. And as you keep up with the times, let your brand evolve slowly. Bands like the Rolling Stones, Rush, and Aerosmith have covered broad territory—but have done it over decades. It's unlikely the Aerosmith ballads of the last decade would've gone over well with their fan base in 1975. That would've been a hard left turn.

CLOSING TIME

Solid brands deliver on a brand promise built from their uniqueness and focus. As you research your competition, target audience, and yourself, decide on what your business uniqueness and focus will be and convey those in a written brand statement.

This brand statement—and the promise it makes—will guide you in your business decisions, help you stay in touch with your target audience, and keep your brand clearly defined for your customers and potential customers.

As you need to make shifts in your brand, do so slowly and carefully. Better to take a small step you can back away from, if necessary, than a giant leap that may be into a bottomless pit. And when you do make changes for the positive, recognize that it's like turning an ocean liner—it takes time.

Ultimately, if you stay true to your brand, your fan base will stay true to you—and like the rockers portrayed in this book, your business will have the "it" factor with people saying, "I've gotta have that."

FRONTING YOUR BAND

Leading and Building Your Team

"I'm a dumb-ass guitar player, you know? But I was smart enough to listen to people with ideas."
–DICKIE BETTS, ALLMAN BROTHERS BAND–

Checklist

What it takes to be a good leader:

___ Setting a good example
___ Leading from the front
___ Being responsible
___ Seeing the big picture (a visionary)
___ Being rational and logical when called for (passionate about the business, but not overly emotional; cool headed)
___ Being business-minded, fiscally responsible, profit-oriented
___ Understanding people and choosing them wisely
___ Embracing the limelight and publicity
___ Understanding all aspects of business (work way up)
___ Being talented

___ Being sober
___ Being team-oriented

Nobody succeeds in business alone. Or to quote the Beatles: "I get by with a little help from my friends." You may have a team directly employed by you, you may have a team of outsourced independent contractors, or you may have a team of supporters who don't work for you in any way. But you can't succeed in business without a team.

Choosing your team carefully is one of the most important things you'll do in building your business. And that includes deciding your style of leadership, whether up front and obvious or more backstage and quiet. Neither is entirely right or wrong; it depends more on your personality and strengths, as well as the team you're leading. Management guru Ken Blanchard calls it "situational leadership."

The power structure is also a critical aspect of your team. Will control be entirely in your hands? Will it be largely in someone else's hands? Will it be a partnership? Will it be democratically shared by all team members? This balance, one way or another, will tend toward a smooth-running business or one that's rife with problems, if not smartly selected.

Now, let's look at each of the items in the above checklist individually.

SETTING A GOOD EXAMPLE

While there are many rockers who set good examples, the first person who came to our minds is Jon Bon Jovi. Here's a guy who came from lower-middle-class New Jersey and paid his dues repeatedly, playing in smoky bars long before anyone heard "You Give Love a Bad Name." Like many celebrities who achieved fame at a young age and faced the shocking world that comes with it, Bon Jovi could've easily succumbed to drugs, alcohol, infidelity, stints in rehab and jail, or all of the above. He could've gone through numerous band members—and wives. And he could've blown his fortune and generally managed his life in a reckless way. But he didn't. (In the interest of full disclosure, the band's breakthrough album, *Slippery When Wet*, was reportedly intended to originally feature a pair of large wet breasts on the cover—so Bon Jovi isn't quite destined for sainthood.)

He's run his namesake band wisely, he's run his life wisely, and he has a lot to show for it. If you're like most people, you probably think of the 1980s' Bon Jovi at first, complete with big hair, tight acid-washed jeans, and high-top tennis shoes. So, you might be surprised to learn that Bon Jovi was the third-highest-earning act of 2006—raking in over $77 million for the year, according to *Fortune* magazine.

True to his Jersey roots, like Bruce Springsteen, he has a strong work ethic. But more importantly, he has a strong people ethic. Like Tom Hanks in the acting world, you don't see Bon Jovi on the cover of tabloids; he doesn't engage in things that the tabloids could even stretch into a story. He also treats his band well, from all accounts, and their stability is indicative of this—except for the 1994 departure of the band's bassist, Alec John Such, the band has remained intact in its twenty-five years in existence. And Bon Jovi was reportedly respectful of Such's choice, saying that he couldn't expect others to hold up to his own workaholic style.

Another indicator of Bon Jovi's good leadership is the ability of the band to go on hiatus while members pursue other projects. Both Bon Jovi and guitarist Richie Sambora released solo albums in the early 1990s; Bon Jovi has appeared in numerous films and TV shows; and in the late 1990s, drummer Tico Torres created a number of paintings, and keyboardist David Bryan composed musicals. The freedom for band members to go their own way and then come back together, repeatedly, *and* maintain an enormously successful career is a testimony to Bon Jovi's good example as a leader, particularly his ability to choose the right teammates.

LEADING FROM THE FRONT

Some rock front people are also their band's leaders and some aren't. Often when the band is named for the front person (usually the singer), it's nearly assured that person is also running the show—the Dave Matthews Band, Joan Jett and the Blackhearts, Bruce Springsteen and the E Street Band, for example. Other prominent rockers fronting and leading bands—but that aren't named for them—include Joe Elliott (Def Leppard) and Ian Anderson (Jethro Tull). Conversely, some strong front people are (or were) not running the show, as you might expect, such as Freddie Mercury of Queen (it was really guitarist Brian May and drummer Roger Taylor, who still perform occasionally under the Queen name) and Michael Hutchance of INXS (it was and still is the three Farriss brothers).

Leading from the front requires an appealing personality, but one that's also commanding. It's not enough to be a fan favorite or be the poster boy or girl. It takes the ability to lead your band, either coordinating and managing all the personalities on hand, or simply directing everyone as you see fit. As U2 singer-leader Bono puts it, jokingly or not, "Everybody argues, and then we do what I say."

Will you lead from the front or back? To lead from the front, you also need to be charismatic, attractive, energetic, magnetic, and talented—but those traits don't conversely indicate a good leader in and of themselves (Vince Neil of Motley Crue, Jim Morrison of the Doors, or Steve Perry of Journey, to name a few). If you see yourself more backstage, leading quietly, then your business will be more successful if someone who has these qualities can be up front (perhaps your general manager). There's a favorite cafe of ours in downtown San Diego that has a quiet, unassuming owner who's rarely seen—but the general manager is an outstanding "face" for the business, giving the place the kind of vibe where you feel welcome, good being there, and want to come back.

The moral of the story is: choose your front person carefully and don't assume it needs to be you by default.

BEING RESPONSIBLE

AC/DC might have a bad-boy image, but they know how to keep their promises. Known as one of the most-responsible acts in rock, it takes a lot for them to cancel a show. And when they have to, they do everything they can to fulfill that show as soon as possible, even if it means an inconvenient and costly change in travel. Their manager remarked one time how no one really knows what the band members go through to put on a show—he's seen them down with the flu and pull it together to rock out on stage for two hours, and then go back to bed for days until their next show. For them, it's a job, and it's their duty to go to work under all but the most extreme circumstances. Even when singer Bon Scott unexpectedly died in 1980, they started recording their *Back in Black* album almost immediately afterward, and released it only a few months later.

SEEING THE BIG PICTURE

A strong leadership trait is having vision. Have you ever met an entrepreneur who couldn't tend to a detail to save her life, but is full of ideas and has a true *vision* for how her business should be? Ideally, this type of entrepreneur needs a detail-oriented person on her team to sweep up the chaos in her wake, but the visionary is vital for long-term success. Detail people usually don't have that view of the horizon and beyond. Why should they? There are things right in front of them to be sorted out.

Gene Simmons of KISS is one of the most-proven visionaries in rock music. (And to be fair, some credit needs to go to co-founder Paul Stanley for seeing Simmons' vision and running with it.) From almost the earliest point in KISS' foundation in 1973, Simmons envisioned the band being akin to super heroes, with a larger-than-life image and stage shows. Although some aspects of KISS happened without intent (Simmons' trademark fire-breathing only came about because their manager suggested it, and he was the only one to volunteer to try it), much of what the band became was the direct result of his vision and tenacity. (Many thought it all a gimmick doomed to be short-lived.)

Simmons did have ideas that were just too extravagant to be realized, such as the band's failed KISS-themed mobile amusement park that would've traveled with their 1979 *Dynasty* tour. But no one could accuse him of thinking or dreaming small, and his over-the-top approach has served the band, especially him, well.

If you're the detail-oriented type of entrepreneur, you will do very well in the logistics of setting up the business. But you may be a bit short-sighted in the long term. Look for someone to complement you in this area.

BEING RATIONAL AND LOGICAL WHEN NECESSARY

Entrepreneurs have crazy ideas. Without them, we wouldn't have most of the conveniences and necessities we take for granted today. And sometimes entrepreneurs can run their businesses in unorthodox ways, defying any sense of rhyme or reason from an outsider's perspective. But somewhere, somehow, there must be a method to the madness—or at the very least, they need to be rational and logical when the need strikes. Although "crazy" enough to dream up Ziggy Stardust and go out on stage as a space-traveler from another planet, David Bowie was actually logical enough to pull from his theater background to find a way to make his stage show exceptional—and that he did. Bowie has also been very rational in his choice of those he works with and how he's handled his business over the decades.

BUSINESS-MINDED, FISCALLY RESPONSIBLE, PROFIT-ORIENTED

Sting is one of those "you love him or you hate him" rock stars. But no one can deny that he's massively wealthy—he makes roughly $2,000 a day *just from the radio play of one song* ("Every Breath You Take"). But Sting wasn't always smart with his money. In the 1990s, news broke that his accountant had run off with several million dollars. Admittedly, given Sting's wealth at the time, this was probably easy to overlook— but as a result of that experience, he's become "one of the music industry's most financially astute figures," according the British magazine, *Hello!* The results speak for themselves: In the decade since that debacle, Sting has leap-frogged over many longer-running U.K. music acts, including Elton John and Mick Jagger, to have the second-highest net worth of any rock star in that country—nearly $400 million—behind only Paul McCartney.

UNDERSTANDING PEOPLE AND CHOOSING THEM WISELY

When Ozzy Osbourne was in Black Sabbath in the 1970s, he would frequently become frustrated with guitarist Tony Iommi. They didn't quite connect, and that made it difficult for Osbourne to get his musical ideas into their songs. Flash forward to the early 1980s. Osbourne had been kicked out of Sabbath and decided to start his own band. Now, having complete control, he could choose anyone he wanted—and one of those people was legendary guitarist Randy Rhoads, who had come from Quiet Riot prior to their own success.

Ozzy saw the young, up-and-coming guitarist as someone he could work with, who didn't carry the baggage he had with Iommi. And Rhoads was a phenomenal guitarist on top of that. Together, they discovered an ability to communicate musically. Ironically, as the story goes, Ozzy was so stoned when he hired Rhoads that he didn't even know he'd done it. However, his decision to keep Rhoads (once he found out) proved to be a smart one, and Ozzy experienced tremendous success through the decade. Ozzy viewed Rhoads as not just a member of the band, but a true equal and friend.

On the flip side, this story would've never occurred if someone hadn't understood *Ozzy* and chosen him. Sharon Arden (daughter of Black Sabbath's manager at the time) was determined to help Ozzy succeed on his own and practically forced him to accept her as his manager. Together, they embarked on finding the members of Ozzy's band to be. And to this day, Ozzy credits her (now Sharon Osbourne) for both saving his career and life, which at the time was at a dangerous low.

EMBRACING THE LIMELIGHT AND PUBLICITY

David Lee Roth was the face (or front) of Van Halen from their beginnings in 1974 until 1985, despite the band being founded by and named after brothers Alex and Eddie. Because Eddie was rather shy and more of the quiet artist type, Roth naturally took to the role of frontman. Always a talker, he would eat up interviews and earn constant coverage in the media with his comments, living up to his nickname "Diamond Dave."

Roth's penchant for the limelight can be traced back to his youth, when he would hang out at his uncle's famous Cafe Wha? in New York City in the early 1960s, when both Bob Dylan and Jimi Hendrix worked there. Although his publicity was not always favorable—he was called "the most obnoxious singer in human history" by the editors of *Rolling Stone* in 1983—the publicity nevertheless kept Van Halen in the public's mind and at the top of the Billboard charts. And when Roth went solo, he maintained his popularity for most of the rest of the decade.

UNDERSTANDING ALL ASPECTS OF THE BUSINESS

Before hooking up with Cher in the 1960s, Sonny Bono toiled on the fringes of the record industry, learning about the business as he worked his way up. He started off as a gofer, then worked in promotions, and eventually became an A&R (artists & repertoir) representative for Specialty Records. It wasn't until he was thirty that he finally became a star with Cher, singing on their 1965 hit "I Got You Babe." From that point on, he recorded a number of hit songs with Cher, became a TV star on their show, and worked in other aspects of the business before switching careers to go into politics.

BEING TALENTED

Trent Reznor is the perfect example of the talented frontman. Having played piano from age five, Reznor picked up other instruments through school (including sax and tuba), and even became an award-winning drama student in high school. In addition, he was fascinated with computers and the promise they held in the early 1980s. (This would later serve him well.) This interest led him to spend a year in college as a computer engineering student before deciding his true love was music.

To break into the business, Reznor moved from his small Pennsylvania hometown and took a job as an assistant engineer and janitor at a recording studio in Cleveland, Ohio. While there, he persuaded the owner to let him record his own music when the studio wasn't being used. Because Reznor was such a dedicated and attentive employee, the owner was happy to help. It's from this modest start that Reznor eventually developed an impressive career as Nine Inch Nails. Being a multi-instrumentalist, Reznor was inspired by Prince to sing and play all instruments on the demos he recorded at the studio. Many of these ended up on his first album (though reworked). And for that first album, 1989's *Pretty Hate Machine*, Reznor produced everything himself, sequencing the tracks on his Mac Plus computer. That album earned gold status (500,000+ units sold) and his one-man show as Nine Inch Nails has continued for the past twenty years, using studio musicians only for limited parts and employing musicians to tour.

BEING SOBER

While we give a lot of credit to the rockers in this book for their business savvy and inspiration, we aren't deluded into thinking many of them can serve as an example for this point. The phrase "sex, drugs, and rock and roll" didn't become popular without good reason. However, it would also be inaccurate to say all rock stars are drugged-out addicts. The truth is, it's a spectrum, ranging from sober to drugged-out addicts. And many rock stars have been thoroughly sober, such as Gene Simmons and Ted Nugent.

The key in music has been that *someone* with control of the band, be it a member, producer, or manager, has to be sober enough to steer things in the right direction. The same goes in any business. Sober can also mean "clear thinking"—and someone with power in a business needs this trait, if not literally sober, to keep it running smoothly.

BEING TEAM-ORIENTED

Although Geddy Lee would probably be perceived by most people to be the leader of Rush, the leadership of the band is really shared by its three members. Their democratic approach is such that if any member doesn't approve of something, be it a creative aspect or business aspect, it doesn't happen. This rigorous leadership style is likely the source of their equally rigorous musical style, which is known for its attention to detail and craft.

Other bands that are highly democratic in their leadership, wherein at least two members share leadership duty, include: ZZ Top, Genesis, U2, the Rolling Stones, AC/DC, Cheap Trick, Pearl Jam, Red Hot Chili Peppers, Linkin Park, and the Grateful Dead. The Dead's figurehead, Jerry Garcia, said in 1991, "You see, the way we work, we don't actually have managers and stuff like that. We really manage ourselves. The band is the board of directors, and we have regular meetings with our lawyers and accountants, and we've got it down to where it only takes about three or four hours, about every three weeks."

Being team-oriented also means recognizing the value in each team member and capitalizing on their strengths. Ideally, the team members complement each other (and compliment each other), creating a solidity as a whole that none have in themselves. Said John Lennon: "None of us would've made it alone. Paul wasn't quite strong enough, I didn't have enough girl appeal, George was too quiet, and Ringo was the drummer. But we thought that everyone would be able to dig at least one of us, and that's how it turned out."

The team-oriented leadership style is a double-edged sword, however, in that the balance of power is very delicate and susceptible to strife. Fleetwood Mac had major internal turmoil while recording their 1977 *Rumours* album; however, it was one of the best-selling albums of all time and earned numerous Grammy awards. Could it be these problems helped fuel their creative juices?

While it's not necessarily advised to encourage friction among team members, there is evidence it does generate positive results—at least creatively. Some other well-known but creatively successful bands that didn't get along: the Everly Brothers (Phil and Don), the Kinks (brothers Ray and Dave Davies would actually fight on stage) and Oasis (brothers Noel and Liam feuded so much they had to cancel their 1996 tour). The Blasters are certainly less well known, but earned a little fame when brother-members Dave and Phil Alvin fought on *The Today Show*. (Hmm . . . come to think of it, maybe the problem is brothers being in bands. Heart's Ann and Nancy Wilson never seemed to have this problem.)

The key is (1) recognizing whether the team-leadership style will work for your situation or not, and if so, (2) agree *how* it will work. Said Herman Rarebell when he was the drummer of Scorpions: "It's just like a marriage. Most bands break up because of ego problems, but we have it under control." And sometimes it means that you put personalities aside for the business. If a band or business can have its members "leave it at the door" when coming to work, the chances for success are much greater. It's a tall order, but it can be done. "We're the Oakland A's of rock 'n' roll," said Glenn Frey of the Eagles. "On the field we can't be beat. In the clubhouse, that's another story. We're completely different people." It's true that the band ultimately broke up, but they put aside their differences long enough to put out some of the best and biggest hit songs in rock, and they've recently put aside their differences to reunite for a new album and tour.

In addition to the items on the earlier checklist, there are a few more things to consider when fronting your band. As mentioned at the opening of this chapter, deciding how people will help you and who those people will be are both critical to your chances for success.

PARTNER AND PROSPER

One key thing to consider is a partnership—formal or informal, temporary or indefinite. Some of the most successful acts in rock history were based on phenomenal partnerships, many lasting for numerous years. While Paul McCartney and John Lennon didn't partner for long (compared to, say, Mick Jagger and Keith Richards), they nonetheless created history and set the bar for collaboration very high for subsequent musicians. Many of the most successful rock partnerships have been between performers, such as Donald Fagen and Walter Becker (Steely Dan), Darryl Hall and John Oates, Gene Simmons and Paul Stanley (KISS), and Joe Perry and Steven Tyler (Aerosmith). However, numerous songwriter-performer collaborations have been longstanding and lucrative as well—Bernie Taupin and Elton John, Michael Utley and Jimmy Buffett.

Partnering can often bring about a result better than either individual could achieve on their own. "Mick Jagger can't even make a successful solo album," said Don Henley, "and the Stones are the biggest rock group that ever was." Many bands in the 1960s featured star musicians who bounced between groups, achieving various degrees of success along the way. For example, Eric Clapton was in the Yardbirds (with Jimmy Page of later Led Zepplin fame), Cream (with Ginger Baker), and Blind Faith (with Steve Winwood who was in Traffic). Likewise, Stephen Stills was in Buffalo Springfield with Neil Young and Jim Messina (who joined later with Kenny Loggins as Loggins & Messina).

This mindset of partnership among rockers wasn't quite as prevalent after the mid-1970s, when a sense of competition was more common; however, it did return in the 1990s with the emergence of rap-metal, rap-rock, and nu-metal. Or in the case of Rob Thomas (Matchbox 20) and Carlos Santana, their collaboration crossed generations with their successful and Grammy-winning song "Smooth" on the album *Supernatural.* (Santana partnered with numerous other artists on the album and has achieved worldwide sales of twenty-five million copies since its 1999 release.)

The most-common traits of a successful partnership are:

✦ Good communication skills, especially under stress

✦ Belief in and commitment to a common goal

✦ Recognition of each other's strengths

✦ Respect for each other and the collaboration

✦ Ability to complement each other to overcome flaws

✦ Compatible beliefs and values

✦ Similar viewpoints about money and business philosophies

✦ Honesty, openness, and a generally trusting

✦ Addiction-free (includes sex, drugs, alcohol, and gambling)

The more of these traits each partner has, the more likely the success of the partnership.

A look at partnerships in rock that fell apart reveals a clear absense or violation of these principles. David Lee Roth and Eddie Van Halen were very different people. Roth came from a wealthy background, believed in flash and showmanship, loved the limelight, and knew how to relate to audiences. He was a real talker. Eddie Van Halen was middle-class and just loved music and playing guitar; he was also quiet, reserved, and shy.

Supposedly, it was Roth who had to convince him to even move around the stage during shows. Initially, these differences led to positive results and huge popularity in the late 1970s and early 1980s, but eventually the detriments outweighed the benefits. Roth reportedly wanted to pull the band toward a more pop style (witness most of *1984* and Roth's following solo album), and Eddie Van Halen was operating in a near-perpetual stupor from drugs and alcohol.

Stewing differences finally led to *1984* being the final album with Roth in the band (until a recent Van Halen reunion with original bassist Michael Anthony being replaced by Eddie Van Halen's son Wolfgang). Likewise, the successful 1970s' partnership of David Gilmour and Roger Waters in Pink Floyd dissolved into legal battles in the '80s over royalties, song credits, and use of the Pink Floyd name.

CONSULTANTS, ADVISORS, MENTORS, OUTSIDE HELP

Knowing when to get outside help and choosing the right help are two other important traits of successful leaders. They realize it's not always possible to have the right answers–an outside person (usually a consultant or business coach) can provide the guidance necessary to get through a particular problem or to keep the business on the right track, especially in the early stages.

Likewise, in the world of rock, many of the most successful bands had a strong guiding hand–their producers. Like a consultant or coach, the producer provides an important outsider's perspective on the band and its music. Said Malcolm Young (AC/DC) of producer Mutt Lange's work on their *Highway to Hell* album: "We learned a lot. You really need an outsider, because we can all go too far and disappear up our own anuses."

When it works, this relationship typically lasts years—Rush and Terry Brown, the Beatles and George Martin, Iron Maiden and Martin Birch, Scorpions and Dieter Dierks, Def Leppard and Mutt Lange, and ZZ Top and Bill Ham. In fact, ZZ Top and Ham worked together for over thirty-seven years, from their beginnings in 1969 until 2006. Sometimes, depending on the dynamics of the band, this guiding hand comes more from the manager, such as with Genesis and Tony Banks. Many times, this person is such an intregal part of the band and its success that he's viewed as an additional member of the band.

Mentoring in the rock world typically happens along the path to success through opening for other acts. Up-and-coming guitarist and singer Jonny Lang sold over a million records in part because he toured as an opening act for Aerosmith, the Rolling Stones, Buddy Guy, and B.B. King. Shawn Colvin recorded one of her records in the home studio of her idol, Joni Mitchell. And 1970s'AM-rock band America was founded by three guys in the Air Force who were so good at what they did that they received the guidance of George Martin after his stint producing the Beatles.

The female band Luscious Jackson were mentored by Beastie Boys— their first show was opening for Beastie Boys, and they were the first band signed to the Beastie Boys' label. Before Colonel Tom Parker took him on, Elvis was mentored by Sun Records' owner-producer Sam Phillips. Other notable mentor-mentee rock relationships include Don Henley and Sheryl Crow, John Lennon and Harry Nilsson, Mick Fleetwood and Rob Thomas, Gene Simmons and Van Halen, and Fred Durst (Limp Bizkit) and Aaron Lewis (Staind).

SELLING OUT

Taking the Mystery Out of Marketing and Sales

"If your album sells, that's cool, more people find out about you, more people get turned on to what you're really about."

–NIKKI SIXX (MOTLEY CRUE)–

Who is the best rock-and-roll band of all time? Before you answer the question, consider that there is one band that did it all–made amazing music, mastered the media and marketing, and sold a ton of records. We're talking about a band that had three number-one records in a single year–over twenty-five years after they broke up. Amazing. Of course, the band is . . . the Beatles.

What can we learn from the Fab Four? Well, when it comes to marketing, it pays to build a buzz and then back it up by being the real deal. And it's important to get the word out about who you are and what you do. The Beatles did it through record releases, public appearances, concerts, interviews, and fan clubs. Yeah, but they're *the Beatles*, you say. Are they really that different than us? If we build a buzz about our business, brand ourselves as a leader in our field, deliver quality products and services to our target market–and are promotable and likeable–what's to stop us from changing the world, or at least making our mark in our area of expertise?

Just like the lads from Liverpool, being able to sell yourself and your business is your ticket to ride. How well you market your goods and services determines how successful your business will be. Promote and profit—it's (almost) that simple. Although it's so easy to neglect this area of your business, it has to be a high priority. Schedule it in. Even if you only spend one hour a day on sales and marketing, you will have a positive effect on your business.

Set aside a portion of your revenues to reinvest in this area. Develop a marketing mindset. This means you are always on the lookout for opportunities to promote your business—and you do it. Why wouldn't a business or a band jump at the chance to make sales and marketing their primary focus? Take your pick of reasons, but "not enough time" tops the list.

There is also a lack of know-how when it comes to promotion. Fear of rejection is always an underlying factor. Another reason is a lack of confidence. A common excuse for procrastinating on promotion is perfectionism. (Don't wait until everything is just perfect—your prototype, business card, or website. It's better to act and react than procrastinate for weeks, months, and years to start promoting.)

Finally, some people believe selling is unseemly and promotion is a slippery slope to selling out. Wrong. Even Frank Zappa bought into sales and marketing: "Art is about making something out of nothing and selling it." Yet bands (and entrepreneurs) can still get defensive about why they don't promote themselves. Guitarist Neal Schon of Journey said, "There's nothing wrong with being commercial. It's just another way of saying you're successful." Amen.

We know, selling is hard, but it becomes a lot easier when you are selling something you truly believe in and know in your heart it benefits others. When you have the right product for the right people at the right time for the right price, why *wouldn't* you want to tell everyone—and then remind them when they forget you told them? When you love what you do and do it well, sales and marketing are not as difficult or distasteful as you might imagine.

Still, not every entrepreneur will master marketing—or want to. You don't have to like selling yourself and your product, but you have to do it—or get someone to do it for you. This chapter is about how to master the art of marketing by focusing on what you do best. Maybe you are good at going online and bringing awareness to what you do, or perhaps you are more of the meet-and-greet type. Either way, by focusing on the areas where you feel most comfortable, you maximize your time and talent to get the word out—and you stay within your comfort zone.

Another way to have more marketing moxie (or at least not to be terrified all the time) is to focus on what's in front of you. Fears come from worrying about an uncertain future—and too many marketing possibilities can freak you out—so only concern yourself with what you need to do now. You do need a (promotional) plan to go with the attack. If you just attack all the time, you waste time and money and usually lack the one thing that matters most—follow-through. If all you do is plan, you'll miss a lot of timely opportunities. That's all part of the plan. The promotional plan. Focus on what you can do now, but think up clever ways to promote later. What do you really want from your marketing efforts? Better brand awareness? Increased sales? Repeat business and referrals? What's the best way to get it? Let's do it.

THE SECRET TO SELLING

Once you realize the secret to selling, you'll never have to actually "sell" anything again—which, for a lot of rock stars and entrepreneurs would be welcome news. Kate Bush once said, "That's hard for me when I have to come out and expose myself and be the salesman of the hour."

The secret to selling is this: selling isn't about you, it's about them (your audience). Joan Armatrading ("Love and Affection") said, "I'd be very uncomfortable if all my songs were about me. I always say you must be a very big-headed person to write everything that you write about yourself." She may be right. That's why it's so much easier when you take yourself out of the equation and see things from the customer's perspective. What do *they* need or want? People buy for one reason and one reason only: they benefit in some way from what you offer.

Find a need, fill it, and solve people's problems. Then be sure to tell them about what you can do for them. It's all about the benefits–for them. Which is good news for you. If you are offering something with a benefit (is there any other kind of product or service?), then all you are doing is informing and educating people about something that will help them in some way. It's a lot easier to wrap your head (and heart) around the idea that you are making a positive impact on others and a difference in their lives, rather than twisting their arm to buy something they don't want or need. You must believe there are benefits in what you do, in order to be believable, and you need to be able to "sell it" to sell it. If you are having a hard time selling something, maybe you aren't sold yourself. Focus on the benefits of what you do and you should be a lot more motivated to sell.

If you're still unwilling or unable to sell yourself (and you make excuses not to market day in and day out), is it possible you aren't as passionate about your products and services as you possibly could/ should be? When you are passionate, you don't have to be pushed to promote. You don't make excuses. You are more willing to try and fail and aren't as afraid of rejection. You aren't as tired, and you do what needs to be done. Tommy Lee, drummer for Motley Crue, said of the band's start, "We were like a self-promotion machine. We went around with flyers and a staple gun and plastered everything." Although we aren't fans of the illegal plastering of telephone poles, we have to admire that kind of effort. The same goes for bands like Metallica, who paid their dues by touring relentlessly to win over fans across the country. One band, Supertramp, would finish a show to thousands of fans and then head off to a small club in the same town to perform covers because they loved playing music that much.

Conversely, Rod Stewart has said it was hard to get behind his music from the '80s. It's hard to sell something you don't completely believe in. "I am not a fan of Monkees' music," said Mike Nesmith, and he was a *member* of the Monkees. And before Nirvana, Kurt Cobain (and bassist Krist Novoselic) were in a Creedence Clearwater Revival tribute band called Sellout. But when they finally had something they could believe in (Nirvana), they had more passion about promoting it.

THE KEY TO MARKETING

When you really *know* your audience–how you help them meet their needs–you can offer them exactly what they want and need at a price they are willing to pay. That's more than half the battle. The other half of the battle is how to best reach your target market. Once again, when you really know them you will also know the best way to put your product (or service) in their path. Tom Waits said, "I still keep one foot in the streets." That's what we should do. Find out as much as we can about our customers by being better listeners. When it comes to target marketing, questions provide the answers. Below are some of the key questions to ask about your ideal clients and customers.

Who Are They?

"I would try to write songs from a woman's viewpoint–that was quite difficult, but rewarding," said guitarist and songwriter Richard Thompson. Knowing the gender of your best customer is a start. (Interestingly, Joan Jett and Joni Mitchell are the only two female guitarists on the list of *Rolling Stone* magazine's greatest guitarists of all time.)

You also want to know how old they are, where they live, where they shop, what they read, who they buy from now and why, how they buy, how much they are willing to spend, and so on. Having the accurate answers to these questions (do not assume you know) will help you to describe your ideal customer in detail. You'll know who they are, who they want to be, what's important to them (Hint: almost everyone wants and needs to be comfortable), and how they want to be reached.

You could and should be able to describe a typical day in your customer's life and then be able to figure out how you fit in. Finding people who need, want, and will pay for what you have to offer (and reaching them) seems so simple, but it takes time. However, it's time well spent. You may even think you know your audience, but through thorough research and test-marketing, you may discover a whole new market or approach to a market. For example, Bob Dorough was a moderately successful musician before he was hired by advertising exec

David McCall to create rock music to help teach kids math—a whole new market for him. *Schoolhouse Rock* ran on ABC from 1973 to 1986 (and has appeared from time to time since) and made Dorough a success.

As we now know from the popularity of *American Idol,* most viewers have their own idea of what a good singer is and like to share that opinion with others—through voting for their favorite contestant. It's the same for people with a product or service. You can learn a lot by sharing your prototype, proposal, and/or product ideas with those who care and can help with insights and ideas—your existing (or prospective) customers. You may also want to confer with your mentor and many other people whose opinions you value. Actual focus groups can also be arranged (for a fee) or you can create your own. As Donny Deutsch, advertising mogul and host of CNBC's *The Big Idea,* recommends: All you need is a pizza and you can get a few people to give you ideas and feedback.

How Many Are There?

The song "Spirit in the Sky" was an attempt by Norman Greenbaum (a farmer at the time) to write a religious rock song. Greenbaum's song about God and Jesus sold two million copies in 1970. Greenbaum isn't a Christian (he's Jewish)—but he surmised a song that appealed to Christians would be a bigger seller than one directed at people of his own faith. The song has also been used in several feature films including *Apollo 13.*

Being able to say everyone is your target market would seem like a good thing—but it's not. It's too overwhelming, too expensive, and too hard to try to reach everyone. (Word spreads a lot faster in a smaller market—such as a regional market or a specific type of customer you want to reach—and it costs a lot less.) You want an audience somewhere between the size of Texas (big) and Topeka (small). If the target market is too big to begin with, you will run out of time and money before you make your mark. If it's too small, you won't earn enough money and will be wasting your time. There must be a market and better yet, a good-sized one. To reiterate what we mentioned before, you need to find enough people (or companies) who want, need, and will pay for your product or service—then find the best way to put yourself in their paths.

The Rolling Stones have a fan base that can only be categorized as huge. Muddy Waters has a fan base that can best be described as modest—at least in comparison to the Stones. The interesting thing is—the Rolling Stones are a blues-based band (like Aerosmith and Led Zepplin), but many of the original blues acts didn't chart or make much money. When the Stones were in America on their first U.S. tour in 1964, they met Muddy Waters (they were fans) at Chess Records studio, and he helped carry in their equipment. Thankfully, later in life, Waters made a nice income from the royalties from his records, in part, because of renewed interest in the blues due to bands like the Rolling Stones.

What Do They Want?

"If you're gonna sell out, make sure they're buying," said Martha Davis, of the Motels. Gene Simmons of KISS adds, "I'm sick of musicians saying, 'I don't care what you want to hear, I'm gonna play whatever I want 'cause I'm an *artist*.' You're an artist? Paint my house." Hmm . . . okay. Let's review: we need to know what people want and then sell it to them.

But how do you know what people want? First and foremost, money talks. They'll let you know by either buying or not buying what you're offering. But there is a better way to know—ask them. It's a cheap way to do market research about what's on their minds, what's important to them, and what they want and don't want. David Bowie has a "Discourse" button on his website where members can ask him questions and vice versa titled "AskDavidAsks." There are also member blogs and message boards that can be monitored and mined for clues about what the audience is interested in. Or just pay attention to trends in what's being bought—or has been bought. Look at past invoices, mailing lists, and e-mails for patterns of who your best customers are.

Even if you know what they are already buying, you want to know what else they might want. What other products or services can you offer that will be snapped up by your fans? The Dave Matthews Band sells posters, calendars, shirts, blankets, hats, bags, backpacks, flip flops, live DVDs, instructional videos–and even Dave Mathews Band gift cards. It could be people will purchase whatever you put out (see above example) or–and this is more likely–you have to figure out what their problems are and solve them with your products and services. It comes down to knowing what your audience wants and then giving it to them.

How Can You Give Them What They Want?

Matchbox 20 guitarist Paul Doucette said, "We caught a lot of shit in our career, but as we've gotten older, we've realized that we shouldn't feel bad about making music that a lot of people like." In 1988, Cheap Trick was about to be dropped by their label after a series of lackluster albums. Their best hits "Surrender" and "I Want You to Want Me" were more their style but their label insisted they record a love ballad called "The Flame." To save their recording contract, the band acquiesced (despite secretly hating the song), and it was added to *Lap of Luxury*. The song went on to become the band's only #1 song.

Go against your customer's wishes at your own peril. Billy Corgan of Smashing Pumpkins asked the audience at the start of a show if they were ready to rock. When the crowd enthusiastically applauded, he replied, "Well, you've come to the wrong place." He was joking, of course, but it could be worse. Limp Bizkit opened for Metallica on their 2003 tour. On one date in Chicago, 40,000 Metallica fans turned on Bizkit lead singer Fred Durst, and those close to the front hurled insults (and objects) at him on stage. He retreated to stage left and continued to yell at the crowd after he was hit in the "nether region" by a lemon. We guess Durst did at least give Metallica fans what they wanted–an early exit.

Many radio listeners probably never realize this, but bands will re-mix hit songs for different formats. They might have several versions of the same song–an adult contemporary version that features more vocals and less drums, another version might be full-length, while still another is shortened, and so on. You may be able to tweak what you already offer to match the needs of the market. Nearly every band will do a sound check before each show and make adjustments depending on the acoustics of the venue. You should do a "sound check" on your business—be your own customer and experience it from their perspective for ideas about how to do what you do even better.

How Do You Reach Them?

In the early days of rock and roll, promoter Alan Freed brought artists to small towns across the country in a traveling showcase. Decades later, on August 21, 1981, a revolutionary way of reaching rock fans debuted— MTV, which appropriately selected as its first aired video, "Video Killed the Radio Star" by the Buggles. Of course, video hardly killed the radio star, but it sure had a massive impact on the rock music business that decade.

The goal of Warner Bros. executives (the creators of MTV) was to reach a demographic under thirty, and the look and feel of the station was designed to appeal to that audience. A few years later, in 1985, MTV launched VH-1 to attract an older audience. And almost twenty years after that, Apple launched iTunes in April of 2003 and sold over a million songs in the first week. Some of the first artists to be promoted were Jack Johnson, Coldplay, and Alanis Morrisette—partly because these artists were the best bet for their target market.

Times change and you have to change with them to take advantage of the best means and methods to reach your target audience. Look at developing trends in your industry (and the media) and ask yourself, how can I benefit from this? Don't fight it. Embrace it. Then ask yourself, if I were my customer, where would I go to look for my products or services? What key words would I use to search for myself online? When would I need to buy? Most important of all, why would I buy from me? The Texas-based band Flyleaf benefited by touring with Korn's Family Values Tour. How do we know? Their debut CD sold over one million copies. Part of that success was because of the exposure and part was because the band's faith-based music is sold in both Best Buy and Christian bookstores.

Who We Want and Don't Want as Customers

In their early days, Van Halen was a promotional machine. During times of a light schedule, they didn't just sit and wait for business—they'd seek out gigs doing backyard keg parties around Los Angeles. To increase attendance, they'd put flyers in the lockers at nearby high schools. This wasn't done without some thought. They even made it a point to attract a following of girls, knowing that would make them more popular to book at clubs and parties. In short, Van Halen targeted a market and attacked it.

You, too, can be proactive about the audience you want. You can also decide what type of customers you don't want. In 1969, the Rolling Stones were the featured performers at a free concert held at the Altamont Speedway attended by roughly 300,000 people. In the days leading up to the event, the date, venue, and the lineup changed. When Mick Jagger announced at a press conference the Stones would be playing (it was supposed to be a surprise appearance), many feared crowd-control problems (the Grateful Dead reportedly pulled out for this reason). The night of the festival, everyone's worst fears were realized. A man (who had pulled a gun) was stabbed and beaten to death by members of a well-known motorcycle gang there to assist with security. It was released recently that this motorcycle gang also had a hit out on Mick Jagger after the debacle of Altamont was over. We're guessing the Stones won't have these individuals on their current VIP list. Ideally, you want customers who want you. This means you are their best bet to fulfill their needs. You can talk about gender, geography, target groups, and different generations, but it comes down to meeting their goals and doing it at the right time, for the right price, and being the right fit (they like you).

What Do I Want Them to Know?

What is the one thing you want people to get from your marketing message? The answer to this question is extremely important. It becomes the basis for your tag line. The best tag lines tell customers and potential customers what you do and what you do for them. For example: "We help [insert your ideal customer here] with [the area you specialize in offering assistance] by/through [the key services you provide] to achieve [the benefits they'll gain]." You can then take this basic tagline and tweak it. Lionel Trains (Neil Young is a minority shareholder in the company) went with the clever tagline, "Lionel Trains make a boy feel like a man and a man feel like a boy," because their trains bring fathers and sons together.

THE MOST IMPORTANT PART OF PROMOTION

When you put yourself out there, good things happen. You never know (or do you?) who's watching. Vonda Sheppard's first break came at age nineteen when Rickie Lee Jones asked her if she would play keyboards and sing backup on Jones' tour. But it wasn't until years later that she had her *big* break, when David E. Kelley caught her act in a small club and wrote her into the TV show he was developing at the time—*Ally McBeal*. He also chose a song from her 1992 album, which had sold less than 6,000 copies, to be the theme song for the show. After the good fortune of making Kelley a fan, she experienced more good fortune in the way of increased CD sales and sold-out concerts. So, get out there and put yourself in the path of your customers.

This is the basic premise of promotion—putting yourself in a position where people will see you. That's why touring is a staple of rock music—always has been and probably always will be. However, you can "get out there" from the comfort of your own home using your computer. There are endless opportunities to show off what you can do using all the online tools at your disposal. Even if you only do one thing a day (e.g., do a Google search related to your business and see where it leads), you may "meet" that difference-maker that makes you millions.

Whether you promote from home or on the road (the Jeff Healy Band played 300 dates a year in the beginning; John Mayall still does 150 shows a year, and he's over sixty), you have to keep yourself out there because "out of sight is out of mind." To make things easier, look for the opportunities that provide the biggest bang for your buck—ones where you'll be in contact with the largest number of people, or ones with a smaller, but better suited group of buyers. This is why bands want to perform on *Leno*, *Saturday Night Live*, and the *Today Show*. This is also true of tradeshows. For up-and-coming musicians, performing at the South by Southwest showcase is a tremendous opportunity to be seen—and heard. Don't be shy. Take advantage of any and all opportunities to show off what you do.

Folk-rocker John Sebastian happened to be in the audience at the original Woodstock. On the second day, the stage filled up with water and organizers couldn't have anyone playing electric guitar in those conditions. They asked Sebastian to play an acoustic set. He was a hit. So, go where the action is. Los Angeles was the center of the universe for rock and roll in the '70s and '80s. Places like Whisky a Go Go and Ninth Street West, as well as the Red Velvet, Pandora's Box, the Trip, and London Fog launched many a band. L.A. was the scene, just like San Francisco was the place to be in the '60s and Seattle was all things grunge in the '90s. And, of course, New York is perpetually important.

MAKING IT LAST

The most-enduring artists have lifelong fans who like them and what they do because, let's face it, for many bands (and businesses) success is a popularity contest and you win with the most fans. But winning fans over takes time. It's a lot like dating. It's possible someone sets you up because they think you would be a good match (word-of-mouth marketing and referrals). Or you spot someone and there's an initial attraction and you want to know more (advertising and promotion). So, you decide to meet for a first date (networking) in the hopes you have something in common and to see if any sparks fly—and they do. Now, you're in the courting phase, trying to win them over (relationship selling). After time together, you fall in love and realize you're meant for one another—so you marry (closing the deal.) When it comes to promotion (and dating) patience is a virtue. In promotion, things are frontloaded—you have to give to get—and it takes time and money to win people over. But when you do, they can be loyal for as long as you faithfully serve them.

It's so much easier to make an existing customer into a better one—so treat them like gold. It's also cheaper (and more effective) to gain leads and clients through referrals and word-of-mouth spread by your fans (your current customers). In fact, it's been estimated that 90 percent of all new business comes from word of mouth. To have long-lasting relationships with your customers, you'll need to do one or all of these things: know and remember their birthdays, send them thank-you cards, give them extra attention, and offer them deeper discounts. Remember they're always right, so always do the right thing and look for ways to win them over again and again by exceeding their expectations. In short, make them feel special.

FANS FOR LIFE

When I first heard the song "Werewolves in London" by Warren Zevon on the radio, I found it interesting, but it didn't make me want to go out and buy the entire album. Then years later, I heard another artist cover Zevon's "Lawyers, Guns, and Money" in concert, and I really liked that song—for obvious reasons. Not long after that, I read an interesting article about Warren Zevon, and I'd reached the tipping point: I went out and bought his greatest hits CD—and loved it. After that, I noticed Warren Zevon was thanked in the credits of a book (*Basket Case*) by one of my favorite authors, Carl Hiaasen. Then I discovered Hiaasen co-wrote the song "Seminole Bingo" with Zevon.

I became a fan of Zevon's, drawn to the offbeat song titles ("I'll Sleep When I'm Dead") and lyrics ("Excitable Boy") and his life (he partied and played with most of the top artists in L.A.). And when I learned he had stage-four lung cancer—like my father—and wrote and recorded an album while he knew he was dying, I felt a deeper connection and went on a campaign to "inform" my friends about Warren Zevon, his song "Keep Me in Your Heart," and his album *The Wind*. When my father passed away, I found enormous comfort in both. This is a story of selling without selling out. I have gone back and bought the entire Zevon back catalog of CDs, a documentary on DVD, a book, and if there was more stuff out there, I'd buy that, too.

–Lee Silber

SHOW AND TELL (AND SELL)

Freebies. Guitar Center was giving away a free compilation CD with a track from Smashing Pumpkins. It also featured undiscovered acts chosen by Smashing Pumpkins. What a great opportunity for up-and-coming bands. Give out samples of what you offer to allow potential customers to experience it.

Demonstrate. At the Margaritaville Restaurant on Duvall Street in Key West, you may meet the Sauce Boss, a guitarist who makes a gumbo between songs using his own sauce—which he sells from the stage while playing the blues.

Show Off. Nowadays, you must have a presence on YouTube, MySpace, and Facebook. Practically every band has a page on these social-networking sites, and many businesses are joining in. Take advantage of this awesome opportunity. Peer-to-peer networking is the new word-of-mouth marketing, and spending time adding friends to your listing pages is promotion. All of these sites have ways you can upload audio and video files that you can use for teaching and training (both great ways of passive promotion), product demonstrations, promotional videos (although they better be cool to get attention), and even contests. (You could have a contest for creating the best promotional video—to promote your product or service. The winner gets recognition, and maybe you could throw in freebies for him or her, and you get a great video.) Virtual touring is becoming a trend with authors.

Test-Market. "Seasons in the Sun" by Terry Jacks was a huge single in the 1970s and has sold over eleven million copies (the most by any Canadian act)—but the song almost never got released. In a strange twist of test-marketing, the songwriter's paperboy (yep, paperboy!) heard the demo and loved it—which prompted the boy to invite his friends over to hear it, and they loved it, too. Jacks then released it on his own Goldfish label, and the song rose on AM radio play to eventually hit #2 in 1974, spending four months on the Canadian and U.S. charts.

Enter Awards/Contests: Past winners at the San Diego Music Awards include: Blink 182, Buck-O-Nine, Lucy's Fur Coat, Jason Mraz,

Jewel, P.O.D., Rocket from the Crypt, Stone Temple Pilots, and Switchfoot. An impressive list for the nation's seventh-largest city. But many bands have risen from smaller places, even small towns, through contests. Your business can either participate in contests or sponsor them. The key, however, is to (a) be creative and (b) maximize your publicity from the contest. Make the contest as interesting and unique as possible, and make sure the media is involved.

Taglines/Labels. The best businesses have (and use) a concise slogan to convey what they do—and what they do for their customers—in a quick and memorable way. Word of mouth is the most effective form of marketing, so your tagline has to be memorable—if they can't remember it, they can't repeat it. To take advantage of this approach to promotion, people must be able to know what you do in a nutshell, so they can tell others. The best way to foster this is to create a concise, catchy, and benefits-oriented slogan or tag line. The best tag lines tell people what benefit you offer in a way they will remember. The best slogans answer the questions, directly or indirectly: "What's in it for me?" and "Why should I buy from you?" When you have a professional-sounding name and tag line that gets people excited about what you do, you'll generate word of mouth. In today's busy, overwhelming, and noisy world, you need a simple and clear message to have a chance at cutting through the clutter. Also, when you have time for a more-extensive pitch than a tag line, expand it with references people know. For example, a band might say, "We're a blend of Rush and the Beastie Boys." Now, that we'd like to hear.

WOW!

To be a successful promoter, you have to be noticeable and memorable. Be extraordinary (but relevant) in some way so that people say "Wow!" when they hear about you or do business with you. Talk about extraordinary—ZZ Top used live longhorn cattle on stage on their 1976 Worldwide Texas tour. Xavier Rudd (an Australian artist) is a solo act who tours with a very unique setup that includes everything from guitars, bass, and banjo to didgeridoos and a stomp box. Of course, bands like Devo and Primus stood out because their stage attire was as unique as their sound. Likewise for a guitarist named Buckethead (Brian Carroll) who wears a KFC bucket on his head while performing live. He's not a novelty act either; he's released thirty-eight solo albums and performed as a guest on a hundred more. Buckethead plays several instruments well, but he is best known for his guitar playing—he's amazing—and has collaborated with everyone from Les Claypool and Tony Williams to Guns N' Roses and Iggy Pop. His music has also been featured in several major motion pictures.

The message is, be good at what you do and don't be boring. In 1964, Pete Townsend inadvertently rammed the neck of his guitar into the low ceiling of a club, snapping off the head. With his friends in attendance and not wanting to look like an idiot, he decided to act like he meant to do it and smashed the rest of his Rickenbacher. This led Keith Moon to trash his drums (it didn't take much to get Moon to break something), and the crowd thought this smash-fest was the coolest thing they'd ever seen. At the time, the Townsend-led band was called the High Numbers, but they soon changed their name to the Who. Another guitarist, AC/DC's Angus Young, experimented with stage antics in the band's early years—only instead of smashing his guitar, he performed in a gorilla suit. Perhaps because it was a little too much (or extremely hot inside), Young changed over to a schoolboy outfit that became his trademark look, befitting his 5'2" frame.

Confidence, knowledge, and being the best can also make people take notice. Barry Mann once said about Carole King, "She was 15, and I saw this confident little broad. She thought everything she wrote was great. And she was right; ninety percent of it was." Billy Corgan of Smashing Pumpkins said, "Great music is still the best marketing." In business this means doing quality work and doing it with a smile (great customer service). This can also mean knowing more about your product, service, or industry than anyone else. *You* are the authority. At the least, you must know your product or service inside and out, as well as what your competition is doing and how you are different and better.

Jimmy Page was not only a fantastic guitarist, but he was also known for playing his Les Paul with a bow. On the low end, bass players are not known for standing out, but over the years there have been some outstanding ones in rock, including Geddy Lee, John Entwistle, John Paul Jones, Flea, Steve Harris, Jack Bruce, Jack Cassady, Chris Squire, Tina Wymouth, Paul McCartney, Les Claypool, Carol Kaye, Billy Sheehan, and Will Lee.

Sometimes people say "wow" because you develop something unique that you've pioneered and mastered. This can be said of Dick Dale, who was the father of surf music with his trademark guitar sound. In 1961, he released "Let's Go Trippin,'" and in 1962 had a hit with "Misirlou," which resurfaced in the 1994 film *Pulp Fiction*. People are naturally attracted to those who are strong and confident. This is no different, and perhaps even more true, in business. We'll let the always-opinionated Gene Simmons have the last word on confidence: "The strong inherit the earth—the meek inherit shit."

Wowing your fans can also mean blowing their minds by going the extra mile and offering exceptional customer service. In a performance at Abbey Road, surfer, singer, songwriter, and guitarist Donovan Frankenreiter went into the crowd for a sing-along with the audience. Those who were there will not soon forget it—plus it's on his live DVD. Get your customers involved. As we mentioned earlier, if you make them feel special, they'll talk about you—and interacting with them is a great way for them to feel exceptional. The band Dashboard Confessional is known for allowing the audience to sing major portions of their songs live. And it's working, since they have three Gold Records to date.

You can also create talk among your customers (good talk) with celebrity endorsements, testimonials, and affiliations. If you look at any rock industry magazine (*Modern Drummer*, *Bass Player*, etc.), you'll see how important product endorsements are in that business. All major rockers have free equipment by virtue of endorsements. And many a young, aspiring rock musician has purchased a certain brand to emulate their idol. (As an interesting side note, Steve Miller ["Fly Like An Eagle"] was taught to play guitar by Les Paul, who also gave him that guitar.) Affiliations that generate buzz can also come in the way of charitable work or connections. Many bands, as do many businesses, achieve good word of mouth (and good PR) by helping out various causes and efforts, from one end of the spectrum (Ted Nugent and the National Rifle Association) to the other (Paul McCartney and People for the Ethical Treatment of Animals).

Regardless of how you wow your customers, keep in mind that it takes a super self-promoter nowadays to make people truly say "wow!"—ordinary and good enough just don't cut it anymore. You have to be extraordinary to make people pay attention.

CLOSE THE DEAL

Early in their career, the members of the Rolling Stones convinced the owner of the Crawdaddy Club in West London that they could bring in more people and hence sell more drinks than any other band. Sure enough, the first time they played the Crawdaddy Club there was a line out the door. That's not the norm. Usually, the world will not beat a path to your door—you'll have to drag them kicking and screaming. But that's what you have to do if you want the business. Whatever your strategy is to get people to sign on the dotted line and hand over their hard-earned dollars, you can't let them leave when they say, "Let me think about it" or "I'm just looking." Instead, you can:

+ make them an offer they can't refuse (a good deal, great terms, added incentives)

+ make it so easy to buy that they do (the process is simplified and streamlined)

+ listen to their objections and be prepared to overcome each one (you have practiced your pitch)

+ make sure you point out all the ways they will benefit by buying, and most of all, make sure you . . .

+ ASK FOR THE SALE.

DON'T TAKE "NO" FOR AN ANSWER

When someone says they aren't interested in your goods or services, your natural reaction may be to get angry, give up, or go too far trying to push it. Instead, turn the situation around and find out why they don't want to buy—or who they plan to buy from—and learn from that. Anyone who watches *American Idol* knows that Paula Abdul is the positive one and Simon Cowell is the negative one. (Randy Jackson falls somewhere in between.) The contestants can learn a lot more from Simon's critical comments (if they develop a thick skin and don't take them too personally) and will ultimately be better performers because they were willing to know (how to improve their performance) and grow (take the advice to heart). It's the same in sales and promotion.

GET HELP

Van Morrison said, "You not only have to write and record, but you have to go out and sell it. Well, I'm not a salesman, and I'm very bad at selling things. If I had to do that for a living, I'd probably be completely broke. I can't sell myself. And I don't even want to. That's something that's not going to change."

Ray Charles adds, "I always tell record companies: 'Let me do the music and you do the marketing.'" Just like many musicians don't always excel at sales and would rather haul and set up their own gear than promote themselves, entrepreneurs can suffer from the same condition—SAPD (Sales and Promotion Deficiency). The good news is—there is a cure and help is on the way. There are plenty of people you can pay to help you promote (consultants, publicists, sales representatives) or enlist for free (interns)—your entourage.

The term "payola" refers to record promoters (illegally) paying to have stations play a song. Disc jockey Alan Freed (an early advocate for rock and roll) had his reputation ruined by payola in the 1950s. Now, few DJs make decisions about song choices. The responsibility falls (for the most part) on program directors and the corporate parents of the stations. The loophole record companies came up with is to pay independent consultants to "promote" songs to radio stations. Now that deregulation allows an individual or corporation to own over a 1,000 record stations (before 1996 it was forty), to have a hit record you need to win over Clear Channel (or one of the other conglomerates, such as Viacom)–or else. You'll need help to have this happen. Perhaps in your industry there's a similar paradigm. There are always people who will help promote you for free–your fans.

Grand Funk Railroad ("We're an American Band" and "The Loco-Motion") had some big hits even though the band received very little airplay and terrible reviews of their music. They achieved their massive popularity through promotion (and touring) and their fans. In the past, bands would ask their faithful to pass out flyers. Now fans can spread the word about their favorite band cheaper and easier using Facebook and other online tools. The concept is still the same–word-of-mouth marketing is still the most cost-effective way to build interest in a band and a business. Some of the other free and easy ways to get others to help you include:

+ Find the one person who knows everyone–who's connected. This person can move mountains with a single call. She (or he) is a mover and shaker who digs what you do. Make sure your mentor or biggest fan is taken care of. In the music business, it means they get the best seats, go backstage and meet the band, and are given free swag (gear and memorabilia). In business you can take your top ten contacts to a ballgame, out for dinner and drinks, or just keep in contact with them (you call them on their birthdays, for example).

+ Friends and family (usually) want to see you succeed. Let them know what you do–and want to do. They likely have a large mailing list and know people who can really help you out. Jack Johnson can count Jackson Browne, Ben Harper, and Eddie Vedder as friends and mentors plus pro surfer Kelly Slater, who produced his *September Sessions* video. Ben Harper even took him on tour in 2001. Just for the heck of it, check out your favorite musician's or band's MySpace page and see who their friends are. You'll likely see some surprising connections.

✦ Get out there and connect with as many people as possible to build your mailing list. Speaking engagements are great ways to meet new people–and give them a sample of what you can do. Socialize more. Contacts come in casual places–your child's playground or preschool, or your country club or golf course. Joining your industry's association and attending meetings is a great (nearly "must") way to meet more people.

FOR FUN

"If you enjoyed my show tonight, please sign my mailing list at the back of the room. If you hated the show, you should also sign up. This way, you'll know where I'm playing next, and you can avoid me with amazing accuracy."–Don White

TALL STORIES

In the band Journey, Steve Augeri replaced Steve Perry when Perry hurt himself hiking and couldn't (or wouldn't) tour. (Augeri was working as a manager of a Gap store at the time.) Augeri was the former lead singer of Tall Stories, a less-than-successful band, but he had "the voice" to replace Perry and toured and recorded with the band until he developed vocal problems. The band eventually hired a forty-year-old singer from the Philippines named Arnel Pineta after guitarist Neil Schon saw him singing Journey covers on YouTube. YouTube! If that doesn't just scream, "Get out there and do it!" we don't know what does.

ROCK THE WORLD

Making a Big Impact through Publicity and Promotion

"Rock journalism is people who can't write interviewing people who can't talk for people who can't read."

–FRANK ZAPPA–

There's a reason "fame and fortune" are often used in the same phrase, as if the two go hand in hand—it's because they usually do. This is why you need the media (and surprise, they need you, too). It's by far the most effective way to reach the most people possible. It may not be "free" press, but positive press can cost a lot less than advertising—and it's much more effective. Where would Elvis and the Beatles be if it weren't for the *Ed Sullivan Show*? (Today, appearing on *Oprah* can have the same effect.)

Your business (and band) needs the massive exposure, instant credibility, and most importantly, increased sales that appearing in print (magazines and newspapers), radio (mainstream and Internet-based), television (network and cable), and other electronic media can provide. Simply put, the media can make or break your business. In this chapter we'll focus on the former.

Smash Mouth's hit song "Walking on the Sun" is a good example of what one well-placed media appearance can do. They began as a ska-punk band that built a buzz at a local level by playing the club circuit. They made a demo in one of the band member's bedrooms and gave it out freely. One copy ended up in the hands of a producer who helped the band make a more polished and professional recording, and eventually a self-financed album. MTV's Carson Daly was a disc jockey at KROQ in Los Angeles at the time, and when he played "Walking on the Sun" from Smash Mouth's demo, listeners loved it. A&R scouts soon discovered the band wasn't signed to a major label and the feeding frenzy began. That's the power of the media, and many a business has benefited by making the most of it.

Here are some things that you can do.

PITCH IT

When your opportunity to garner media attention arises–or you make it happen–be ready. One of the main tools you'll need is a press kit (online in your website's media room, and a physical one as well). Include in the kit whatever prototypes or samples you have (just like a band's demo)–and let the media try your product or service for free. Photographs, media clippings, fact sheets, and bios are included in a press kit as well.

The most important part of a press kit is the press release–or a pitch letter for the electronic media. Writing press releases and pitch letters (that work) is an art. The people in the media get pitched day in and day out–they've seen it all–so you must avoid being boring. You must make them say "Wow!" to get their attention–and hold it. An exceptionally good story idea (pitch letter) or press release has an irresistible quality to it and begins by having one heck of a headline. Following the headline is front-loaded copy that is compelling, clever, timely, newsworthy, witty, and most of all, well-written.

Bands know that media exposure means more butts in the seats at shows and buyers flocking to iTunes to purchase their latest release–and that means more royalties. In fact, the goal of being on radio and TV isn't only fame for fame's sake (brand awareness); the goal is to increase sales. Many reclusive rock stars (and other celebrities) will suddenly seek out the media spotlight when they have something to promote. It's how the game works—and it works for both parties.

Businesses can learn valuable lessons from bands that know how to work the mainstream media. When a band's album receives rave reviews, more people will purchase it—the same goes for your product. When a band is coming to town on tour, they will pursue the regional media to get the word out to their fans (and work the Internet). A businessperson speaking at a conference or at a college could do the same thing. The similarities between a business and a band are numerous. For example, a business (like a band) will let the media know when they reach a major milestone (an album goes gold or makes the charts), donate to a worthy cause (do a benefit concert), land a new client (switch record labels), launch a new product (a new album), move to a new location (record in an exotic locale), open another office (start a side band), win an award (Grammy), or celebrate an anniversary (ditto). Let the media know what you are up to because you never know when they may use your news.

HIRE A PRO AND/OR GET MEDIA TRAINING

You may want/need to put your money where your media is and hire a professional publicist. To do a cost/benefit analysis, you have to take into consideration what your time is worth (it takes a lot of time to pursue the press), how valuable it is that your business appears on major media (an appearance on *Oprah* or the *Today Show* is priceless), and whether you have what it takes to do it yourself (it's nice having a publicist in place who has editors and producers on her speed dial, who with one call can do it all).

Maybe you will decide to do it yourself, which will be a LOT less expensive, but you'll be doing a lot of work to put press releases out and researching the Internet to get contacts for e-mail submissions. One thing you may want to consider is media training, so you can really shine when the time comes for you to appear on talk shows. It's easy to forget why you are there—to promote your product or service—and easy to get caught off guard and say something foolish. It's much better to be prepared for the obvious questions–ones *you* provide–and come off as believable, knowledgeable, and personable.

The bottom line is the bottom line, when you factor in what it costs to advertise versus garner free (positive) press–and it works. In the early days of MTV, in every market where MTV was shown, album sales went up substantially for artists with featured videos. Where would Kelly Clarkson, Chris Daughtry, and Taylor Hicks be if they weren't seen by millions on *American Idol?* (Hint: It probably would be more like "Do you want fries with that burger?" than "How's everybody doin' tonight? Let's rock!")

There are a lot more media outlets today than in years past, but the principle is the same–the more exposure the better for business (assuming it's positive, and sometimes even when it's negative). In the early days of Genesis (the band, not the Bible), Peter Gabriel took being the front man of this progressive rock band very seriously. Every time the band performed, he would outdo himself with his theatrics on stage, including some pretty outrageous outfits. (One night, Gabriel came out in a woman's dress and a fox-skin cap to the surprise of the band.) This made for interesting reading, and *Melody Maker* would always do a write-up about Genesis–and more specifically what kind of get-up Gabriel was wearing. This led to a lot more interest in the band and, as you know, Genesis (and Peter Gabriel) went on to become mega stars.

DEVELOP A MEDIA MINDSET

Developing a media mindset can be as simple as flipping the channels on your television (watch every news station in your hometown to see what they like to cover), tuning the stations on your car radio (the stations that have talk shows), thumbing through as many magazines as you can (as well as all the newspapers in your area), and surfing the Web for anything that might be relevant to your product or service. Then, figure out how your business fits in with what these different media outlets like to cover.

Entrepreneurs with a media mindset also pay attention to trends (to see if their businesses relate to what's happening now—or in the future), actively watch the news to look for connections to their businesses, and notice how other businesses find a hook and use spin to garner good PR. Of course, an entrepreneur with a media mindset accepts any chance to showcase what she can do and actively seeks out opportunities to get media coverage.

If people don't know you exist, *do you exist?* Good question. If you are trying to make a name for yourself as a rocker or own a start-up business, the answer is no. Both need to inform the public about the positives in what they do, through public relations, or the media will profile someone else—the competition.

"Personally, being somewhat envious of Richard's songwriting and guitar playing, it's somewhat satisfying he's not yet achieved house-hold-name status. It serves him right for being so good," said Talking Head's David Byrne about guitarist Richard Thompson. Fairport Convention was one of the first British folk-rock groups, and members Richard Thompson and Sandy Denny (vocals) have received critical acclaim, but the band got very little press and recognition. Talent (or a great product or service) will not get you far without press coverage. The Flying Burrito Brothers (and Gram Parsons) were virtually unknown during the time they were active, but they paved the way for mega country-rock acts like the Eagles and Poco (who both received good press). Ry Cooper is considered one of the best all-around guitarists in rock, but most people have never heard his name. They know the names of the people he's played with, though, including Taj Mahal, Eric Clapton, Neil Young, the Rolling Stones, Randy Newman, Little Feat, and Gordon Lightfoot.

AVOID ALL-TOO-COMMON MISTAKES

It's nice when you can reach the most people for the least amount of money and effort. Paul McCartney (2005), Rolling Stones (2006), Prince (2007), and Tom Petty and the Heartbreakers (2008) performed during the Super Bowl halftime show because it reaches millions of viewers.

It's also important to be consistent and never out of the public eye for too long. This requires a businessperson to make PR a priority and take some time to work on it regularly. You can save time by jumping straight to the major media, but what you do needs to have that kind of appeal. To do this, you will need to be on top of your game when it comes to pitching producers and editors.

Here are some tips to help you avoid the common mistakes most people make when approaching the media. First, not knowing the rules of writing a press release guarantees it will end up in the trash. Not knowing the correct person to pitch or misspelling their name will have the same result. Members of the media are overworked and underpaid. They are also overwhelmed with story ideas, so they're looking for ways to exclude your press release rather than include it. Elimination is their main survival tool. Don't give them the chance. Being that they are busy, don't waste their time. Watch the show, read the magazine, listen to the host before you pitch, to ensure it's a fit. And when you do pitch your idea, get to the point fast and lead with your best material–your hook. In short, don't waste their time, know the rules, and be nice. It sounds obvious, but people get ticked off when the media aren't interested. Gaining publicity is a marathon and a sprint–you will need to do both before you get to the end of the race.

You can say you're great until you're blue in the face, but it's much more believable–and people tend to listen more intently–when a member of the media is espousing you or your product's greatness. Third-party endorsements and credibility are invaluable for a fledgling business. For rock stars, good reviews are worth their weight in gold (records). It's instant credibility. Elvis Costello once said, "I can't actually play any instrument properly. I can't read music. And here's the *New York Times* calling me the new Gershwin." Almost every successful band or solo artist has had good reviews. Otherwise, they wouldn't be where they are.

Now with interactive media, recording artists not only have to worry about what professional reviewers think, but also must win over the public. (Comments on YouTube and other social networking sites can be seriously harsh.) It's also important to get endorsements by leaders in your field or even celebrity endorsements. "I get the Shuffle and then I shuffle the Shuffle" is what President George W. Bush said in 2005 after accepting an iPod Shuffle from Bono of U2. Winning an award for being outstanding in your field is not only newsworthy, it can also be your ticket to better sales. It's like opening a Willy Wonka Bar and finding the golden ticket. Winning a Grammy Award helped Bonnie Raitt's *Nick of Time* album reach multi-platinum status.

PUBLICITY INTO PROFITS

You can't pay your bills with publicity, so you must turn publicity into profits. Here's a good example of how that happened for one band. Sometimes going against the grain can lead to media interest. In the early '90s, Blind Melon's sound was a breath of fresh air—they were able to mix their classic rock roots with the alternative sounds of the day to create a retro, straight-ahead style all their own. And they conveyed it well on stage and on their four-song demo, titled *The Goodfoot Workshop*.

Capitol Records signed the group in 1991, but the studio sessions didn't turn out as the band had hoped, and the EP wasn't released. In the meantime, singer Shannon Hoon was providing backup vocals on tracks for Guns N' Roses and even appeared in their video for "Don't Cry." The good news was, the added exposure helped Blind Melon land a featured slot on MTV's *120 Minutes Tour*, and they began to build a buzz about the music. The bad news was, they didn't have a record to promote or sell. The band had to go back to the studio and finish recording, but their debut didn't get released in time—and they missed out on the hype that had been created.

Blind Melon continued to tour and their record was finally released, but it was an uphill battle to regain their earlier momentum. Finally, the band's album cover photo (a girl dressed in a bumble bee costume) came to life in the video for "No Rain" and interest in the single and the *Blind Melon* album shot it to the top of the charts. The album would go on to become a multi-platinum seller.

GENERATE BUZZ

Good reviews can be used to get retailers to carry your product or corporations to use your services. It's like a stamp of approval. But it's up to you to turn it into something profitable and productive. The pursuit of reviews (from professionals and the public) should be a part of your publicity plan. You should also ask for and use testimonials from your satisfied customers. Ultimately, reviews are invaluable in the eyes of your customers–and potential customers.

When you hear the term "buzz," what do you think of? From a band's standpoint, it's a positive thing–as long as you can live up to the hype. The same goes for a business. When the name of your product or service is on the tip of everyone's tongue, you have a big edge over your competitors. (Hey, when we said "buzz" what did you *think* we meant?) Bruce Springsteen appeared on the covers of both *Time* and *Newsweek* in 1975. He was hailed as the latest and greatest thing. His first three records were not strong sellers at the time (though his song "Born To Run" was selling well), but there was plenty of buzz because "The Boss" delivered the goods and exceeded expectations.

Patti Smith was a pioneering poet and punk rocker in the '70s–and in the early days of her career, she benefited from both major label support (Arista) and consistent coverage in magazines like *Creem*. To build a buzz about your business or product, work backwards from the time you want the interview or article to appear. (Magazines have long lead times, and TV and radio producers are often hard to get a hold of.) In the early '70s, Lynyrd Skynyrd was discovered in Atlanta by producer and keyboardist Al Kooper; he signed the band and produced their debut album for MCA Records. The label really got behind the band, and used the media (and touring) to help make "Gimme Three Steps" and "Free Bird" major hits when released in 1974.

Don't let being a newbie at something inhibit you from trying to generate interest in either yourself or your product. When interviewing for a job in a new field (or your first job), it's always ironic to hear the interviewer say something like, "Well, you're perfect for the job, except you don't have any experience." You say to yourself, "Duh. How can I get any experience if nobody will hire me without it?" It's the same with the media. Publicity begets more publicity. Once you get that first article, review, or radio interview, it gets easier to get more. Fred LaBour was a journalism major at the University of Michigan when he wrote a review of the Beatles album *Abby Road* for the student newspaper. In his review, he observed that if you played the album backward, it gave clues indicating that Paul McCartney was dead. National papers picked up the story and interviewed LaBour extensively. (He went on to become a songwriter.) And of course, the Beatles benefitted immensely from all the resulting coverage.

CREATE YOUR IMAGE (BRANDING)

How we see ourselves may be very different from how we are perceived by others. Using the media, you can actually create the image you want the world to see. In business, it's called branding–creating a unified message that communicates your focus, uniqueness, and benefit. We use Jimmy Buffett as an example often in this book because, quite frankly, he is at the top of the list of business-savvy solo rock stars. And that's the irony. The public image Buffett wants everyone to see is that of a laid-back guy who sips margaritas on the beach when he's not sailing, surfing, fishing, or flying his seaplane to tropical locales all over the world. The truth is, yes, he does all those things–but he also does a lot more. Buffett goes on tour each summer and sells out large venues everywhere, playing to adoring fans who hang on his every word. He still writes and records relevant records. He has written four best-selling books. He owns *two* very successful chains of restaurants (Margaritaville and Cheeseburger in Paradise) and markets his own line of tequila and shrimp. You get the idea–he's making millions and living the life of a rock star.

What *isn't* publicized is the real Jimmy Buffett–a workaholic who is very involved in his businesses and takes touring very seriously. (He has a strict no-drugs policy for his band, for example.) Interestingly, in 1996, the Jamaican government shot at Buffett's seaplane–mistakenly thinking he was smuggling drugs into the country–prompting him to write a song about it ("Jamaica Mistaica"). He also opened a Margaritaville Cafe in the airport there. Maybe the Jamaicans had come across an old copy of *High Times* magazine featuring a candid interview with Jimmy Buffett (December, 1976) and believed he really was the drug-smuggling pirate he sings about in "A Pirate Looks at Forty." Little did they know.

Decide now what you want your business image to be before someone else decides for you. Use the media to send the message you want. This begins by looking at all the points of contact you have with your customers, including your website, newsletter, brochure, and blog. Make certain they reflect what you want. In the formats we just mentioned, you can include articles, stories, interviews, examples, and other tidbits that the media may pick up on and use. It's also perfectly fine to interview and/ or write articles about you and your business. Don't lose sight of the fact that being in business for yourself makes you a (minor) rock star in some people's eyes. And those who hold down regular jobs may just be interested in a podcast about the life and times of an entrepreneur—you.

WORK THE WEB

Back in the '70s, media was a one-way form of communication. Now, through interaction online, an artist or entrepreneur can test-market and gain valuable feedback before launching a project. The use of the Internet to build a buzz is awesome. Viral marketing is all the rage, and for good reason—it works. The term "media" now must include the Web as one of the most cost-effective ways to get the word out about who you are and what you do. FaceBook and MySpace are amazing tools— in the right hands—to the savvy entrepreneur. In the past, direct mail was an expensive and often ineffective method for reaching your customer base, and it can now be entirely avoided. Simply put, there has never been a better time to build a buzz, because the new media are easier to use, less expensive, and much more effective.

THINK GLOBALLY

In advertising you want to narrow the focus of your audience (your target market) so you don't end up paying to reach people in places where your products and services aren't needed or sold (or reach people who don't care about them). When it comes to publicity, however, the more people who read and hear about you the better. That's why you can now go worldwide with Internet-based media (and mainstream media are online for millions of people around the globe as well). This opens up a literal world of possibilities and opportunities.

Here's a great example of what going global can do. In the 1970s, Cheap Trick had released three albums that all went nowhere. After failing in the U.S. and Europe, they tried out Japan. (Japan has always been enamored with American rock stars.) Their record company taped two of the concerts in Japan and released a live album to capitalize on their overseas popularity. The live version of "I Want You to Want Me" somehow made its way back to the States and became the band's first hit. Suddenly, Cheap Trick was popular in Japan *and* the U.S. There are fewer geographic boundaries for businesses now, and it has never been easier to sell stuff almost anywhere in the world. With digital music, it's the same—sales are calculated for the U.S. numbers and internationally and, in some cases, more music is being sold abroad.

The same tool you would use to find international media opportunities (the Internet) is the same medium you want to appear on. Explore the endless possibilities of the World Wide Web.

BUT START LOCALLY

Most bands became famous in their hometowns before being discovered by the world. One reason is the familiarity and proximity of your local reviewers, reporters, and producers. (Get to know your local media.) Another reason is the obvious angle of "homegrown talent/business does well." It works almost every time. It's also good to get your media experience on a small scale before going big time, so you're more prepared and polished when you appear on national TV. In addition to maximizing local and regional media, don't forget to target your trade publications. True story: a heavy metal band pitched a steel industry trade magazine and got a feature written about them.

MAKE A DIFFERENCE AND BE CHARITABLE

Greg Emerson of Emerson, Lake, and Palmer: "As I said to Ringo [Starr], I was in a successful rock-and-roll band. He was in a band that changed the world. That's the difference." You can likewise use the media as a platform for greater good. Bob Geldof (Boomtown Rats and star of the film version of *The Wall*) organized Live Aid. Frank Zappa took a stand against Tipper Gore's parental advisory stickers. Pearl Jam used the media to crusade against Ticketmaster's monopoly and ever-increasing concert ticket fees. Bono appeared on *60 Minutes* and expressed his views on relieving third-world countries of their debt. (By the way, Bono is the only person who's been nominated for a Nobel Peace Prize, Oscar, Grammy, and Golden Globe.) There are hundreds, if not thousands, of examples of rock stars doing good deeds—many through their own charitable foundations.

Businesses that give back to their community (and society) are usually rewarded with extra exposure in the media—and much good karma. Assign your business to a cause. Perhaps your business can support the cause through pro-bono services. Or maybe (if the cause is youth-oriented), your company can fund a trip for the kids to a pro basketball game. Or how about giving your employees a day off—as long as they dedicate that day to helping a non-profit group? The possibilities are endless.

Lastly, it feels freakin' great to see your name in print. There aren't many bigger boosts to your ego like appearing in the media. It's everything you need and want in one package. As an entrepreneur, you get a little sense of celebrity, you reach a larger audience of potential customers, you have instant validation from a respected third party, and your family and friends are dripping with envy—not to mention your competition starts feeling a little inferior.

BE ACCESSIBLE

To increase your chances of becoming a media star there are a few things you can do. The most obvious is to be available and easy to reach. Playing hard to get is for superstars or those rare people in life who seem cosmically tapped for greatness. The rest of us have to play nice and work it.

Consider Scott Ian of Anthrax. It seems he is *always* on VH-1 and MTV, as well as other reality shows—which makes us wonder if it's his knowledge of rock music or his accessibility that make him a frequent guest. Having a system to track what press kits or prototypes went to whom is necessary to be a frequent guest. The most important part of getting media exposure isn't sexy, timely, convincing, or compelling human interest stories (although that helps)—it's follow-up. Without follow-up something terrible happens: nothing.

Handling your own PR requires organization and a thick skin. You'll hear "no" a lot, but it only takes one "yes" to get your campaign off the ground. Once you land an interview, make sure to be the best guest you can be (before, during, and after the interview) so you're invited back. A reporter asked John Lennon, "Was your family in show business?" Without missing a beat, he answered back, "Well, me dad used to say me mum was a great performer." Lennon was almost always a great interview, and the Beatles earned much air time as a result.

True story: In 1972, Electric Light Orchestra was about to release their debut album with United Artists, but when the label's representative was unable to reach their manager, he wrote a note that read, "No answer." And that's what ELO's album ended up being titled.

HOW ROCK STARS MASTER THE MEDIA

The Plan

When you take a look at what happens behind the scenes of a major rock band, you quickly realize why members thank everyone and their brother when they win a Grammy. It takes a small army to run the business of a band. In addition to the lawyers, accountants, techs, roadies, personal chefs, drivers, and managers, there are the publicity people. With really big bands there will be a person handling publicity for the label, another for the band, and in some cases, individual band members will have their own publicists. These efforts are usually coordinated

WHY THE MEDIA NEEDS YOU

You may not realize it, but being in business for yourself (rather than working for the man) makes you special. Ask anyone working a 9-to-5, dead-end job who earns what feels like minimum wage and has to deal with Dilbert-like management and they'll tell you, being your own boss is better.

Business people are a little like rock stars because it's a gutsy and cool thing to own your own company. (I know, it's not all glitz and glamour, but the media doesn't know that–they have real jobs.) So when you can pitch your product or service in a way that makes sense for the news, a radio talk show, or a publication, you have a legitimate chance to publicize your business. Why? They need interesting stories (content) and good guests– and they don't have the time to go out and get them. So, if you contact them with an interesting, compelling, timely, newsworthy, informative story idea, they may just take you up on it.

There are more media than ever before and they all need content. Add to that a short-age of editors, writers, and producers, and that means the media wants ready-to-roll story ideas that fit their format. They need to fill up the space between ads (I know, that sounds so crass, but it's true) and if you can help them do that–and increase their audience share– you will be on the air faster than you can say "Gene Simmons."

with a publicity plan. (Publicity usually doesn't just happen; it's an organized, synchronized, and strategized effort.)

Record companies lay out an elaborate plan for the release of an album–much of the effort being focused on building a buzz before the record even ships. This is nothing new, though. In 1969, Columbia Records signed unproven guitarist Johnny Winter for an unprecedented amount–hundreds of thousands of dollars. (It should be noted he was discovered, in part, due to a favorable review in *Rolling Stone* about his band, Winter, and the Texas music scene.) Obviously, Columbia planned to get that money back from record sales. So, to ensure the success of their newest (and most expensive) act, the label pulled out all the stops and embarked on a massive media campaign. Even though the album didn't produce a hit single, the publicity led to solid sales.

Now, almost thirty years later, with more media outlets than ever before, a choreographed and concerted effort is made to launch everything in rock music, from a new release to a worldwide tour. When Todd Rundgren went out on the New Cars "Roadrage" tour, he and original Cars' member Ric Ocasek appeared on *The Colbert Report*. They appeared to be feuding because Ocasek wasn't going on the road with the band, but the truth is, it could all have been an act. Ocasek had actually approved of Rudgren as replacement for Benjamin Orr because he sounded so similar. The appearance and argument were timed just before the tour started. Hmmmm . . .

The Hook

A hook is used to describe a catchy chorus—and a well-conceived approach to promotion and publicity. It can be something as simple as tying the release of an album to a timely date, like Black Sabbath did when they released their first album on Friday the 13th, February 1970. Or, you can take something unique about your brand and tie it in with something related, like Queen did when they rented the Queen Mary for the release party for *Innuendo*.

Many rock stars mine their past for memorable and personal "human interest" stories. A story about a band that's touching, inspiring, or interesting becomes the hook and is repeated and retold many times over. Vincent Furnier renamed himself Alice Cooper and dressed in ghoulish drag because—here's the hook—he was a "reincarnated witch." The story, very bizarre in that era, was eaten up by the press and his shows literally took on mythic proportions.

Mixed Media

There was a time when doctors and lawyers weren't allowed to advertise on television. Ahhh, the good old days. There was also a time when a rock star would never pitch a product unless they were desperate. Now recording artists are not only lending their music to commercials, they are appearing in them, including: Gwen Stefani (HP), Alice Cooper (Staples), Ozzy Osborne (I Can't Believe It's Not Butter), and Little

Richard and Peter Frampton (Geico). As far as we know, none of them are exactly desperate.

Truth is, it can be great exposure for an artist–and they get paid. Sheryl Crow was quoted in a *60 Minutes* segment as saying she made $40,000 on her McDonald's commercial alone (she sang)–and this was *before* she was a big star. This makes us wonder what a relatively unknown reggae band like Common Sense (they are regulars at a place called the Belly-Up Tavern in San Diego) made from having Ford use one of their songs in a commercial? It seems common sense is good business sense.

Here's a good example of mixed media making a name for an obscure artist. (If an unknown artist from Israel, living in Paris, can make it in the U.S., so can you.) Yael Naim recorded a modest album in her Paris apartment in 2005 and released it in Israel only. But Apple Computers discovered and used one of her tunes, "New Soul," in an ad for their MacBook Air in early 2008. As a result, it shot up the chart to #7 on Billboard's Hot 100 and #1 on iTunes. (Some longtime rock stars haven't even done that.) Apple also helped Feist by using her song "1234" in an iPod Nano spot. If she was using a Windows computer before, we bet she's an Apple fan now.

Awards and Contests

Alanis Morisette appeared on *Star Search* in 1989, but didn't win. Lynyrd Skynyrd got their first record deal from winning a local Battle of the Bands contest. *American Idol* is a lot like a *Star Search* or a Battle of the Bands, where the winner (and often runners-up) gets a recording contract and a solid fan base. The difference is in scope. *American Idol* winner Taylor Hicks (2006) has sold 700,000 copies of his first album. Chris Daughtry (who didn't win) has sold over 3.8 million copies of his debut album. Season-one winner Kelly Clarkson, however, has sold over sixteen million records– as much as many bands who've been around longer than she's been alive.

On the other hand, you can always create and publicize your own contest like Carly Simon did. Her closely held secret about who is the subject of her famous song "You're So Vain" became a major media event–and a contest. Is it one of her ex-beaus: James Taylor, Warren

Beatty, Cat Stevens, or Kris Kristofferson? Is it Mick Jagger who also sings on the song? In 2003, she auctioned off revealing the name for a charity benefit and the highest bidder took the prize for $50,000. He was sworn to secrecy, but did slyly say the person's name has an "e" in it. Every news media covered the story, did polls, speculated, and created lots of exposure for Carly Simon and her song. Lastly, when it comes to awards (at least in music), nothing is more coveted than a Grammy. And no band has won more of them (and received the media attention that results) than U2, with twenty-two and counting.

Affiliations

It's nice when you can name drop Elvis Presley and say he's into your music. That's what Wanda Jackson, a rockabilly star in the late '50s was able to do. Elvis was her mentor and boyfriend and helped her with her hit "Let's Have a Party." Speaking of hooking up, when obscure Austin-based recording artist Bob Schneider started dating actress Sandra Bollock (who had moved to the Texas town), he saw a rise in his career. And it certainly didn't hurt the Cars' Rick Ocasek and his credibility when he dated and married supermodel Paulina Porizkova.

Crosby, Stills, Nash & Young was a side band for Neil Young while he was still in Crazy Horse. Mostly he was an instrumentalist in CSNY and sang a few songs, but he loved working with the talent of the other three without having to be out front. The result, however, was greater exposure for Young (being in not one, but two significant bands), and he made sure the "& Young" was part of the band's name. (Not one to shy away from publicity, during Young's days in Buffalo Springfield, he drove around in a hearse as a way to make a big entrance.)

There are hundreds of examples of rock stars opening for larger acts to get their name out (and in the paper), but a notable one was Def Leppard opening for Billy Squier in the early 1980s. After some time, Def Leppard was so popular (and upstaged Squier) that they became a headliner themselves. And many bands in the late '70s didn't want the up-and-coming AC/DC to open for them for fear of being out-rocked. (Good publicity for AC/DC, but not for the main band.)

Being the best at what you do is a worthy goal in and of itself, but it also can lead to more media opportunities. Take Alan Holdsworth, for example. Eric Clapton may be a guitar god, but Holdsworth is a guitar hero's guitar hero. A fearless improviser with a finely tuned sense of texture and dynamics, he is a master musician. It was his guitar virtuosity and industry media attention that prompted Eddie Van Halen to help get him a record deal.

Gossip Is Good

Couplings involving rock stars that made the "news" over the years include: Jackson Browne with Daryl Hannah; Linda Ronstadt with Albert Brooks, George Lucas, and Jerry Brown; Joni Mitchell with Graham Nash; Paul Simon with Edie Brickell; David Coverdale (Whitesnake) with Tawney Kitaen; Eddie Van Halen with Valerie Bertinelli; Tommy Lee (Motley Crue) with Heather Locklear and Pamela Anderson; Pamela Anderson with Kid Rock; Adam Duritz (Counting Crows) with Courtney Cox and Jennifer Aniston; Fred Durst (Limp Bizkit) with Britney Spears; Chris Martin with Gwenyth Paltrow; Sheryl Crow with Lance Armstrong; and Gwen Stefani with Gavin Rossdale (Bush).

All of these romances generated moderate to major publicity in both tabloids and standard news outlets, and some were rumored to have occurred (or were faked) purely for the publicity. Next time you hear of a rock star romance, check further and you may just find they (or their partner) have a current project to publicize.

Touring

Bands go on tour for a number of reasons—most obviously for money, fun, and adulation—being out on the road performing also leads to PR. In 1994, Rod Stewart performed a free concert in Brazil for 3.5 million people, which has got to be some kind of record, and was covered in most major world media for it. Simon and Garfunkel's famous free performance in Central Park (in the rain) was more than memorable and publicized—it was recorded and sold. The Rolling Stones pulled out of

THE COVER OF THE *ROLLING STONE*

Jan Wenner borrowed $7,500 from his wife's parents to start a magazine about the music scene. *Rolling Stone* launched in November of 1967 with John Lennon on the cover. Although 40,000 copies were printed, only 6,000 sold. With a groundbreaking approach to journalism and coverage of the booming rock music scene, the magazine slowly gained a following among rock fans and musicians. By 1973, *Rolling Stone* had achieved legitimacy, as immortalized in the hilarious ditty by Dr. Hook and the Medicine Show called "The Cover of the *Rolling Stone*." The song marked the honor it was, and still is, to appear on the magazine's cover. Today, *Rolling Stone* has a readership of over a million fans, and the magazine's estimated value is around $2 billion.

the Glastonbury Festival in Somerset in 1995, and the band Pulp stepped into the headline spot and had the 40,000 audience members singing along to their song "Common People." How much press coverage would Pulp have likely gotten had they not found themselves in such an extraordinary situation?

Whether a rock band or a business, getting out "on tour" is a good path to publicity. In 2007, Tim Westergren, CEO and founder of the Internet radio service Pandora.com, went on tour to speak to many of Pandora's six million customers through presentations all across the U.S. Not only did that result in local media coverage (which presumably led more people to discover Pandora), it also gave him a chance to get valuable feedback from Pandora fans. The events were even complete with much of the same memorabilia you'd see at a rock concert— T-shirts, hats, and other items—though, unlike at a rock concert, they were given away.

Be Different, Daring, and Controversial

Nothing, and we mean nothing, tops the story involving Ozzy Osbourne and a dove. (He bit the head off the little bird during a meeting with record executives.) The doves were to be released to signify the launch of the new album, but Ozzy had other ideas. Which makes us think of Alice Cooper, who once quipped, "I've never killed a chicken on stage. Well, not purposely, anyway."

Cooper was first signed by Frank Zappa's label (aptly called Bizarre) but moved to Warner Bros. for his *Love It to Death* and *Killer* albums in 1971. In 1972, he wanted to wrap each copy of his new album *School's Out* in disposable panties. The panties weren't up to code (they were flammable) and the publicity surrounding this was priceless. He then dumped thousands of panties from a helicopter at a Hollywood Bowl concert later that year.

In addition to biting the heads off small animals or bombing your fans with panties, blowing up or lighting your instruments on fire has been newsworthy in the rock world. Keith Moon of the Who blew up his drums during an appearance on *The Smother Brothers Show*, using triple the explosives originally meant for the stunt. And one of the most memorable moments in rock history certainly is Jimi Hendrix setting fire to his guitar at the Monterey Pop Festival in 1967. Less radical, but still worthy of media interest, can be your hobbies or part-time pursuits. Donovan Frankenreiter and Jack Johnson are professional surfers. David Lee Roth has worked as a New York City paramedic. And that rock star of an entrepreneur, Richard Branson, is a licensed pilot. Speaking of which, both Bruce Dickinson and Nicko McBrain of Iron Maiden are licensed pilots—in fact, Dickinson is a part-time pilot for British Airways.

Hometown Heroes First

Tori Amos is a winner. In 1977, she won a county "teen talent" contest by singing a song called "More Than Just a Friend." And during her high school years, she became well known in the Washington, D.C. area—and was elected Homecoming Queen, Most Likely to Succeed, and Most Talented at her high school. During this time, Amos also co-wrote "Baltimore" with her brother Mike for a competition involving the pro baseball team Baltimore Orioles. The song won the contest and became her first single. Since then, the singer-songwriter (and pianist) has gone on to sell over twelve million records worldwide and enjoys a large following here and overseas.

Most artists start out as hometown heroes and then branch out. Before becoming a national sensation, Kid Rock first won over the Motor City, Nirvana was big on the Seattle scene, and No Doubt were the darlings of Orange County, California. Taylor Swift was first featured in *Sea Ray Living* magazine, a publication for the owners of Sea Ray boats. (Her parents own a Sundancer.) So, don't forget the trade mags.

The threesome of Rush frequently appear in rock music magazines—Neil Peart in *Modern Drummer*, Alex Lifeson in *Guitar Player*, and Geddy Lee in *Bass Player*. Hometown followings are often built by doing "meet-and-greet" events with fans or industry insiders. For her debut album, singer-songwriter Treana performed live acoustic sets at music industry magazine offices and radio stations, blowing them away with her passionate music. The result: numerous excellent write-ups and positive reviews.

Be the News

Perry Farrell, the lead singer for Jane's Addiction was frustrated by the lack of media attention and airplay for independent artists, so he started the Lollapalooza tour in 1991—which reached 600,000 fans in twenty-one cities that year and included many prominent bands of the year, such as Living Colour, Violent Femmes, Nine Inch Nails, and Butthole Surfers. Farrell later sold the rights to the festival to the William Morris Agency for a tidy sum, and the announcement made the news.

Almost every band has a way to communicate with their fans—via websites, blogs, and newsletters—and create their own news. Linkin Park even has its own online news outlet, *LP Times*. And more than a few rockers were members of the media before becoming stars, including Mark Knopfler (who was a reporter and music critic for the *Yorkshire Evening Post*) and Jimmy Buffett (who wrote for *Billboard* magazine). But maybe the most involved in the media is Mark McGrath, lead singer of the band Sugar Ray and currently the host of the television entertainment show *Extra*. (McGrath majored in Business Communication at the University of Southern California's Marshall School of Business.)

Set Records

The world record for deepest underwater concert ever performed in front of an audience is held by singer Kate Melua and her band. They were flown by helicopter to an oil-drilling platform off the coast of Norway where they then descended by elevator to a depth of nearly 1,000 feet for their show. The gig was an anniversary celebration of the platform and the audience was the oil workers. Her feat has put her in the *Guinness Book of World Records*, which sells over a million copies a year.

NOT ALL PUBLICITY IS GOOD PUBLICITY

We're sure you've heard that any publicity is good publicity, but that's not always true. In 1966, John Lennon half-joked that the Beatles were more important that Jesus. Hmmm, not good. This led to quite a backlash, and Beatles' albums were burned by angry Christians (and some non-Christians) throughout the U.S. (Ringo Starr had the best line, though, when he joked that "they have to buy them to burn them.")

And then there's the worst publicity. In 1974, a fourteen-year-old girl died at a David Cassidy concert in London, and, five years later, eleven people died at a Who concert in Cincinnati. No one wants a tragedy like that to occur under any circumstances. But it's also true that no one wants their name and brand associated with tragedy either.

On the lighter side, since reality shows have become so popular, rock stars have jumped on the trend with Ozzy Osbourne, Travis Barker (Blink 182), Tommy Lee (Motley Crue), Brett Michaels (Poison), Gene Simmons (KISS), and Vince Neil (Motley Crue) all gaining exposure through their own shows. But there's a balance, and it's questionable whether the shows are actually good publicity. After all, isn't Ozzy's stature diminished just a little when we see him shuffling around his mansion, reminding you of your medicated grandfather? Or how about watching Vince Neil get a facelift? It's nice to see your name and face in the media, but not when it's attached to negative perceptions.

Speaking of negative perceptions, after successful albums like *Stand Up, Aqualung, Thick as a Brick,* and *Living in the Past,* the media lambasted

Jethro Tull's next release, *Passion Play*. But despite the poor reviews, it still sold very well, and the band sold out virtually every date on the accompanying tour. However, the hostile attack on the album did have a negative effect on the band members.

And lastly, be aware of the "law of unintended consequences." In 1967, San Francisco band Moby Grape had become one of the premier psychadelic bands to come out of the Bay Area and even experienced a bidding war from record labels to sign them. Columbia Records won, and work began on the band's self-titled first album. Once it was released in the summer of that year, Columbia wanted to capitalize on the popularity of the psychadelic rock movement and released an unprecendented five singles from the album at once. (They eventually released ten of the thirteen songs on the album as singles.) Moby Grape experienced much success that year, including a coveted slot at the Monterey Pop Festival, but their second album the following year didn't fare well at all. Even though it charted at #20, sales were not as expected, and the band never regained their initial popularity.

Although no one can be sure exactly what happened, the prevailing theory is that there was simply too much hype and overexposure at first with the multitude of singles that Columbia released. Nearly a decade later, a similar thing happened with KISS when their label shipped five million copies of the members' simultaneous solo albums. Although an apparently clever publicity move—no band had ever released solo albums by each member at the same time—the flood of albums resulted in massive returns of unsold albums from stores and the first-ever appearance of KISS records in bargain bins. They went from being the most-popular and highest-earning band of 1978 into a rapid decline that they wouldn't recover from for many years.

RAVING FANS

Achieving Lasting Success through Loyal Customers

"You can be out of tune or play the wrong note, but if you can put a smile on someone's face then I figure we're successful."
–GEORGE THOROGOOD AND THE DESTROYERS–

It's been said in business that it's less expensive to retain your existing customers than it is to recruit new ones. The mantra is to build a solid base of customers and make them happy. Not to say you can't or shouldn't go after new ones–but make sure you cultivate those you already have.

Savvy rock stars are keenly aware of this. They've worked very hard, perhaps playing in smelly bars night after night for years, to build their following. Fans may come and go due to radio airplay or what's popular at the moment, but the true fans are where a rock star's perennial income is derived. The most successful businesses build a solid following of raving fans. The word "fan" comes from "fanatic"–and you need customers who are fanatic about your business.

TALKIN' 'BOUT MY GENERATION

Perhaps there's no better way to have raving fans than to give them plenty of reasons to talk about you or your products. And there aren't many things rock stars excel at more than this.

Going back to Elvis's gyrating hips and the Beatles' mop-top haircuts, rock stars have done what it takes to get people to talk about them. Most people hadn't heard of Bruce Springsteen in 1964, but when *Rolling Stone* columnist Jon Landau saw him that year in Boston, he declared in the magazine, "I saw rock and roll's future, and its name is Bruce Springsteen." It was the legendary rocker's energy and passion, not clever theatrics, that were so impressive. It doesn't always have to be Jimi Hendrix lighting his guitar on fire to get people to talk (though it doesn't hurt). And you also never know who's watching, so give it your all.

On that end of the spectrum, you have the performers who didn't (or don't) rely too much on theatrics, but blow you away with other aspects of their show—Springsteen, Sevendust, Peter Frampton, Cream, the Grateful Dead, Nirvana, and Foo Fighters, for example. And then on the other end, you have those who took the show to a whole new level—KISS, Queen, David Bowie as Ziggy Stardust, Pink Floyd, Alice Cooper, Jimmy Buffett, Hendrix, Slipknot, and the Who. How can you blow away your customers or take your show to a whole new level?

What it comes down to is putting on a show, whether it's "showy" or just a great experience. The most talked-about rock stars, and almost invariably the ones with a massive fan base, are those who truly put on a show. Nowadays, with so much competition for nearly any product or service, customers are drawn to the experience. Starbucks recognized this and capitalized on it. Instead of a cup of decent (or not-so-decent coffee) served in a plain-white Styrofoam cup from a grumbly waitress in a diner (the pre-Starbucks' experience), you can now get an exceptional cup of coffee or at least a trendy coffee drink in an environment that's inviting, welcoming, and classy. And we're not just talking about Starbucks—its competitors on the national, regional, and local level have all done the same to some degree. As a result, you have *teenagers* drinking coffee, something that was unheard of just over a decade ago.

When Apple opened its retail stores, including its ingenius Genius Bars, no one had quite seen a store like that. The stores were sleek, stylish, high-tech, ultra-modern—you almost thought you'd stepped into the Starship Enterprise. And, of course, it fit the Apple brand, matching the artistry with which Apple redefined (and redesigned) the personal computer. Gone was the boring beige world of PCs, and gone was the uninspired computer store.

Even Apple product releases are an event (once Steve Jobs thankfully returned to the helm). With showmanship worthy of the best concert, even a product as physically small as the iPod is launched on a huge scale with a big event to match. Apple has created a rock-star image around its brand that other PC and software companies have yet to match. And talk to the devotees of Apple and its Mac computers (such as the authors of this book), and you'll talk to truly raving fans.

Speaking of raving fans, there is perhaps no better testimony than having a tribute band. When that happens, it means a band's fan base is so big and so demanding that the band itself can't even satisfy the desire. Out of this crops up a tribute band—not just a cover band, but one that endeavors to capture the live show of the original band in all its glory. Of course, it's literally the next best thing, but that doesn't mean it isn't great. Fans worldwide love Led Zeppagain, an impressive and faithful tribute to Led Zepplin.

Zeppagain and many other bands rise above the typical small-club tribute status and develop raving fan bases of their own, playing before hundreds of thousands of people on tours all over the world. Some tribute bands become so numerous (for one original band) that they have to get clever to develop their own niche—of the many Zepplin tribute bands, there's one called Dread Zepplin, which plays with a reggae beat and features an Elvis impersonator as singer.

Among the many KISS tributes is one called MiniKISS, with members who are all little people. And yet another niche is all-female tribute bands, such as AC/DShe and Iron Maidens. Needless to say, the tribute band members themselves are raving fans, creating their ventures as a way of honoring their favorite bands and doing something they love for a living. One such fan, Tim Owens, went from being the singer for British Steel (a Judas Priest tribute) to being the singer for the actual Judas Priest when their longtime singer, Rob Halford, departed.

Owens' tribute performance was so good he was a natural replacement. And all of the contestants on the 2005 TV reality show *Rock Star: INXS* were huge fans of the INXS, especially the winner, J.D. Fortune.

Okay, but what does this all have to do with your business? Well, more than anything (besides doing what you can to create raving fans), it means do what you can to replicate yourself or your business. In some ways, tribute bands are like franchises. Instead of one McDonalds, Ray Kroc knew there would be more profit if there were clones all over the U.S. (And smartly, part of that plan was owning the land under all those stores.) And while tribute bands aren't (usually) created by the original band, they pay licensing fees for the music and certainly promote the original band in the process.

In the "real" business world, another form of this replication is licensed contractors. PrePaid Legal is a company that has spread like crazy because of its model, licensing the use of its name and services to individual entrepreneurs. In the world of corporate training, many aspiring trainers sign up with a major training company—Tony Robbins, Ken Blanchard, et al.—go through their certification program and become official "Robbins Company" trainers. Despite his larger-than-life persona, Tony Robbins can't be everywhere, but he sure can spread his name and wisdom (and reap the profits) through this approach.

YOU WANTED THE BEST—YOU GOT THE BEST

Being a fantastic rock star doesn't always mean an extravagant show—some of the best have had long stretches without touring. But, when it came to their musicianship, you were simply in awe. (The Beatles didn't tour after 1966, during which time they released some of their most acclaimed work.) If you're over forty, that moment of feeling awestruck probably first came sitting in front of a turntable with clunky headphones engulfing your ears; if you're under twenty, that moment could've come anywhere, but you probably had your iPod in your pocket with your earbuds in your ears.

Perhaps it was a Jimi Hendrix or Led Zepplin album in 1974. Or perhaps it was an Iron Maiden or Rush cassette tape in 1984. Or possibly it was an Oasis or Nirvana CD in 1994. Or maybe it was a 3 Doors Down or Puddle of Mudd download in 2004. Regardless, the connection was made through the amazing product you were experiencing. Bands and musicians who have pushed the boundaries and dedicated themselves to the craft of music are well represented among the most successful. (Doing so doesn't guarantee success, of course, but rockers who *didn't* think outside the box artistically or mastered their music are noticeably absent from the rock-and-roll hall of fame.)

Success in business requires bucking trends, or at least bending them. Guns N' Roses literally exploded onto the scene in 1987 by injecting a harder and authentically angry edge back into a genre that had become "lite" and too pop. But it didn't happen without a little push. MTV initially rejected their video for "Welcome to the Jungle," but with the band manager's persistence the influential network finally decided to air the video—just once at 4 a.m. eastern time. Nonetheless (and perhaps because it was still only 1 a.m. on the west coast), calls flooded in requesting more of the video. Very quickly, riding on heavy MTV rotation, the song was picked up by radio stations nationwide, and the album *Appetite for Destruction* made Guns N' Roses one of the few bands to experience over a million sales of their first release.

Nirvana, Pearl Jam, Soundgarden, Alice in Chains, and the Seattle grunge movement were counter to the glam-rock trend of the mid-late 1980s. Gone was the look of guys who apparently spent hours getting dressed and made up for a concert and in came the look of guys who apparently slept in their clothes and just got out of bed. But it worked. And numerous bands who were knocking on the door of glam-rock success in 1990 or 1991 suddenly found themselves yesterday's news.

Similarly, Black Sabbath's dark style and sound was an intentional effort to differentiate themselves from the popular "peace, love, and flower-power" bands of the late 1960s.

First, strive to be great in your business. Perfect your craft, whatever it may be. If yours is a knowledge-based business, such as consulting, your knowledge should be honed on a daily basis, just as a drummer practices timing on a daily basis. If yours is a service-oriented business, streamline your processes and strive to deliver outstanding service with a smile. Second, watch what's going on around you, especially your competition. Observe the trends. If everyone is doing the same thing, how will your business stand out just doing more of that same thing? While it may not be possible, at least consider going completely counter to the trend, as Black Sabbath and Soundgarden did. You may just find your business being the leader of a whole new trend.

BEING ELUSIVE OR EXCLUSIVE

An age-old technique to pique attraction is elusiveness or exclusivity, and many savvy and successful rock stars have used this approach to build and hold onto their fans.

Perhaps the most extensive example of this is KISS. Although their use of makeup was more of a branding effort on the part of founder Gene Simmons, the accompanying mystique led to a truly raving fan base for years. Rock and teen magazines in the mid-late 1970s willingly went along with the plan, not publishing photos of the band without makeup to perpetuate the interest (and magazine sales). It was even said at the time that photos of the band without makeup didn't exist or had been destroyed, although this was later admitted to be purely a ploy. But what a successful ploy that was. And in 1983, when KISS's popularity had already waned for a few years, the band's "unmasking" on MTV was a huge event, earning significant ratings for the network and setting up the band for another stretch of success through the 1980s.

More than any other band, the Beatles were who Gene Simmons based his commercial vision on, and they had their own flavor of elusiveness. In 1966, following a successful show at Candlestick Park in San Francisco, the Fab Four did no more paying concerts. The move, normally a death knell to any band's success (touring is considered imperative), only solidified their legendary status. Sales of their subsequent albums were significantly greater, and their less-public presence even allowed them to cleverly perpetuate the rumor that Paul McCartney had died—leading to plenty of gossip, fan talk, and media speculation.

Like the Beatles, other bands generated fan frenzies by being unavailable. Promoting their new album *The Wall* in 1980, Pink Floyd only performed in two cities in the U.S. (New York and Los Angeles) and only three others in the world, generating quite a buzz among fans and boosting the value and prestige of tickets. And Steely Dan went for a stretch of years without doing a show, creating quite a demand.

How can your business be more elusive or exclusive? Many service professionals have discovered that being unavailable actually creates more demand. A consultant we know is typically booked two to three months in advance; however, it doesn't slow the numbers of clients who hire her. Not being *too* available tends to make potential customers think, "Wow, they must be good." Some restaurants and clubs have special rooms reserved only for VIPs and clientele that run high tabs. This air of distinction not only boosts the egos of those with access to these rooms, but it also rubs off on patrons who can only get into the "normal" sections. At least they are in the same establishment.

While being unreachable can lead to fan engagement and loyalty, being partially available ultimately seems to work the best.

Many bands do this through backstage passes, VIP lounges, and after-show mixers—allowing just enough concert-goers to have access to them to make them (the fans) feel special and talk about the experience with others. Other public events such as signings in record stores (are there any of those anymore?) and promotional parties allow select fans to meet the band, and many more to wish they could. Veteran rocker Ronnie James Dio (Black Sabbath, Dio) earned a reputation for sticking around after every show, sometimes spending up to five hours meeting people and signing autographs.

Some band members extend this availability by heading out to clubs and bars after their concerts where they mix and mingle with fans. Supertramp took this one step further, playing entire sets at nearby clubs after concerts.

Other bands make themselves partially available to fans by playing "anonymous" shows. Putting these concerts on under a pseudonym, usually at small venues, allows them to put the word out to chosen fans and offer limited tickets. Iron Maiden reportedly did this in a British town, masquerading under the name "Free Beer." Having this name on the marquee of the club certainly attracted attention.

THE CARE AND KEEPING OF FANS AND CUSTOMERS

Some of the previous examples—backstage passes, exclusive shows, hanging out with fans at clubs—certainly go a long way toward fan retention. But successful bands know they have to be dedicated to keeping their followers loyal.

Perhaps the most obvious mechanism is the fan club. Now there are fan clubs and then are *fan clubs*. One of the most well known are the Deadheads, devotees of the Grateful Dead. The most fanatic of Deadheads traveled the country following the tour from city to city. But this wouldn't have lasted long had the Dead not returned the favor with stunning shows. Knowing they had the most exceptional of fan bases, the Dead did everything they could to deliver—extensive jam sessions in concert, variations on songs, allowing fans to record their shows, and generally creating an atmosphere unlike any other. As a result, they played before stadium-filled crowds on their tours year after year.

A similar culture of fans has followed Jimmy Buffett as well. Known as Parrotheads, they are a dedicated bunch, and Buffett never lets them down. Like a Dead concert, a Buffett concert is an *experience*, often lasting all day and night with fan-organized activities running peripheral to the actual show.

And lastly, mention of extreme fan clubs would be incomplete without mentioning the KISS Army, at its most popular in the late '70s. Serious fans of the larger-than-life band weren't just in a club, they were in an *army*, complete with ranks and officers. Unlike Deadheads and Parrotheads, the KISS Army was officially created by the band to engage the fans. Following the credo of "give them a little something extra," the KISS Army bestowed upon its members all sorts of cool memorabilia unavailable elsewhere, such as exclusive patches and posters.

People need to feel connected, especially in this digital-online age. Have you ever noticed how concert-goers scream when the singer says, "Hello, Cleveland!" (or whatever city or town the concert is in). Listen to the live version of Journey's song, and you'll hear the crowd go wild when Steve Perry puts their city's name (Houston) in place of Detroit in the lyrics. So, give your fans (customers) an experience and make them feel special. Connect with them. This is why so many bands and musicians (and entrepreneurs) have jumped on the social-networking sites MySpace and Facebook. It allows them an easy, free, and hip way to interact with their fans.

YOUR WEBSITE

Does your website interact with your customers, or does it just sit there blabbing sales information at them? What could you do to make it more cool? For answers to these questions and more, check out the websites of some of the big rock stars.

We mentioned Jimmy Buffett and his Margaritaville culture earlier, and if you're not familiar with it, you can check it out at www.margarita ville.com. What an incredible way to interact with fans—there's a radio station, exclusive videos, contests, the latest news, discussion boards, recipes (using Buffett's products, of course), and more.

Korn's website (www.korn.com) is another great example of fan involvement. Aside from providing all their music videos (good product sampling), they invite fans to submit photos they've taken at concerts. Korn also has a music club (paid members only) that offers exclusive music and behind-the-scenes videos, collaborations, backstage passes, a special fan discussion board, and pre-sale concert tickets.

The key is offering cutting-edge interaction, online exclusivity, and attitude. At first glance, the Monster Energy drink website (www.Monster Energy.com) could be mistaken for a rock band's. While this definitely fits their target market, it's important to realize the rock-star approach can work for most any site. A good example is the site for the TV show *The Big Idea with Donnie Deutsch* (www.BigIdeaDonny.com). Lastly, we humbly submit for your approval an example of a website that has what we're talking about—this book's site (www.RockToRiches book.com).

DELIVER THE GOODS

"Dimebag Darrell" Abbott was so enthralled with KISS that he had a tattoo of guitarist Ace Frehley on his chest. And he ultimately did well for himself as the co-founder of Pantera, a metal band that sold millions of records. Do you think KISS delivered the goods as far as Dimebag Darrell was concerned? Most certainly. Ultimately, regardless of how (and how many) ways you connect with your fans, your business needs to deliver the goods.

You can create the best product in the world, but if customers have a hard time with your ordering process and are abandoning their online shopping carts, then it doesn't matter. Conversely, you can have the best website in the world, but if your product is inferior in some way and your customers don't buy or recommend it, then it doesn't matter either. You must deliver on all counts. In Chapter Three, "The 'It' Factor," we discussed your brand promise. It's this promise that you need to honor to keep and cultivate your customers (as well as gain new ones). *Nothing* in this book matters if you don't do this. Yes, profit is the lifeblood of any business, but without keeping your brand promise—without delivering the goods—there will be no profit.

SUMMING IT UP

Most of your customers are hard-earned. With the ever-increasing array of choices they have nowadays, customers are more fickle than ever. Advertising and promotional budgets—or at least promotional creativity—need to be higher than ever. Even Starbucks, having gone for years without advertising, is now running spots on radio due to market intrusion (by McDonald's of all companies!).

It's imperative that customers be converted to raving fans. Merely providing a good service or product is not often enough; customers need to interact with your brand. And to be a true rock star of a business, it's necessary to think beyond what's currently being done. Sure, have a discussion board on your website, but what can you do to break out of the pack? What can you do with your customers that's super cool and never been done? A contest where the winner "runs" your company for a day? A website where your customers can choose from a dozen looks of the site (goth, fun, cartoony, industrial, animals, etc.) to suit their styles? Only you can decide. But if you want truly legendary rocker status, start thinking outside the box.

FROM ROCK TO RICHES

It's the Profits, Stupid

"I would rather be rich than famous. That is, slightly more rich and slightly less famous."

–JOHN LENNON–

What They Earned (2007)

$88 Million	The Rolling Stones
$67 Million	Bon Jovi
$30 Million	U2
$150 Thousand	Singer in Led Zeppelin Tribute Band
$45 Thousand	Average Indie-Rock Musician
$40 Thousand	Average Touring Musician

Source: *SPIN*, April 2008

Tom Petty is quoted as saying, "The more you get, the more you get." That is so true for both bands and businesses. Sales numbers are to bands like batting averages are to baseball players–everything. When it comes to a lasting career in the music business, you're only as good as your most recent record sales. Many prominent bands were dropped or threatened with being dropped by their record company due to slow sales. Labels cut unprofitable acts faster than you can say Slash. The reason for this is obvious; it's called the music BUSINESS. The goal is to make money, and strong sales usually mean the record company (and the band) earn more.

For a business owner, sales are important, make that very important, but not the best barometer of success. There is nothing *more* important to a business than the bottom-line. It's all about the PROFITS (as long as they're ethically earned). And if it's not, it should be, because breaking even (or losing money) isn't going to lead to lasting success. It doesn't take an accountant to figure out that the difference between what you earn and what you spend is your profit–and being in business is about profits. And if you aren't earning a profit, you are doing something wrong–it's that simple.

This basic idea seems to escape a lot of smart people. So does the principle that your focus should be on earning as much as you can, spending as little as you have to, and then investing the rest (either back into building your business or something else that will earn you more money on your money.) No matter what you want to do with your business–build it bigger, sell it, go public, pass it on to your kids–profit is of the utmost importance.

Make a commitment to be prosperous and profitable from this day forward, because being profitable starts in your head (your mindset) and is manifested in the decisions you make. And making more than you spend isn't only important for a business; this same approach should also be applied to personal finances. If you struggle managing money in your personal life, chances are, you'll also have financial trouble in your business endeavors as well.

"John and I literally used to sit down and say, 'Now, let's write a swimming pool,'" Paul McCartney was quoted as saying. We know they wrote dozens of "swimming pools," but being in business doesn't guarantee a profit, not even for the Beatles. The Beatles' label, Apple, was a mixed bag. On one hand, they signed James Taylor–but his success came after he left the label. On the other hand, Badfinger (originally called the Iveys) had hits on the Apple label (including some written or produced by ex-Beatles McCartney and Harrison). It might've helped that they sounded a lot like the Beatles. In fact, some fans even thought they were the Beatles under an assumed name. Regardless, they had significant success with hits such as "Come and Get It," "No Matter What," "Day After Day," and "Without You" (which went to #1 when later recorded by Harry Nilsson in 1972).

However, Badfinger's success took a bad turn. It was discovered that their manager allegedly had mob ties, and the band saw very little of their money. Bandmember Pete Ham had a wife and child, with another child on the way, and was unable to pay his bills. On April 23, 1975, he hanged himself in his garage studio and left a note that said he would take his crooked manager with him. Another bandmember, Tom Evans, killed himself in 1983, due to money and legal problems.

MAKE MORE

The most common cause of business failure is poor financial management–typically, not earning enough revenues to meet expenses, or conversely, spending more than you make. Making more money (especially a lot of money) begins in your head. You have to first believe that you deserve to be paid well for your time, talent, and the products you produce. (And your time, talent, and products should be worthy of that belief.) You then need to find people who'll pay you what you want and ask them for the sale. This is easier said than done. The secret to making it big in business is the belief that what you do (and sell) has value. If you truly believe in what you're doing and are passionate about it, it's much easier to go after the big bucks. If you don't feel that what you are doing is really beneficial to buyers, or you are only mildly interested in your product or service, it will be that much harder to get others to pay a premium–or anything at all.

So let's assume you love what you do, and you've built the best possible widget that benefits a large number of buyers. This is actually more than an assumption–it's a directive. Now that we've worked that out, let's make the most of the possibilities and explore some ways to make more money from your widget.

UPSELL

The secret to building a bigger business is to offer more products and services to your existing customers. It's a LOT cheaper and easier to market new and improved products or add-on services to an audience that's already sold on you—and that knows you understand their needs and fulfill them. This can be done by bundling things together. Prince did this a few years back when he bundled his new CD with concert tickets. Bands have been recording live shows and selling them on the spot for a few years now—you purchase a CD of the concert you just experienced on your way out. Long before technology allowed bands to do this, there was merchandise being sold in the back of the room (T-shirts, hats, programs, and more—John Mayer even has his own line of clothing and shoes he sells at his shows). This is still a very important and lucrative source of revenue for bands. The White Stripes sell an estimated $19,000 to $25,000 of gear a night at their shows, which sounds impressive until you learn that U2 rakes in as much as $150,000 a night in merchandise sales.

REPACKAGE/RESELL

In the book business, a title that tanked and is now relegated to the "deep-discount" bin (to recoup at least some of the costs) is called a remainder. Likewise, in your business, there may be products that don't do well—and rather than write them off as a loss for tax purposes, there may be a better way to get your money back. Sometimes repackaging items can breathe new life into a dead product line, or you may find new markets (or new uses) for old products.

The ultimate example in rock and roll is the "best of" or "compilation" CD. These comprise songs that are already recorded so they cost less to produce than new CDs; in some cases, however, they outsell the current offerings of a band. (Some compilation best-sellers include those from Elton John, the Eagles, the Rolling Stones, Steve Miller, Aerosmith, Billy Joel, and Journey.)

A live album is more expensive to produce than a compilation, but still a bargain for a band compared to recording new material—and they can be super sellers as well. Led Zeppelin did a live album and a movie (*The Song Remains the Same*) based on the group's concert at Madison Square Garden in the early '70s. They then re-released material from that same concert several years ago, again selling a substantial number–now that's successful repacking and reselling.

RAISE YOUR RATES

"If you don't go for as much money as you can possibly get, then I reckon you're just simply stupid," said Mick Jagger. We agree; get the most money you can without pricing yourself out of the market (or being unethical)–or create more expensive versions of the things you already offer for a more "upscale" clientele. Think about concert tickets–one price allows you to be up close and personal with the band (front row); another price has you front and center, but several rows back. Or, for those who don't want to pay (or can't afford to pay) over $100 per ticket, there may be lawn seats available. This way nobody is turned away and more money is made from the premium seats.

Similarly, for the Nine Inch Nails' 2008 album, *Ghosts I-IV*, there were several versions available, ranging from a free partial album to a $300 deluxe set. At one time, it was possible to compete on price, but in today's market this is rarely true. Unless you're a behemoth like Wal-Mart or Amazon.com, you can't compete on price and hope to make a profit. (And Amazon.com spent a decade in business losing money before they finally reported a profitable quarter.)

Nevertheless, the bottom-line is–you do need competitive prices. To do this and make a profit, focus on value-added extras you can sell to the same customer that generate additional revenue. The "loss leader" approach attracts traffic to a retailer or service with a low price on one or more items (that the retailer takes a loss on), and then the attracted customers are upsold on more profitable items. A similar example is the ink-jet printer. The printer itself is fairly cheap; it's the replacement ink that is relatively overpriced–but it's a consumable, so the long-term value for the manufacturers, wholesalers, and retailers is much better than it would be for the printer, even if it were more expensive.

Regardless of how you approach pricing, you also must learn what others are getting paid, to be sure you aren't charging too much or too little. Or in the case of the 1969 Woodstock festival, the producers had to pay a premium to get performers to sign on—because the producers had never put on such an event. But the performers were a reliable draw, and the producers knew if they could just get the first few, they could get the others. It worked. Being reliable often means you can make more. You've probably never heard of Nathan East, but in the music business he's known as "Everybody's Bassist." He's worked with Eric Clapton and Phil Collins and is one-fourth of Fourplay. Talented? Yes. Likable? Yes. Reliable? Yes. Busy? Yes.

LICENSE YOUR PRODUCTS

KISS is the king of merchandising. There are thousands of products featuring the band logo and likenesses of the band characters, but no licensed item can compare to the Gene Simmons' Vomitizer, which spits fake blood just like the real rocker. (The KISS Kasket does come a close second, however.)

Another way rock stars can pad their bank accounts is with the licensing of their songs for commercial use. Carly Simon's song "Anticipation" was used in Heinz ketchup commercials long before it was cool to license songs for ads. Moby turned licensed music into a cottage industry and has raked in over $16 million dollars from it, reportedly having licensed over a thousand commercial uses of his songs. In the twenty-first century, it's become not only acceptable but common practice, as everyone from the Beatles to Led Zeppelin have rented out their music for commercials.

You almost can't attend a pro sporting event nowadays without hearing licensed music urging the fans on, whether it's "We Are the Champions" by Queen, "Start Me Up" by the Stones, or "Hell's Bells" by AC/DC. (In the interest of accuracy, however, it should be noted that the *owner* of the music has the licensing rights, which may or may not be the artist. And as a result of selling their rights to songs, some artists have found their music being used in ways they wouldn't approve of.

So, when you have intellectual property, or property of any kind, be careful to whom you sell your interest in it.)

INCREASE EXPOSURE

The more marketable you are, the more money you can make. When someone sees an article about your business in the *Wall Street Journal*, you can probably raise your rates—or at the very least land more gigs. John Sebastian had hits with the Lovin' Spoonful ("Do You Believe In Magic?" and "Summer in the City") before he was hired by TV producer Alan Sacks in 1970 to write a theme song for a coming sitcom called *Kotter*. Sebastian wrote "Welcome Back" and not only did Sacks like the one-minute song, he changed the name of the show to *Welcome Back, Kotter* to match. The extended radio version of the song became a #1 hit. Cha-ching.

Awards are another path to more exposure, and more money. Maroon 5 has won two Billboard Music Awards, one MTV Video Music Award, one Teen Choice Award, one World Music Award, and three Grammy Awards—and their debut album, *About Jane*, went triple platinum based on the hits "Harder to Breathe," "She Will be Loved," and "This Love." Or, if you're really savvy, you can increase your exposure (and get paid at the same time) by signing an endorsement deal.

In the 1950s, Chubby Checker endorsed Thom McAn as "twist shoes" and Elvis did print ads for RCA. In the 1960s, Jefferson Airplane did an ad for white Levi's and the Yardbirds and the Who did radio ads for Great Shakes. Other bands with endorsement deals in the '60s and '70s included Vanilla Fudge, the Bee Gees, Moody Blues, and Tom Jones. Then in the 1980s, the Pet Shop Boys took it to yet another level and sold advertising space on the packaging of one of their albums.

MAXIMIZE/LEVERAGE

Once you're established in business, you are automatically an expert. Other entrepreneurs will want to know the secrets to your success, and you can sell your talents and skills for additional revenue. This means you can consult, write a book, take side jobs, accept paid speaking engagements, or start a second business. To make the most of your success, strike while the iron is hot—or use it as your exit strategy. In the 1980s, R.E.M. was one of the most-popular indie-rock bands, cranking out an album a year and touring extensively. In 1987, they had their first hit with "The One I Love," and a succession of hit songs and multi-platinum albums followed before the band signed a five-record deal with Warner Bros. for a reported $80 million. They would have never gotten such a lucrative deal had they not leveraged their success.

Led Zeppelin uniquely leveraged their popular epic song "Stairway to Heaven" by not releasing it as a single. This resulted in a LOT more albums sold (an estimated 500,000 extra) because people had to have that song. Cirque du Soleil created a production based on the Beatles' music—which was a very lucrative deal for the surviving members of the band. Some artists also use their leverage with their label to land their own division, as Madonna did. She then signed an unknown female artist who later became one of the best-selling artists of the 1990s. Her name? Alanis Morrisette.

CREATE/INVENT

"I Write the Songs" is thought of as a Barry Manilow tune, but it was actually written by Bruce Johnston of the Beach Boys (about bandmate Brian Wilson). Manilow only performed it. (By the way, we KNOW Barry Manilow isn't a rock star, but the Beach Boys were.) The person who pens a song gets more than the person who simply plays it. (Of course when you write, record, perform, and produce your own songs that means you make the most money.) In business, when you are the inventor or creator of something, there's more money to be made than by simply selling something—usually.

Plus, you may be in line to receive royalties and residual income for life. Just one well-timed idea can leave an inventor set for life. You remember how you used to see stereo systems with the Dolby Stereo symbol on it? Well, the inventor of Dolby sound would get paid each time his technology was used. Speaking of Dolby—Thomas Dolby, that is—although he is best known for his song "She Blinded Me With Science," Dolby is also a successful inventor and entrepreneur. His company, Headspace, was heavily involved in making music downloadable, as well as partnering with technology companies and products like Beatnik, Retro Ringtones, and RetroFolio, which specializes in ringtone asset management software. Dolby (whose real last name is Robertson) has also created hundreds of the digital ringtones now found on mobile phones everywhere and is a frequent speaker at technology conferences around the world.

FOCUS ON PROFITABLE PRODUCTS

Don't be afraid to drop what isn't making money to focus more time, energy, and resources on what is. That could mean dropping clients who don't pay on time (or pay at all) and going where the money is—your profit centers. Bands that understand they have two parallel careers—first as recording and songwriting artists, second as live performers—will realize the greatest growth.

But as times change, successful bands adapt. Unlike in the past, there is far more money to be made now from touring than from recording. Paul McGuinness, longtime manager of U2, estimated the band made $154.2 million during one tour after selling out more than 100 arena and stadium shows around the world. "Our recording income is not insignificant, but it's less than we make from touring. The figures used to be closer together." While U2 "only" make an estimated $15 million in advances for each album they release (plus any additional royalties), they grossed $139 million on the road in North America in 2005—including as much as $150,000 per night in merchandise sales.

Touring is simply far more profitable than selling CDs. You have to go where the most money is. The Rolling Stones grossed $500 million from their 2006–07 tour, but made far less in record royalties during that same period. And according to Billboard, Madonna's 2006 *Confessions* tour was the highest-grossing tour for any female artist in history. We're guessing her CD royalties were much less than her tour revenue. Where you tour can also be a factor in how much you make. These mega-acts usually only tour the major cities and do more shows in those cities—since they've already incurred the expense of getting there. (Lesser-known acts, however, aren't enough of a draw and need to tour the smaller cities and towns to build their followings.)

Yet another profit center that's become a trend of late is corporate concerts. Big bands like Aerosmith, as well as retro acts like Pat Benatar, are doing private gigs for big bucks. Reportedly, Benatar and her band were paid $50,000 to perform a very short show at a technology conference, during which she replaced the words of her hit "Heartbreaker" to be a more relevant "Codebreaker."

FIND A LARGER AUDIENCE

The New York Dolls (as the name would imply) were a glam band that wrote and sang about New York life. Their songs "Jet Boy" and "Personality Crisis" were underground favorites, but their albums didn't sell well outside of New York. Bachman-Turner Overdrive (BTO) was from tiny Winnepeg, Canada, but found a larger audience by expanding into the U.S. Although Queen was one of the most popular bands in the world in the mid-'70s, their popularity eventually waned in the U.S. and Britain. So, to cultivate and expand their fan base, they began touring foreign markets most bands were ignoring, including Latin America, Asia, and Africa.

Sometimes finding a larger audience is not geographic but rather a matter of what you're selling. Paul Weller was in two popular U.K. bands, the Jam and Style Council, but because of the subject matter of their songs, they only had modest success in America.

TEAM UP FOR ADDITIONAL REVENUES

Since the beginnings of rock and roll, bands have brought opening acts on the road with them. The fact that bands are more predominant (versus solo artists) implies people can be more successful by pooling their resources and talents. We've already mentioned in this book several musical festivals where a collection of artists, all performing in one venue, is the big draw. There are also many examples of individual artists teaming up to record together to reach new markets–such as Santana on his *Supernatural* album–or just to explore new creative avenues.

In business, it may be better to take the "if you can't beat them, join them" approach and work with others in your industry. That's how we came to write this book together. You can do bounce-back promotions, refer people back and forth, share projects, and cover all the bases easier by working together.

GENERATE PASSIVE INCOME

"I've been living off the royalties from 'Sister Morphine' for ten years, which is really bizarre–don't tell me drugs don't pay," said Marianne Faithful. Technically, you can only be in one place at a time. That's why it's so nice to be in bed sleeping while money is being made on your behalf. (Consider this: Elvis Presley earned $49 million dollars in 2007– and he'd been dead for thirty years.)

It's called residual or passive income, and quite frankly, it's a lot more lucrative than fee-based earnings where you trade your time for money. Which segues to an important point: The expression "time is money" isn't completely accurate. Sure, you trade your time for a fee, but in reality, you are trading a piece of your *life* for a fee. You get a finite amount of time to live and when you use it (for whatever reason) you can't get it back. That's why it's so much better to create something once that's so good (and desired) you can just sit back and watch the money roll in.

Screamin' Jay Hawkins only had one hit with "I Put a Spell on You," but the song has been covered by several artists, including Nina Simone, the Animals, and Creedence Clearwater Revival. Each time the song was re-recorded, Hawkins (and now his estate) earned money from those versions. You can work hard for your money or you can make money by hardly working.

SELL OFF PART OR ALL OF YOUR BUSINESS

When David Bowie went public (not about *that*) and offered to sell stock in himself by creating "Bowie Bonds," he substantially increased his net worth when Prudential bought the entire $55 million offering. Even if you're not in the position to sell it now, you may have begun your business with the intention of selling it for a huge payday after you built it up. If that's the case, timing is critical—you don't want to sell out too soon. Richard Berry wrote and recorded the original "Louie, Louie," but it became a hit for the Kingsmen—because Berry had sold all his song rights in the 1950s when he needed money. As a result, he missed out on millions from that one song alone.

But there's another avenue to "selling" your business, at least in part, and it doesn't involve multi-level marketing. What do Subway, McDonalds, Domino's Pizza, Holiday Inn, Dunkin' Donuts, and RE/MAX all have in common? They are all franchised. Franchising has been a formula for success for years, allowing you to pull in capital while essentially only selling the name, model, and reputation of your business. Even if you don't franchise, you should run your business as if you were—that's the advice in the book *The E-Myth* by Michael Gerber.

SEEK BETTER TERMS

"It was the only band where, as a rock drummer, you could play in 17/16 time and still stay in decent hotels," boasts Bill Bruford about being in King Crimson. There are things more important than money—okay, that's a stretch, but there are non-monetary things that can be as valuable. For example, if there's no more money to be had during a negotiation, maybe you could seek something in trade instead. Or, you could get better terms and more time to pay—or more money up front, if you are selling something.

Apple co-founder Steve "Woz" Wozniak had millions of dollars and a dream. He wanted to do a better-than-Woodstock music festival in the '80s. His plan was elaborate—to mix the world of computers and rock. He got some land east of Los Angeles and on Labor Day weekend in 1982, the U.S. Festival was held. (Woz lost $10 million on the event, but his son was born there, and Apple stock rose $18 million that day.) Then, he held another one in 1983. The list of performers was LONG, and the cost was astronomical. The reason: the top acts (such as David Bowie and Van Halen) knew Woz had bucks, so they held out for more money and got it. Bowie reportedly got $1.5 million.

The Sunset Strip has always been an important part of the rock music scene. The Trip, the Red Velvet, the Whisky a Go Go, and Starwood were a few of the places you had to play if you wanted to make a name for yourself, and it's still true to some extent today. (The Byrds, Frank Zappa and the Mothers of Invention, the Doors, Los Lobos, Black Flag, X, Van Halen, the Knack, and many heavy metal bands made an impact on the strip.)

By the time heavy metal hit the scene, the clubs had put a pay-for-play policy in place. Promoters rented the club for the night and charged the band to play there, paying them back from the profits made at the door. Obviously, a better deal would've been to get a set amount to perform—regardless of the turnout. Or perhaps a cut of the bar take, since bar sales can easily match or top the ticket sales.

Jim Guerinot, who manages Gwen Stefani, said, "With CDs, you're making between fifteen and twenty-five percent royalty. On the road, you get a royalty of eighty-five to ninety percent [from ticket sales]." Look at deals from all angles to see if there are ways to increase value by adding to or removing from the deal. Band members get a per-diem while on the road and can add other items to their contract rider (e.g., free booze) so they have less out-of-pocket expenses—which is almost as good as money earned.

Are you in a similar situation, accepting a lesser deal without having even tried to negotiate better terms? Always try for better terms, whether it's on your credit card rate or your rent. Savvy negotiators can "make" hundreds, even thousands, of dollars an hour—with regard to what they gain in negotiation. Asking can take almost no time at all, and yet can reap very worthy rewards.

GO FOR VOLUME

In addition to profits, big sales numbers make you more marketable. Poor sales may mean your time is coming to an end. Consider Peter

Frampton. He was on top of the world when his 1976 album, *Frampton Comes Alive*, was selling millions of copies. However, one year later, his follow-up *I'm in You* sold only a million copies. Though successful by most standards, it was a relative flop, his career never recovered, and he had serious financial trouble for years. It didn't help that the album strayed from his formula for success–happy music played live.

PROJECT CONFIDENCE

When Jack Johnson first met with a record executive interested in his music, he said he couldn't start working on an album until after he got back from a lengthy surf trip (which he was filming). That kind of confidence and walk-away power usually translates into a better bargaining position–and more money. Sometimes, you need to be able to walk away from something to get it, a difficult stance to take when in reality you can't afford to walk away.

When you have (or present the image of) confidence, people gravitate toward you. It's kind of like a long line at a restaurant–the longer it is, the more you may say, "I gotta try that place sometime."

PERSIST

Singer and songwriter Bill Withers ("Just the Two of Us" and "Lean on Me") didn't get his big break until he was over thirty years old. In 1971, he was working for an airplane parts manufacturer, assembling toilet seats for 747s, when Booker T. Jones produced his song "Ain't No Sunshine." The song was a hit and won a Grammy in 1972.

PRODUCE AND PROSPER

As obvious as this sounds, it can easily be overlooked: If your business isn't growing at the rate you'd like, could it be you aren't doing all you can do? In many businesses, how much you make is in direct proportion to how hard you work. It's also true in some types of businesses that you have to produce to prosper. Brian Eno is known for taking a minimalist approach to producing. He played keyboards in Roxy Music and then teamed up with Robert Fripp in King Crimson. Following that, he produced David Bowie, the Talking Heads, and then took his production approach to songs for U2, including *Joshua Tree* (a huge success for the band). While recuperating in a hospital after a car crash, Eno came to appreciate the ambient sounds outside his hospital room—rain. So, he created soothing ambient music that reflected the environment and the eventual tapes sold very well.

WORK SIDE GIGS

The term "moonlighting" originally meant your second job was more of a night shift and started after your day job ended. Nowadays, moonlighting can mean you take on an additional project or client between other projects, or start a business on the side. This works well because you earn more money, make more contacts, and gain new knowledge.

In the late 1950s, Carol Kaye was a jazz guitarist performing in clubs around Los Angeles. She took a gig to record for a Sam Cooke record, which led to more studio work as a guitarist. However, in 1963, a bass player failed to show up for a session at Capitol Records, so she stepped in and the rest is history. From that point, Kaye became the go-to bassist and played on more than 10,000 recordings including tracks for the Beach Boys and the Doors. You just never know where something can lead with a side gig, and you'll make some extra money in the process.

Travis Barker, drummer for Blink 182, founded Famous Stars and Straps (a clothing company) in 1999 and LaSalle Records in 2004, and opened a Wahoo's Fish Taco restaurant in Norco, California. Companies such as DC Shoes and Zildjian cymbals have also co-designed products in his name. Regardless of how things go with his band, Barker has a number of avenues to keep an income going, not to mention the extra streams of income in the process.

GET PAID

Charge whatever you want, but if you can't collect it, what does it matter? It's not "show me the money" as much as it is "pay me the money." Unless you own a coin-operated laundry mat or a self-service car wash (cash businesses), you will be faced with the challenge of collecting on outstanding invoices. It's an art form made easier by being organized, diligent, and having the right tools. Dolphin Records founder John Dolphin had made many enemies in the music business—mostly over unpaid royalties. One of those unhappy artists was Percy Ivy, who shot and killed Dolphin in his office—in front of two fledgling teenage musicians, Sandy Nelson and Bruce Johnston.

Not dissuaded from the music business, Nelson (a drummer) went on to record "Teen Beat" and "Let There Be Drums," and Johnston made surf music before joining the Beach Boys in 1965 as Brain Wilson's replacement on stage. As mentioned earlier in this chapter, he also wrote the Barry Manilow hit "I Write The Songs." While people may not get shot over money in most businesses, collections and cash flow are a fact of life. Think your cash flow is bad? Bands on tour may not get paid for months. Queen once played a gig in Rio de Janeiro for a promoter who was notorious for not paying. Not only that, he also had a reputation for holding band equipment for "ransom" after concerts to get them to accept less pay. But savvy to his ways, Queen landed their own plane next to the concert stadium and quickly loaded their gear immediately after the gig and flew off. When the promoter attempted to pull his usual trick, the band and gear was gone. Hopefully, you'll never have to resort to such measures, but be prepared to get crafty when it comes to a slow or nonpaying customer or client.

SPEND LESS

Take a twenty-dollar bill out of your wallet, tear it up, and throw it away. Can't do it? Then why would you waste money on things that simply do not pay off or produce a profit for your business? A few of the reasons (rationales) for this are:

✦ "It was tax deductible," as if the item were free because you can write a portion of the purchase off your taxes.

✦ "It was a better deal if I bought in bulk, so stocking up seemed like a good idea"—and it can be, if you have the space to store the stuff and the money couldn't have been used for greater good.

✦ "I got a coupon for $10 off a new leather chair at my office supply superstore." This is an example of being penny-wise but pound-foolish if you didn't need a new chair or you ended up buying a $500 chair instead of the $100 one because you had to use your $10-off coupon.

✦ You are too busy running your business (into the ground) to find the best deal or even check and see if you already have the item you are about to buy. Or, you are running late, so you absolutely, positively need a package sent using the fastest (and most expensive) method.

✦ You say you need a new computer, but the truth is, you don't really *need* one—you *want* one. Knowing the difference between needs and wants is the difference between spending hundreds of dollars—and not.

One of the biggest reasons businesses don't make it is a failure to watch the bottom-line. And one of the biggest reasons businesses succeed is an obsession with the bottom-line (and finding creative ways to make more and spend less). Remember, money saved is money earned. Unfortunately, many rock stars didn't get this memo and have been almost as famous for their lavish (and foolish) spending as they were for their music.

In 1971, it was reported that Rolling Stones' guitarist Keith Richards was spending—each week—roughly $1,000 for food, $1,000 for booze, $2,500 for illegal substances, and $2,500 for rent. (It should be noted, in all fairness, this was well within his means.) There are many more examples (too many to mention) of rock stars who spent every last dime they had on fancy cars, big boats, opulent homes, exotic vacations, and private planes—only to lose it all when they experienced a slowdown in their record sales.

In the case of the late-1980s' glam-metal band Warrant, when their record label dropped them (in favor of the blossoming grunge movement), some of the band members had to declare bankruptcy due to excessive spending. And do you think all the current aging rockers, in their fifties and sixties, are reuniting to tour just for nostalgic reasons? We don't know, but we certainly suspect some of them haven't managed their money well and are facing tough times as senior citizens. So, let's learn these lessons the easy way and look at some ways to cut costs with this premise in mind–spend money on things that make you more money.

LIVE ON LESS

As mentioned elsewhere in this book, Jewel lived in her van so she didn't have to pay rent and could focus on writing and performing, and Metallica lived in their rehearsal room to save money. Those examples are the extreme when it comes to living on less–and were done when the artists were paying their dues and may not have had a choice. So, it's more interesting when an established star chooses to live on less. That's why Jack Johnson is one of the most unassuming rock stars.

Jack and his family live primarily in a simple home (they don't even have cable television) in Hawaii–even though his latest release ("Sleep Through the Static") reached #1 on the Billboard album chart, and he has sold more than fifteen million records since his debut album, *Brushfire Fairytales*, came out. He loves surfing, camping, and living a simple life, despite his tremendous wealth–and giving back is very important to him. (He and his wife founded the Kokua Hawaii Foundation to bring environmental education into the classroom.) Johnson's business (Brushfire Records) is based out of a building in the back of a Los Angeles home he owns. And having his own recording studio and record label allows him to record, package, create, and edit music and videos there. By forsaking the trappings of wealth, Johnson certainly has more money to put back into his business, art, and foundation.

Kim Deal (bassist and guitarist for the Pixies and the Breeders) drives a 1995 Volvo and has owned the same modest suburban home in Dayton, Ohio, since 1990, even with the success of the Pixies reunion tour. Longtime star Linda Ronstadt lives in a modest home with a big garden where she grows fruits and vegetables. And current superstar John Mayer lives in the Los Angeles suburbs with a roommate.

"People say I am a millionaire, but that's not true–I only spent millions," said Robert Plant of Led Zeppelin. (We have no doubt Robert Plant spent millions, but we do doubt that he *isn't* a millionaire.) John Entwistle of the Who, on the other hand, did make and spend millions and ended up with next to nothing. As fast as the Who made money, he spent it. And the main reason for his financial woes was his inability to live on less when the band wasn't making millions. In fact, one of the main reasons the Who reunited and toured was to help Entwistle earn enough to pay off his debts.

"Avoid a major drug habit; don't have kids before you're ready to raise a family; and stay out of debt," advised James Taylor. Dennis Wilson, co-founder of the Beach Boys made all the mistakes Taylor advised against, and then some. Wilson made a ton of money as a Beach Boy (and solo artist) and had a home in the prestigious Laurel Canyon (which Charles Manson and his "family" took over at one point, including $100,000 of his money). He had his beautiful and beloved yacht "Harmony," which he kept docked in Marina Del Ray. He earned plenty of money from his music, yet ended up broke and homeless. While staying on a friend's boat in the same marina, he would dive down and look for expensive items he had thrown overboard years before. Sadly, on one of those dives, he hit his head on the bottom of a boat while coming up, passed out, and died.

So what is the lesson to be learned? Look up when surfacing from a dive. Yes, true, but also invest back into your business first. While you do need a place to live, a way to get around town, and clothes to wear, spending most of your money on these things (at the expense of your business) is a mistake too many people make. While a home can appreciate, a new car and clothes do not. Investing in your business is the best bet for your money for the long run.

CUT (BUSINESS) COSTS

"Most bands don't make money–they just squander it on producers and cocaine and lots of other bullshit, and it's disgusting–there is so much idiotic excess," said Sting. He was also quoted as saying, "I've given up tantric sex. I'm trying to get Trudie [his wife] into tantric shopping. That's where you shop for five hours but don't buy anything." Obviously, Sting has some strong opinions about how money should be spent. For a business interested in making a profit, it should be obvious that less money going out can mean more money going into your bank account–you know, making you wealthy. Whenever you purchase a piece of equipment for your business, ask yourself if this item is going to make money or just cost money? By buying only things that boost your bottom-line, you will build your business a lot quicker.

Most entrepreneurs underestimate how much money is spent each month. Expenses are almost always higher than you think. So cutting back wherever you can may help compensate (somewhat) for a lack of understanding of all the costs of doing business. If a band eliminates a couple of trucks from a tour, they can save money–and probably still put on a great show.

Emerson, Lake, and Palmer had an incredible sixty-three roadies on their 1977 tour. The Tubes ("She's a Beauty") began as a band that put on an elaborate stage show requiring props, costume changes, choreography, and theatrical presentations. With only one big hit (though "Don't Touch Me There" could be considered another), the band later became a straight-ahead rock band with a stripped-down show.

In 1992, U2 created a multimedia extravaganza with forty-foot video walls and 1,200 tons of equipment. Pink Floyd had such an elaborate stage show for *The Wall* that they only performed it in five cities worldwide. It included video screens, fireworks, giant inflatable objects, and a wall gradually built by roadies out of cardboard bricks during the show. The Who's Keith Moon (a.k.a. "Moon the Loon") would wreck cars, trash hotels, and even restaurants–not to mention his drums–while on tour. It was estimated that the total damage of his actions was over a quarter of a million pounds.

Okay, so maybe your business doesn't tour with 1,200 tons of equipment or trash restaurants, but as with these bands, there are certainly expenses that you need to monitor. And you must cut back when it's not bringing in money. This happened to KISS in 1979. Expecting a huge response to their new *Dynasty* album, the band took their already renowned stage show to yet another level. The army-like amounts of equipment and logistical needs became cumbersome and expensive and had to be scaled down. Recognize when costs are exceeding expenses and not creating a return. It may be that you'll have to scale back—which, depending on what it is, can be an ego buster. But don't let your ego get in the way of good business, or you may find yourself out of business.

FAST FACT

The Animals recorded their famous "House of the Rising Sun" in one take. The eight minutes it took included one four-minute rehearsal. Amazingly they got the song on tape for a total cost of just $5.

SHARE EXPENSES

The cost of doing business has never been higher—and this will be true whenever you are reading this book. The cost of leasing retail or office space is extremely expensive. Higher fuel costs have driven up shipping fees. Labor costs almost never go down—unless you move your business to another country. And necessary goods and services are always subject to inflation. So what's a business (or a band) to do? Teaming up is one way to reduce costs. Sharing equipment, office space, and even labor just makes sense, if you can make it work.

Bands are always on the lookout for ways to maximize their celebrity and share expenses. Some touring acts have recently turned to corporate sponsors (Honda, Lexus, Southern Comfort, Corona) to help offset costs. A Nordstrom or Victoria's Secret can also help defray the costs of producing and distributing music by including the rights to put their brand on the music—as Josh Stone agreed to. Endorsement deals are another way to save money on your gear when you go out on the road. Almost every rock star has one—or twelve. It's great exposure (artists are featured in the product ads), and they get free stuff to boot.

John Mayer is one artist who embraces this concept. He has his own line of Martin and Fender guitars. He also teamed up with Steve Jobs of Apple and appeared on stage with Jobs at more than one MacWorld Conference and Expo to help launch Garage Band and iPhone. Mayer also has endorsement deals with VW and Blackberry.

Businesses should not overlook the co-op money made available by manufacturers and suppliers to help with advertising, signage, or point-of-purchase displays. At the beginning of their career, U2's live appearances were operating at a loss, but the band got tour support from their record label—which paid off because the band's records went to #1 nearly everywhere they went. And it never stopped from there as, over two decades later, they've sold roughly 150 million records. When Sammy Hagar wanted to open his own cantina in Cabo San Lucas, he turned to his Van Halen bandmates for money and got each to invest $40,000 in his business. He bought them out later.

START INVESTING

Cher: "My mom once told me, 'Honey, you marry a rich man.' I said, 'Mom, I *am* a rich man.'" There are a lot of rock stars who have become rich beyond their wildest dreams by being smart with their money. (Unfortunately, there are many more who should've been set for life, but squandered enormous sums of money.) For every Rod Stewart, who became rich (despite his divorces) through royalties and his investments in real estate, there are many others—Mick Fleetwood and Meatloaf to name a couple—who had to declare bankruptcy.

What's a good investment? It depends. Eric Clapton collects guns. Sebastian Bach collects comics and KISS memorabilia. Rob Morrissey collects 1950s' wrestling magazines. John Entwistle of the Who collected tea pots and expensive cars. Ian Anderson of Jethro Tull invested in salmon farming and made millions (more). And Jewel decided that putting her money in the bank was the best investment: "When I first got signed I put $100,000 in the bank." On the other hand, Mick Fleetwood found himself $2 million in debt after some bad investments in Australian real estate and restaurants in the mid-1980s.

So, let's look at some investment options for entrepreneurs, with this thought always in the back of our minds—in business, when it rains it pours, but it's usually followed by a long and arduous drought. It's good to have something saved up not just for a rainy day, but for the dry spell that follows. (We will not go into the obvious tried-and-true investments like money markets, the stock market, and other practical and proven places to put your money. That would take up the entire chapter, and there are many other (excellent) books on the subject. Instead, we'll look at a few other ways to have your money make more money.)

Invest in Yourself

Stephen Perkins, the drummer for Jane's Addiction and Porno for Pyros, used his Bar Mitzvah money to buy his first drum set. Brain Setzer made decent money from Stray Cats, but spent most of it. He then struggled for six years, wanting to make a big band album. The problem was, big-band music requires a BIG (expensive) band, and his was over eighteen people. As a further challenge, there was no market for big band at the time. But he believed so much in what he was doing that he invested the last of his money in the project. The result: *Jump, Jive, and Wail* sold over two million copies, was a chart-topper, earned Setzer a Grammy Award, and started a resurgence in big band and swing music. Frankie Valli bought back the master tapes for his 1974 song "My Eyes Adored You" and released it on the small Private Stock label. His investment in his own music landed that song at #1 on the charts with very profitable sales.

When it comes to investing in yourself, nothing's better than owning your own business. Righteous Babe Records was founded by Ani DiFranco with $1,500 of borrowed capital. The folk-rocker is fiercely independent—and it's paid off. With her musical integrity intact, she has sold more than a million of her own records and has expanded beyond a one-person shop to include releases from other musicians. She now has a fully staffed record label, and she's proof there are viable options to the more-conventional methods of making it in music. (And this is most likely true in your industry as well.)

Another female rocker who took the independent path is Aimee Mann. The critically acclaimed singer-songwriter (formerly in 'Til Tuesday) found it so frustrating working with record executives that she bought back her album *Bachelor No. 2* and released it on her own Superego label. (Cool name.) It may sound risky doing it all by yourself, but which sounds more risky: (1) you control your fate and make the decisions about marketing your work, or (2) you have someone else making those calls? That's what we thought. Doing it yourself allows you to be in charge of your destiny.

Carole King didn't do it all herself, but she found similar success striking out on her own. She started out as a staff songwriter in the famous Brill Building in New York City, where she penned over seventy hit songs—for other artists. But when she finally recorded and released her solo album, *Tapestry*, it was on the charts for over five years, making her one of the best-selling female solo artists of all time.

For do-it-yourself rock stars, more money can be made (and kept) by writing, recording, producing, and selling their own stuff through their own record labels. Jimmy Buffett owns his own record label, Mailboat Records, and earns as much as $5 in royalty per record sold (compared to the standard $1 to $2.50 seen by artists signed to a label not their own). Led Zeppelin established their own record label, Swan Song, to release all of their albums beginning with *Physical Graffiti* in 1975. Swan Song went on to release records by other rockers, including Dave Edmunds, Bad Company, and the Pretty Things.

Invest in Your Future

U2 understands how important it is to be good at both the music *and* the business, and they've always been prepared to invest in their own future. They never wanted to join the long (and humiliating) list of regrettable artists who made lousy deals, got exploited, and ended up broke—with no control over how their life's work was used and no say in how their names and likenesses were bought and sold. That's why

U2 owns all their master recordings and most of their copyrights–which are licensed long term to Universal.

There are plenty of other artists who've also thought about building a true legacy that would ensure their financial security for years to come. Despite smart decisions in the 1970s about retaining the rights to all things KISS, Gene Simmons and Paul Stanley almost wrecked the ship in the 1980s with a lack of cohesive purpose. Smartly, however, they regained their focus on the KISS vision and regained their financial security with lucrative tours in their original make-up and regalia.

As you think about investing in your future, think about strengthening your industry. If you intend to stay in your industry, it's in your best interest to keep it strong. Jerry Jeff Walker penned the song "Mr. Bojangles," which became a hit for the Nitty Gritty Dirt Band in 1970. Walker then used the profits to move to Austin, Texas, the following year to record his own album for MCA. He employed local musicians and, in doing so, helped to develop the now-famous music scene in Austin. His album *Viva Teralingua* contained the song "Getting By," from which he is doing much better than just getting by.

Diversify

The saying goes, "Don't put all your eggs in one basket." And this is so true when it comes to investing. You may not have much to go around now (perhaps only the ability to open a basic savings account), but when your investment funds grow, so should the number of ways you invest them.

Many bands (or band members) have diversified by building their own recording studios and then renting them out. Not only does this save money when they're recording, it earns them money when they aren't. Jimi Hendrix owned Electric Lady Studios. Phil Ramone opened his own recording studio and produced and/or engineered albums for Paul Simon, Billy Joel, and Bob Dylan. Iron Maiden founder-bassist Steve Harris and the Band's Levon Helm both own studios, while Jimmy Buffett owns Shrimpboat Sound in Key West. Gil More, the drummer-singer for the Canadian trio Triumph, used his earnings from the band to build Metalworks Studio, which is a respected recording studio that also trains new engineers and technicians for Canada's music industry. He then expanded the business to include Metalworks Production Group for concerts and corporate events.

Another way to spread out your investment money is to open a side business (ideally, once your main one has become successful and stable). Guitarist and avid bow-hunter Ted Nugent ("Cat Scratch Fever") has his own line of beef jerky called Gonzo Meat Biltong. And though the Monroes only had one hit ("What Do All the People Know"), keyboardist Eric Denton put his proceeds into starting a music store in San Diego called Guitar Trader.

When a band or a business has a solid hit, they should manage their money as if they won't have another–chances are they won't. Unfortunately, it's hard to curb your enthusiasm and optimism (or celebrate, if you've been living lean for a long time before that hit). Rockers who splurged, but fortunately had more hits to come, include: Paul Simon, who bought a red Impala convertible with his first royalties from "Hey Schoolgirl," (the car burned to the ground) and Bob Dylan, who bought a seventy-foot yacht that later sank in the Caribbean after hitting a reef. Conversely, Joan Jett diversified *and* invested in her future when she bought stocks in companies she knew, liked, and consumed, like Snapple and Starbucks–and made money.

GET FINANCIAL HELP

"I used to think that letting others handle my finances gave me more creative freedom. I have discovered that you can actually have more creative freedom when you control your own financial and business matters," mused David Bowie, one of the smartest men in rock. You can do it yourself if you're comfortable working with numbers–like Huey Lewis, who had a perfect score of 800 on the math portion of his SAT. Having a business degree helps (Dave Mustaine of Megadeth), as does a background as an agent (Dido).

But more often than not, handling the counting all by yourself leads to a loss. That's why when Mick Fleetwood was managing the band's

Tusk tour, it didn't go so well. (And the album only sold four million copies, far short of what they did with *Rumours*.) When the lengthy and well-attended tour's final accounting came in, the band realized they had been on the road for a year for next to nothing, largely due to the elaborate expenses of their big show. Mick Fleetwood's reign as band manager came to an end.

Get a Good Accountant

Put money aside for taxes. Musicians (and the self-employed) must allocate a portion of their royalties, performance income, and other earnings for taxes. A good rule of thumb is a *minimum* of 15 percent and, more safely, 25 percent. A band's business manager will usually handle this task. And once you've set aside the money for taxes, make sure they are paid.

At one point, the Treasury Department claimed James Brown owed $4.5 million in back taxes, so the IRS filed liens of $2.2 million on his land. He had to sell everything to get them (and his ex-wives) off his back. Marvin Gaye also made millions, but side-stepped his taxes—and ended up filing for bankruptcy and living with his parents after his home was repossessed by the IRS.

While it's good to know how taxes work and to be at least capable of doing them, it's always smart to get a reputable accountant to handle this task. Invariably, they have an awareness of the tax code (which changes every year) that results in at least one deduction that far exceeds their fees. Typically, a small business earning under $100,000 a year will have a tax-preparation fee of $200 to $500. It's well worth it.

Get a Good Lawyer

Protect your intellectual property. It's valuable and, depending on your business, may be your best asset. As mentioned elsewhere, founders Gene Simmons and Paul Stanley own the rights to the KISS logo and looks. Steve Harris is the sole owner of Iron Maiden and its intellectual property. But neither of these ownerships could happen (at least not at that level) without a good lawyer. Ultimately, you need to protect yourself, because it just takes one lawsuit to kill a business (and a band). Stories abound of bands that were unable to release albums due to contractual issues.

Prince couldn't even use his name and had to become "The Artist Formerly Known As Prince" (before his identity became a symbol). Ozzy Osbourne was sued by the parents of a teenager who killed himself after listening to the song "Suicide Solution." (It actually carried an anti-suicide message and was written about Bon Scott, 1970s' lead singer of AC/DC, who drank himself to death.) It should be noted that the case was rejected by the courts. Judas Priest was also sued in Reno, Nevada, by the parents of two teenagers who attempted suicide (one succeeded, the other survived) while listening to one of their songs. The suit claimed backwards messages in the music instigated the teens, but a trial ultimately exonerated the band. (Singer Rob Halford said that if they were to put subliminal messages in their music, it would be "buy more records.")

In 1987, Tom Petty sued a tire company for $1 million for using a song very similar to his song "Mary's New Car" in a TV commercial. The ad agency that produced the commercial had previously sought permission to use Petty's song, but was refused and instead used a soundalike. The judge issued a temporary restraining order prohibiting further use of the ad, and the suit was later settled out of court. Some have claimed that the Red Hot Chili Peppers single "Dani California," released in May 2006, is very similar to Tom Petty's "Mary Jane's Last Dance," but *that* didn't bother him. He told *Rolling Stone* magazine: "I seriously doubt that there is any negative intent there. And a lot of rock 'n' roll songs sound alike . . . If someone took my song note for note and stole it maliciously, then maybe [I'd sue]. But I don't believe in lawsuits much. I think there are enough frivolous lawsuits in this country without people fighting over pop songs."

Get a Good Business Manager

Paul McGuinness has been managing U2 for thirty years. The Rolling

Stones and the Beatles both used Allen Klein to manage their business affairs. It's important to pick the people who will manage your money wisely. But DO YOUR HOMEWORK. Harry Nilsson got a five-album/one-million-dollar deal with RCA and invested the money wisely, becoming very wealthy. Unfortunately, that was until his business manager reportedly stole all Nilsson's money and forced him into bankruptcy in 1992. He died two years later of a heart attack at the age of fifty-two.

Similarly, Murry Wilson of the Beach Boys sold the band's publishing rights to Irving/Almo for less than $1 million and kept the money, after being fired by Brian Wilson. (The band had ceded rights to him when he was their manager.) Brian Wilson then sued Irving/Almo and got $10 million.

Lenny Hart (father of Mickey Hart, the Grateful Dead drummer) was an absentee dad, but came back into his son's life in late '60s after the band's success. They entrusted him to handle their finances, and he reportedly stole it all. That same decade, the Animals wrote "House of the Rising Sun" (as a group) but their manager said all of their names "wouldn't fit." He suggested they credit keyboardist Alan Price with writing the song, and Price would then split the royalties. He never did.

The band known as the Band has been furious for decades that Robbie Robertson is credited with writing many of the songs they claim were actually collaborations. And then there's the Billy Joel story. His music business career got off to a bad start, so he sold the rights to his royalties for quick cash before he made it big. Part of the deal meant Family Productions (who had purchased his rights) got a quarter of every dollar Joel made from subsequent albums. When Joel signed with Columbia Records and released *Piano Man* in 1973, it sold over one million copies—but after Columbia's cut, Family Productions' cut, and other expenses, Joel reportedly only made $7,763.

His wife at the time was a graduate of UCLA's school of management and worked on sorting out his financial affairs, before they divorced in 1982. From 1974 through 1989, Joel had a number of hits and should have made a lot of money. But when he had his manager (also his former brother-in-law) audited, he reportedly discovered millions of dollars had gone missing. Joel filed a multi-million-dollar lawsuit.

APPLY FOR GRANTS

Performance artist Laurie Anderson had to support herself early in her career by teaching poetry at Riker's Island prison, among other things. ("Roses are red, violets are blue. I'm gonna kill you.") But it was after she started to attract grants (including from the National Endowment of the Arts) that her career began to take off. Her commercially successful "O Superman" was self-produced in 1981 and sold 800,000 copies via mail order, before she signed with Warner Bros. and sold many more. Grant money does take effort to secure—but it's out there, often sitting unclaimed because it does take effort. But if you learn how to write grant proposals (or hire someone to do it) and are diligent about the process, you can find capital for all sorts of projects or business purposes.

YOUR MONEY OR YOUR LIFE

You probably have never been forced to choose between your money or your life. Or have you? To pay the bills, many of us have to choose between what we *love* to do and what we *have* to do. Sure, we've heard that if we do what we love, the money will follow. But we have to ask— How? How much? How soon? Many rock stars seem to have it all—the coolest job on Earth and riches beyond what many of us will ever see. Is it all glitz and glamour to be a rock star? No. Being cooped up in a studio for weeks on end to work on a new album can be nearly torturous. There's also a tremendous amount of pressure put on rockers by record companies to have a hit, and then to replicate that success on every release.

Consider this quote from Peter Buck of R.E.M. about the making of *Around The Sun*, which was not the band's best work but took an inordinate amount of time to record: "I'm always obsessed with the passage of time. How much more do I get? I just couldn't imagine ever again spending that much time doing something I didn't like the end result of."

Then there is the false impression that rock stars are making millions. If you read "Royalties" at the end of this chapter, you'll know the music business is the business model from hell—unless you're the label. Okay, you say, but what about being on stage in front of screaming, adoring fans. That's the life. Right? Yes, being on stage can be a dream come true. However, the time it takes to get to that point—getting from gig to gig can be lonely, boring, and long. Listen to Bob Seger's ode to the road, "Turn the Page," for a firsthand account.

And that's not the worst of it—think about all the rockers who died in plane crashes, bus accidents, and even onstage mishaps. So get this: the "rock star" image is really for musicians who've made it. Many who have yet to break through would trade a valuable body part to be in a real studio recording an album or on the road getting paid to play.

If you reread the above paragraph and insert "entrepreneur" and "business" for "rock star" and "band," there are a lot of parallels. Being your own boss can seem lucrative and glamorous. But you may also be stuck in your store or restaurant day in and day out, or have orders out the wazoo and still be in debt, or travel around the country drumming up business when you'd rather be home with your family and friends.

Have we bummed you out? Don't worry. That you're still reading is good; it means you have hope. Go through the above examples again, and read them with the eyes of someone who simply wouldn't want it any other way—they love what they do, and they get to have their money *and* their life. Figure out where what you love to do intersects with what enough people are willing to pay for. And then you can truly do what you love, and the money will follow.

ROYALTIES

Most of the record-buying public (especially those who pirate music without paying) don't know how royalties work. So let's take a look. First, the bad news: when a CD is sold everyone gets a cut, and the artist is only one of a dozen entities with their fingers in the pie. The good news: music generates royalties when it is performed in public (performance royalty), which includes music played in concert, radio, TV, commercials, films, and even in elevators, cafes, retail stores, malls, and bars.

This performance money is paid to the songwriter and the music publisher. Rockers also get paid "mechanical royalties," which are payments from the record company/label to the songwriter, publisher, and performers of the music based on units sold. This includes CDs, downloads, videos, ringtones, computer games, sheet music, and more. (And this is the point of contention regarding pirated or shared music.) Mechanical royalties (8.5 cents for songs less than five minutes in length) are split between the songwriter and the publisher, while the recording artist gets paid a variable rate based on the terms of their contract. So, on a typical CD sold, the biggest percentage goes to the record label, the next largest slice goes to the store, with the recording artist, songwriter, and publisher splitting the rest.

In the end, the average band will make about a buck on a CD with a list price of $15.00. A song sold on iTunes for 99 cents will result in the songwriter and publisher sharing 8 cents and the artists and producers splitting 10 cents. Keep in mind, however, that when a band makes that buck on a CD, they have managers, roadies, equipment, and other expenses to pay out of that amount. As if that isn't bad enough, the record labels pay upfront recording, promotion, and touring expenses as "advances" against future royalties—so if a band racks up $300,000 in these costs (not hard to do), they'll likely need a gold album (500,000 copies sold; *not* easy to do) to make decent money on it. A band with five members in this scenario could see an income of only $30,000 each, hardly enough to be set for life.

"Most performers make roughly a high school teacher's salary," said Dennis Oppenheimer of the Performance Group, an artist's management agency. Indeed, Throwing Muses once asked a stagehand to take over on bass guitar during a tour when they were popular. He was excited for the opportunity to be in the limelight, then discovered he'd have to take a pay cut.

Donald Passman, author of *All You Need to Know About the Music Business*, states that a band needs to sell nearly half a million copies of an album before it sees any royalties. Jamie Kitman, manager of They Might Be Giants, told the *Washington Post* in 1995: "[The band] have sold about 1.5 million albums for Elektra. But we've never seen a single royalty check from the company since we joined it in 1990." What money they made came from touring and merchandise.

It's not all risk for the rockers, however. Record execs say, out of all acts signed, they only make money on about 15 percent (with other money made from the back catalogs of bands no longer performing or recording). Of course, the records are stacked, so to speak, against the bands. Labels can spread their losses and have been known to drop acts after one poorly selling album. Artists, on the other hand, unless they diversify as described in this book, typically find themselves in debt to the record labels or worse: multi-platinum Warrant was dropped in the early '90s and then sued by their label for the cost of unsold concert T-shirts.

THINK LIKE A ROCK STAR

The Makeup and Mindset of Success

"I never set out to be weird. It was always
other people who called me weird."

– FRANK ZAPPA–

As you'll learn in this chapter (and much of the book), success begins in your head–and in your heart. You need an inspired vision, and you need the persistence to stay true to that vision no matter what others may say (or think) about you.

The trials and tribulations rock stars go through to reach success are not unlike those of entrepreneurs. Perhaps entrepreneurs don't have to suffer smoke-filled bars and beer-soaked club floors–but more than enough have slept in their cars, run up credit card debt, and eaten ramen noodle dinners night after night to achieve their dreams.

The most successful rockers have displayed a clear and unwavering desire for fame and fortune. And what appears to be overnight success was always the result of years of obscurity, often at below-poverty levels. But because they had the qualities revealed in this chapter, they reached goals most people only dream of. Except, that is, for entrepreneurs, who–believe it or not–share similar drives, goals, and imagination.

HAVING A CLEAR VISION

Sting once said, "Being intelligent is not a prerequisite for being a rock star." Perhaps being "intelligent" would lead someone to make a more safe and sane choice for a career path than rock music. But make no mistake, legendary rock stars are no dummies. And we certainly have found plenty of exceptions to Sting's comment.

First and foremost, rock stars are visionaries. Not necessarily in the drug-induced way (though that's been known to happen), but rather knowing *exactly* what they want to be. It's easy to think we know exactly what we want to be, but when truly grilled on the topic, most people waiver. They either have an unclear vision of themselves in the future or it's a myriad and kaleidoscopic vision—"I'll be a successful poet-crafts-man-cafe-owner-real-estate-agent." Rock stars never answer like that. Often from a very young age, they pictured themselves onstage, wailing out killer guitar solos and then catching a limo to their private jet to fly to the next show. Granted, being a rock star is often surprisingly mundane compared to that vision—but the vision was extraordinary, in the literal sense of the word, and crystalline.

According to Eddie Van Halen's older brother Alex (drummer of their namesake band), Eddie slept with his guitar and played it every day after school instead of doing homework. Ironically, when they were growing up, Alex started out playing guitar, and Eddie started out on drums. However, when Alex began to prove himself a better drummer than Eddie, Eddie became annoyed and took up the guitar. And the rest is history. But throughout it all, Eddie maintained a vision that surpassed his brother's (and a vision that should inspire any entrepreneur).

When asked in a 1996 *Guitar World* interview how he went from his first chord to being a virtuoso of the electric guitar, Eddie replied, "Practice. I used to sit on the edge of my bed . . . my brother would go out at 7 pm . . . and when he'd come back at 3 am, I would still be sitting in the same place, playing guitar. I did that for years." That determination and intense desire to prove himself eventually led him to start his first band, Mammoth, at the age of seventeen.

KISS chief visionary Gene Simmons was extremely clear about what he wanted as well. Frustrated that his prior band, Wicked Lester, had no clear image ("We looked like a bunch of guys at a bus stop," Simmons once quipped), he set out to create a band that was iconic. His vision was a combination of the Beatles (whom he admired for their merchandising success as much as their musical talent) and superheroes. As an immigrant from Israel in the 1950s, he was fascinated by the uniquely American superhero concept and wanted to incorporate this comic-book element into his band. Now, nearly four decades later, Simmons' clarity about his vision of KISS has proven itself the masterful foundation of a $100-million-plus empire (with total licensing revenues reportedly exceeding a *billion* dollars).

One of Simmons' other early influences was Alice Cooper, who had a similarly clear idea of what he wanted his own band to be. Although his band's horror-oriented image could be traced back to 1965, when they performed as the Spiders with a huge black web strung behind the stage, it wasn't until 1968 that Cooper (then named Vincent Furnier) decided they needed something more to succeed and observed that most bands weren't making the most of their stage presence.

Thus was born Alice Cooper, originally the band name, but what later became Furnier's legal name. Playing off the gimmick that he was a reincarnated witch, Cooper correctly banked on the idea there would be controversy over his performing in drag (as a witch) and incorporating horror-show theatrics into performances. With the help of exaggerated tabloid reports of stage antics, which he exploited, Cooper became credited with establishing the "shock rock" genre and stayed true to his vision for years, raising the bar with his increasingly horrific performances and evil persona. Just as Black Sabbath's dark music intentionally represented a sound and image counter to the peace movement, Cooper's gore and grim appeal stood out among the sweet AM-radio sounds of much of the hippie rock of the time.

Sometimes, the vision may not be preconceived, but the mindset to hold true to the image that emerges is nonetheless crucial to success. The Australian band AC/DC has stuck to a formula of simple blues-based rock throughout the many trends of four decades. Holding true to their stripped-down sound has been one major component of their success, which includes being one of the best-selling bands of all time and creating the best-selling rock album of all time (1980's *Back in Black*).

One of the most important traits of successful rockers is the stubbornness and conviction to hold their vision when those around them don't see it. KISS was repeatedly told to drop their makeup and image during their early years when success seemed impossible–but Simmons and co-founder Paul Stanley would have it no other way.

Likewise, Detroit up-and-comer Kid Rock spent years proving to countless naysayers, including his father, that a white kid could succeed in the rap-music business. His dedication was so strong that he did the unthinkable–he asked his father for a $5,000 loan to fund his record production, *after* he had moved out of the house in frustration. Then, once he was successful in that genre, he dedicated himself to proving he could transition to rock-star status. Rock's next transition, moving into the realm of country music, required no convincing of anyone. By that point, he'd sold millions of albums and proved his vision of being a multi-talented musician and performer. Another Detroit rap-rock crossover success, Eminem, faced a similar struggle that lasted a decade.

As with these rockers, successful entrepreneurs hold a firm and positive vision of their businesses. But vision alone is not enough.

TURNING FANTASIES INTO REALITY

Singer Joe Elliott of Def Leppard envisioned his future band in high school, even writing imaginary reviews of his band's shows. The fictional band's name? Deaf Leopard.

PASSION AND PERSISTENCE

Not only do the stories above reflect the vision these rockers had, but also their passion and persistence. Every successful rock tale is fueled by these two traits, with endless accounts of doing whatever it took to make it through early tough times:

+ Guns N' Roses ate at homeless shelters and lived with "girlfriends" in Los Angeles.

+ Aerosmith guitarist Joe Perry washed dishes at a restaurant in New Hampshire.

+ KISS, Judas Priest, Aerosmith, Jewel, and many others toured and slept in beat-up vans and station wagons.

+ Duran Duran worked as doormen, disk jockeys, and glass collectors at the club their managers also owned (where the band also rehearsed).

+ Jimi Hendrix moved between at least seven cities in the U.S. and England in less than five years, trying to get steady work as a guitarist.

+ AC/DC spent twelve to fourteen hours on the road each day—in the back of a truck—on their early tours of Australia, because the distance between cities was so long.

+ Even though their album *Number of the Beast* was #1 on the U.K. chart and #3 on the U.S. chart in 1982, Iron Maiden members were only making 100 pounds a week (equal to less than $100 at the time) while touring Europe (which included frequently having to jump-start their old bus).

And the list could go on. The question is: how bad do you want success?

Take soft-rock/country singer and songwriter Kris Kristofferson. He was a Golden Globes boxer, a Rhodes Scholarship recipient (to Oxford), a captain in the Air Force, an instructor at West Point, and a commercial helicopter pilot. While sweeping the floors of a recording studio in Nashville just to make contact with industry names, he gave Johnny Cash his demo tape. Cash promptly dumped it in a lake. Not to be dissuaded, Kristofferson made use of his pilot's license and surprised Cash by landing a helicopter in his yard to give him another demo tape. Undoubtedly impressed (or frightened) by the aspiring songwriter's moxie, Cash eventually recorded Kristofferson's "Sunday Morning

Coming Down"—which was voted Song of the Year in 1970 by the Country Music Association. Kristofferson went on to write countless country and rock hits (including Janis Joplin's "Me and Bobby McGee"), win numerous industry awards, and appear in dozens of films.

More than almost anything else, success in the rock world and as an entrepreneur (after all, rockers *are* entrepreneurs) requires confidence and guts. Standing up to the unbelievers, standing up to the many obstacles, standing up for your vision, and having a high level of tolerance for discomfort—being comfortable with being uncomfortable—are almost daily requirements.

Do you have it too easy? Do you have escape routes, so that you don't *have* to make it work? While not a rock star in the sense that most people in this book are, Cher has always had a strong rock-star sense. When asked how she made it in her early years, she replied that she had no other choice. (Her parents divorced when she was a child, she lived in a foster home for a while, and she dropped out of high school at sixteen due to severe dyslexia.) This *need to succeed* fueled her for years to come. She is the only person to have won an Academy Award, a Grammy Award, an Emmy Award, a Cannes Film Award, a Golden Globe Award (three), and a Billboard Music Award (numerous). Having sold over 100 million records since 1964, she's one of the best-selling artists of all time.

Lastly, passion and persistence also mean adhering to your principles. "I refuse to slap some stupid words on the stupid paper just so we have a stupid song finished," said folk-rocker Suzanne Vega, known for her strong and intelligent lyrics. Are you this passionate about your product? There's a fine line between commerce and integrity, and you need to decide where to draw that line (other than where it's legally drawn).

In whatever business you run, refuse to just "slap it on the paper" to get it done. Freddie Mercury of Queen once said, "We were adamant that 'Bohemian Rhapsody' could be a hit in its entirety. [It was considered too long for radio.] We have been forced to make compromises, but cutting up a song will never be one of them." Keep your standards high, and you will have a greater likelihood of success in the long run.

DETERMINATION AND BELIEF

While these two traits may seem the same as passion and persistence, they're subtly different. Determination and belief are the foundations of persistence. You persist because you are determined and have an unwavering belief in your goal. And you believe you are entitled to this success—it's there waiting for you, but you're just not there yet—and, regardless of what's in your way, it's just around the corner. You've just gotta get there. As Police drummer Stewart Copeland recounted, "I had to talk Sting out of leaving in 1977, by saying 'Look, success is just around the corner.' I had to keep his morale up."

One band for whom success was literally right around the corner was Linkin Park. By 1999, while going by the name Xero, they had been rejected by every major label and numerous indie labels after playing forty-two label auditions (called "showcases") in three years. By late 1999, they decided to try again for Warner Bros. Records—which had already rejected the band three times itself. Only this time, due to a key contact there, the band was signed and renamed Linkin Park.

A year later, in October 2000, they released their first album, *Hybrid Theory*. By Christmas of that year, only two months later, the album had achieved gold status (500,000 copies sold) and then went on to become the best-selling album of 2001 with sales of nearly five million copies. Within only two years, the band went from being without a deal and having a lot of frustration to being the biggest band of the year and winning a Grammy award. Said guitarist Brad Delson in 2002: "We hit a lot of roadblocks—we could have easily given up, but we said, 'We know what we have is great. We're gonna keep going until someone else thinks so.' It should be inspirational for people to know that if you really go for something and are willing to bust your ass, then you can make it happen." Spoken like a true entrepreneur.

From Linkin Park's base in Southern California, we travel to Georgia almost a decade earlier. Then-unknown Ed Roland had been working at a recording studio in Atlanta, doing production and engineering work for local artists. Having studied at the Berklee College of Music, however, his aspirations were more toward songwriting and publishing.

As such, he submitted his demo songs to numerous labels in the early 1990s and received uniform rejection from them.

By 1993, a small indie label picked up Ed Roland's collection of demos and released them as *Hints, Allegations, and Things Left Unsaid* under the artist name Collective Soul. At this point, despite the release, there was nothing to indicate that success was on the horizon for Roland. But unknown to him, his song "Shine" from the album was becoming hugely popular at a college radio station in Orlando, Florida. Soon, the buzz was getting around and the song's popularity spread. Within months, although numerous labels had rejected the songs, Atlantic Records caught wind of the grassroots success of "Shine" and signed Roland–releasing the album nationally in March 1994 using its existing name and recording (a rare move) minus one song. Roland quickly formed a band to support the release; the result was "Shine" hitting #1 on the Billboard charts, the band playing at Woodstock 1994, and the album reaching #15 and achieving double-platinum status (over two million units sold).

But wait, there's more! This tale so far would serve well to demonstrate Roland's determination and belief, but his will would soon be tested even more. The following year, Collective Soul's eponymous album reached triple platinum, spawned three #1 singles, and they were headlining a national tour. But they weren't making any money. Their manager had reportedly diverted their funds into his own hands and gained control of the publishing rights. (Details are unavailable due to a later court order.) Left with no choice but a legal battle, Roland and his band suddenly found themselves with no money (the funds were frozen pending the lawsuit), with a cancelled tour, and unable to afford studio time to record their next album.

As a result, while the court case dragged on through much of 1995 and 1996, they had to rent a cabin in a cow pasture and record into a computer. Their determination paid off–the court case was settled, the album (*Disciplined Breakdown*) was released in 1997, went platinum, and generated two #1 hits. Following that, Collective Soul went on to generate ten more top-40 (mainstream rock) hits and sell a total of roughly eight million albums in the U.S.

Rejection, and the determination to overcome it, is a repeated ingredient in the rock-star recipe. Joan Jett's self-titled debut solo album in 1980 (after her stint in the Runaways) was rejected by twenty-eight major labels in the U.S., leading her to release it independently with the help of producer Kenny Laguna (and his daughter's college savings). Selling the album mostly out of the trunk of Laguna's car after shows, they couldn't keep up with the demand. But that "problem" impressed Neil Bogart, the founder of Casablanca Records (and longtime friend of Laguna's), and he signed Jett and Laguna to his new label, Boardwalk Records. The following year, Joan Jett and the Blackhearts recorded their first new album on Boardwalk, *I Love Rock and Roll*–and it shot to #2 on the strength of its title song, which topped the charts for seven weeks in 1982. From there, Jett had numerous hit songs in the '80s and parlayed her success into roles as a music producer and as an actor in film, television, and on Broadway. Interestingly, her independently released *Joan Jett* album makes her the first female performer to start her own record label. And none of this would've happened had she decided to give up after those twenty-eight rejections.

Rejected even more than Joan Jett, the songwriting duo of Felice and Boudleaux Bryant had thirty artists (including Elvis) decline to record their song "Bye Bye Love" (not related to the Cars' song). Finally, the Everly Brothers picked it up in 1957, and it became a huge hit, topping the pop, country, *and* R&B charts and selling over a million copies. (Selling a million copies in 1957 was a much bigger feat than it is now.)

Sometimes, determination is a key component of success later in a career or a business's lifespan as well. Numerous bands have had to fight and overcome addiction problems in the midst of stardom, such as Stone Temple Pilots, Guns N' Roses, Metallica, and Aerosmith. According to the band's autobiography, Aerosmith's manager promised them in the mid-1980s (at the lowest point in their career) that he would make them the biggest band in the world by 1990 if they all completed rehab programs. It was a wise incentive, as the outcome proved, but also indicative of the band members' determination to not let fall apart what they'd worked so hard to build.

Following Scorpions' world tour in 1981, singer Klaus Meine lost his voice during the recording of the *Blackout* album. The problem was so bad he couldn't even speak, and his doctor said he should change professions. But, not one to give up, Meine (and the band) stuck it out—and after therapy and surgery on his vocal cords, he returned to the microphone and Scorpions enjoyed mega-success through the rest of the decade.

FAKE IT 'TIL YOU MAKE IT

Another interesting similarity between rock stars and entrepreneurs is the ability, and sometimes necessity, to . . . well, let's just say, stretch the truth until it becomes reality. As is often said, and is often true, nothing breeds success like success—and sometimes you need to create that image of success first.

Three examples come from KISS (no surprise, considering image was critical to the band). Back in 1973 when they were first getting started, they produced some of their own shows in New York City. And to attract people and industry reps, they would bring in bigger-name bands to share the bill. But since KISS was producing the show, they made the tickets and posters and they would put their own name at the top of the bill. During that time, they would also play limited shows in the area and tell people they were on tour. Lastly, when they were beginning to enjoy some success a few years later, they put the KISS logo on a chartered plane to give the impression they had their own jet.

Sometimes faking it 'til you make it means jumping on opportunities even if you're not ready for them. You see that it's the thing to do, you know it's the right thing to do, and you'll just have to figure out later how to make it work. Los Angeles, 1981. An aspiring seventeen-year-old drummer named Lars Ulrich catches wind of a compilation album being put together featuring up-and-coming metal bands. Ulrich secures a spot on this album. Ulrich has no band. No problem. Before the due date for delivering his song, Ulrich puts together a band that includes singer-guitarist James Hetfield and records the song "Hit the Lights"—under the name Metallica. After the success of the metal compilation album ("Hit the Lights" was considered by many to be the best track),

Metallica moved to San Francisco (the L.A. scene was too glam for them) and ten years later were one of the most popular metal acts of all time. The original Woodstock in 1969 was born out of a bit of fakery. The producers, four men operating under the name Woodstock Ventures, had *never even put on a concert before*–but sought to put on the biggest concert of that year. Among the many hurdles was securing big-name performers. Recalls one of the producers, Joel Rosenman: "To get the contracts, we had to have the credibility, and to get the credibility, we had to have the contracts." (Every entrepreneur knows some form of this Catch-22.) To solve the problem, they just needed to get the first few acts to attract the rest, so they offered to pay fees as extraordinary as the festival they envisioned. And it worked. Jefferson Airplane signed up, followed by Creedance Clearwater Revival and the Who. The credibility of those bands then led to the signing of the others. Ironically, the actual intent of the festival was to raise money for the four entrepreneurs to start a recording studio, and due to the losses they incurred (most of the half-million attendees never paid) the studio never came to be.

If you're just getting your business going, look at how you can create the impression of success–even if you're still borrowing from one credit card to pay the bill for another while you wait for that big check your client owes you. Are you dressing the part? If your industry values physical appearances, you may need to invest in a decent suit or business outfit. If your website is sub-par, what can you do to make it more impressive? Perhaps, if you don't have the thousands of dollars to pay for a professional design, it means hiring a savvy kid from the local high school. Maybe you could barter with a website designer. Or how about a highly publicized contest in which you generate a lot of media coverage for the winner in lieu of a market-rate design? Regardless of how you do it, a stellar website is one of the best ways to appear to be bigger and more successful than you are.

JUST GET OUT THERE

Al Kooper started his career in the Royal Teens and had a hit in 1958 with "Short Shorts" when he was fourteen. Following that, he co-wrote a #1 hit song ("This Diamond Ring") for Gary Lewis and the Playboys. Then, when he heard Bob Dylan was doing a recording session nearby, he found a way to get an invitation in the hopes he could play guitar on a track. Guitarist Mike Bloomfield was much better, however, so Kooper offered to play keyboards. He actually couldn't. But he did well enough on "Like A Rolling Stone" to help make rock history. (Talk about faking it 'til you make it.) In the years to come, Kooper accomplished much in the business: he toured with Dylan; formed the band Blood, Sweat and Tears; played on cuts of the Who's *The Who Sells Out*; and discovered and produced Lynyrd Skynyrd. Not bad for just putting himself out there–and *creating* the opportunity to appear on one of Dylan's biggest hits.

Because the business world is built on connections, you need to get out there and make them. (See the section on networking in Chapter One.) By putting yourself in front of others, putting your work out to the public, or offering your services to others, you meet people and discover opportunities.

BRINGING IT ALL TOGETHER

Being a rock-star-like businessperson takes a lot of unique traits. But regardless of how many you have, it all begins with a firm belief in yourself and that success is yours to create.

The path to the top in rock and in business is not an easy one; it's pitted with holes, often overgrown with brush to be cut through, and occasionally perched dangerously along a cliff. But as you'll learn from this book, more than anything, just keep going. Don't dwell on setbacks any longer than necessary to figure out another direction–and of course, to learn from them.

As you keep going, remember that only persistence will get you to your goals. Success may be right around the corner or it may be a ways off–but it's only those who give up who don't get there.

BUSINESS-MINDSET CHECKLIST

Below are examples of artists and bands we think embody a particular trait necessary to making it big in business. It's not a complete list. Other bands certainly have some of these qualities. But these examples capture what we mean when we discuss having the right "business mindset."

Passion (Scorpions)–Most bands pay their dues and exhibit immense passion to reach stardom. But few have had a road to success as long as Scorpions. Founded in Germany in 1965, it wasn't until 1979 that they achieved modest success with their album *Lovedrive.* And it was *seventeen years* after they started before they reached stardom with their first platinum album, 1982's *Blackout.* Now, still going after more than forty-three years in business, they're one of the longest-running bands performing.

Vision (Rush)–Exploring the progressive-rock movement made popular by bands such as Yes, Pink Floyd, and Genesis, Rush released *Caress of Steel* in 1975 to little acclaim and sluggish sales. As a result, their record label pushed the band to create their next album in a more commercial and radio-friendly format (i.e., shorter, catchier songs). Unwilling to give up their vision, the Canadian trio composed their epic 1976 album, *2112,* which became their first platinum record and began their ascent to superstardom.

Ethics (Coldplay)–In addition to their ongoing and outspoken support of numerous causes, especially fair trade, the band has refused several multi-million-dollar product endorsement deals. Says leader Chris Martin, "We wouldn't be able to live with ourselves."

Talent (The Beatles)–Need we say more? Okay, we will. The Beatles broke ground in many ways very early in the development of rock music, from use of exotic instruments to recording techniques to style to songwriting to composition. As a result, they laid the groundwork for nearly every genre and style of rock that followed–and are still the standard many musicians aspire to.

Flexibility (Kid Rock)–He started out as a teenage rapper in Detroit, succeeded in that field, moved on to rock, succeeded there, and then moved to country and succeeded there as well. And along the way, he's proved himself a versatile performer on the turntable, behind the mic, playing rhythm and lead guitar, and playing bass and drums.

Ideas (Trent Reznor of Nine Inch Nails)–Another multi-instrumentalist, he's mostly a one-man show. But Reznor most exemplified being an idea man when he released his 2007 album, *Year Zero* . . . and released all the songs as GarageBand tracks for free for any Mac user to mix and play with. (GarageBand is a consumer digital studio for the Mac.)

Hard work (Jon Bon Jovi)–Cited by many to be a nonstop worker, he once said of himself: "The fact that I'm a workaholic, studio in, studio out, stage on, stage off, want to be dealing with music day and night, doesn't mean everyone else has to adjust to that pace."

Risk (Sharon and Ozzy Osbourne)–The married metal couple decided to make their long-running Ozzfest tour free in 2007 and were predicted to lose a ton of money. Instead, they found all the sponsors necessary to give away every ticket, nearly a half million, to fans via the Internet.

Money mindset (Jimmy Buffett)–While most rock stars are inclined to party after concerts, Buffett was more content to retreat to his hotel and do business, tallying up receipts and calculating expenses. As an entrepreneur, not only do you need a money mindset but you almost always need to put profits ahead of partying.

Promotional thinking (Gene Simmons of KISS)–Recognizing the commercial value of the KISS name, logo, and band-member characters, Simmons trademarked all of these early on and has capitalized on them to the tune of over 2,500 licensing deals.

Persistance (Aerosmith)–Down and out in the early 1980s and on the edge of fading into rock history, the "Bad Boys from Boston" stuck it out and were rediscovered by the MTV generation when they collaborated with Run DMC on a rap-rock video of "Walk This Way" in 1986. Following that, the band members all went through a rigorous rehab program for a few years, ending the 1980s with two smash albums, *Permanent Vacation* and *Pump*. Since then, they've risen to legendary rock status as one of the best-selling rock bands of all time and were one of the top-grossing touring acts of 2007.

Leadership (Bono of U2)–You can't name any other rock star who's reached true dignitary status. From his early days with U2 raising social consciousness from behind the microphone to meeting with leaders of numerous nations to solve world problems, Bono has demonstrated unparalleled leadership on and off the stage.

Confidence (Sarah McLachlan)–No one could make money on a festival featuring only female musicians; they aren't popular enough. Or at least that's what McLachlan was told in 1996 when festivals and radio stations rarely played two female acts in a row. But despite the naysayers, she moved ahead and started Lilith Fair, proving them wrong when the first festival raked in over $16 million. The popular festival continued for three years and broke numerous female artists into the mainstream.

DEAL WITH IT

Staying Positive in Negative Times

"I feel there is a curse on rock stars."
–(THE LATE) MARC BOLAN–

Do you have any idea how many people would love to . . . ? You could end this sentence with either (or both) answers below:

a. Be their own boss.
b. Be a rock star.

So many of us dream of making millions working for ourselves. And many of us also wonder what it would be like to rock out on a stage with thousands of fans screaming their appreciation. Both remain a pipe dream for most people because it's just plain hard work to build and maintain a thriving enterprise, or make your mark in the music business. Those who've "been there, done that" in both business and rock music have the scars to prove it. It ain't easy–if it were, all of us would quit our jobs and start a business or take up the guitar.

If you're wondering whether we're trying to scare you out of your dream, the answer is no. We want you to go for it. We want you to be thinking to yourself, "I don't care how difficult it is to be in business. I'm different. I'm determined. And I'm gonna make millions and change the world." That's the kind of attitude rock stars and entrepreneurs share—and in many ways, your *attitude* determines your *altitude* in business. Otherwise, most people would give up before they got going or quit when the going got tough.

Instead, if you see a lack of capital, competitors moving in on your turf, or a "spirited" employee as interesting problems to solve, then you will do well running your own company. Even if you'd rather not have to deal with difficulties (and who does?), you'll be a better entrepreneur if you meet each new challenge with one belief—"What doesn't drive you out of business will make you stronger." In fact, you'll be a better person, too.

Read on to be inspired by the trials and tribulations faced by some of rock's biggest stars and how they survived and thrived *because* of them. Pay special attention to the lessons learned by those who have paid their dues. When you hit these same bumps in the road, you'll know there's a light at the end of the tunnel, and you can confidently move toward it.

START ME UP

Aimee Mann (formerly of the 1980s' hit band 'Til Tuesday) found it so frustrating working with record executives that she bought the rights back to her album *Bachelor No. 2* and released it on her own Superego label. That's one reason to start your own business—dissatisfaction with your current career path. And there are a million more reasons—like the potential to make a million dollars—why going out on your own is the way to go. But there are also a million excuses why potential entrepreneurs don't do it. Here are three of the most common:

1. Fear of Losing Your Safety Net

There's a lot to be said for having medical and dental benefits, a retirement plan, profit sharing, and a weekly paycheck. But it's even better when your *own* company is providing you these things. It's not easy—or even necessary—to give up your day job to begin building a business. But keep this in mind: outside of investing in the stock market, owning real estate, or having a rich relative leave you millions, owning your own business is one of the few ways to create serious wealth.

In rock and roll, there are examples of band members leaving a hit group to go solo—and succeeding. Take former front man Peter Gabriel: he left Genesis to go solo and opened the door for drummer-turned-singer Phil Collins—who later experienced some of *his* greatest success as a solo artist. Michael McDonald was in *two* super groups, the Doobie Brothers and Steely Dan, before making it on his own. And Sting and Dave Grohl were one-third of two of the biggest bands of all time (the Police and Nirvana) before branching out and hitting it big.

There are also plenty of people who left good jobs to go for the gold (record). Bob Seger worked on a Ford assembly line but wanted to make his mark on—and money from—music. For ten years, he toiled for an annual salary of around $7,000 while logging thousands of miles in an old station wagon traveling from small gig to small gig. (He couldn't afford a hotel so he would have to drive all the way back home after each one.) But he enjoyed it more than his conventional job—and it paid off, literally, when he was finally able to quit Ford and became a hit rocker.

Some people, however, can't quite get up the nerve to quit their job and "join the circus" so the decision has to be made for them—they get laid off. Don Henley was devastated when the Eagles broke up, but he never would have had a successful solo career had they stayed together. Or, you can keep your day job and "dabble" on the side. Fleetwood Mac was like a dysfunctional family in many respects, but they were still a family, and this included colleagues and crew. When Fleetwood Mac associate Robin Anderson (one of Stevie Nicks' closest friends) died of leukemia in 1982, Stevie used her grief to write some of her better solo songs for the album *The Wild Heart*—while remaining a member of the band.

As serial entrepreneurs ourselves, we have started a dozen different companies. One visual best explains what it's like to make the big jump—

imagine standing at the edge of a very tall cliff overlooking a churning sea below. If you look down or think about it too long, your fears will get the better of you. So you have to take a leap of faith. So far, neither of us has drowned, so our advice is go for it–but check to make sure it's deep enough before you take the plunge (meaning there are enough people willing to pay for your goods and services).

2. Fear of Obstacles

Maybe you've heard how many businesses fail within the first few years (the Small Business Administration states that just about half of all new businesses make it five years), and you're afraid to take the chance. Well, keep in mind, this is the same success/failure rate for marriages–but that doesn't stop people from tying the knot. The reason is, couples believe love conquers all and see the cup as half full (half of all marriages *do* make it). It's the same in business. If you truly believe in what you are doing, absolutely love it, and are willing to work at it, you will see success. Still, excuses abound as to why being in business is a scary thing. These include (in no particular order):

It's too late. Singer/songwriter Shawn Colvin spent a decade plying her craft in coffeehouses and bars across the country and didn't release her debut album until she was thirty-three years old. (It went platinum, won a Grammy Award, and got rave reviews.) And her biggest hit song came when she was forty. It's never too late.

I'm too old. Shawn Colvin could've said this, too. But the Traveling Wilburys were mostly older–formed in 1988 by Roy Orbison (fifty-two), Bob Dylan (forty-seven), George Harrison (forty-five), Jeff Lynne (forty-one), and Tom Petty (thirty-eight). Despite their ages, the band's first album is considered by many critics to be one of the best in rock history. In 2007, the remaining members released *The Traveling Wilburys Collection,* which reached #1 on the UK charts and #9 in the U.S.

But I have kids to think about. Showing the courage to start and run a business is a lesson your children can learn a lot from. One of the best behind-the-scenes stories on TV's *American Idol* occurred during season five when fourth-place finisher Chris Daughtry's wife explained what a good father and selfless person Chris has been. She had encouraged him to go for his dream and try out for the show. Good thing. After *Idol,* Daughtry enjoyed amazing commercial success with his band–their first release sold over three million copies, it was the fastest-selling debut album in Soundscan history, and the band was nominated for four Grammy Awards.

But it's too hard and/or there is too much competition. Tina Wymouth, bassist for the Talking Heads said, "It's a cruel and heartless world out there in commercial rock 'n' roll." We agree. If you knew what it took to get a song on the radio–and keep it there–you would be shocked and horrified. So, if you're tempted to say your industry of choice is difficult to break into, just remember, it could be worse–you could have rock music aspirations.

I'm worried someone will steal my idea. "People copying us doesn't bother me at all," said Peter Hook of New Order. "Some of them probably do it better than we do." In 2002, Peter Gabriel released *Up*. Shania Twain and R.E.M. also released records titled *Up*. Don't let the fear of someone stealing your ideas stop you. Better to keep going, be the best you can be, and forget the rest. And when necessary, you can always sue them–and win.

Led Zepplin had to pay the estate of Richie Valens for lifting lyrics for their song *Boogie with Stu*. Bob Dylan sued Rod Stewart over the song (by the same title) *Forever Young* and won. Likewise, George Harrison was sued by the writers of the Chiffon's hit song *He's So Fine* because *My Sweet Lord* sounded too similar. And Chuck Berry sued the Beach Boys for *Surfin' USA* sounding a lot like *Sweet Little Sixteen*. Berry won back royalties and was awarded sole songwriter credit. Sure, imitation is a form of flattery, but we're betting you'd prefer they just send a nice card. The best defense against others illegally using your ideas is to stay one step ahead of the competition. And get a good lawyer.

I don't have the right equipment. Singer/songwriter Stephen Bishop (*On and On*) penned a book called *Songs in the Rough*, which included examples of how and where many songs were written–on envelopes, napkins, and even toilet seat covers. In the beginning of a business you can beg and borrow (but don't steal) much of what you need to get off the ground. In their first few years in business, Rhino Records wouldn't buy a copier until they exceeded a million in sales, so they walked to a nearby copy shop instead. The goal is to spend money to *make* money–not to make your life easier.

I don't have any money or I'm deep in debt already. Lack of money is probably the biggest stumbling block to building a business. Most people don't know where to get money to start and are afraid to risk their savings on a (probably) risky venture. So don't.

Grammy winner Beck Hansen was working for $4 an hour at a YMCA and a video store–and living in a rat-infested shed behind a friend's house–while making *Mellow Gold* for $500. Lynyrd Skynyrd got their start when they won a local "battle of the bands" contest and used the prize money to record their debut single.

During the dot-com bust, everyone witnessed what happens to businesses when money is thrown at them by venture capitalists. It's usually more prudent to start small and grow slowly, building it with your proceeds and profits. Many bands began their rise to glory in a garage, as did big companies like Apple, HP, and Disney.

"Those who can, do. Those who can't, bitch," said Kenny Rogers, who decided not to fold 'em after the break up of New Edition in the 1970s, leaving him in a financial mess. And that was despite the band's run of hit records and sold-out shows. So Rogers began his solo career over $65,000 in debt, but "the gambler" paid it off, and he ended up in the black.

Sure, any business is a risky business and you could wind up in the red. But with a good chance to be your own boss and create a thriving enterprise you can later sell or pass on to your kids, you owe it to yourself to find the funds and give it a go. If you don't do it, however, you'll have a *zero* chance of success.

3. Discouragement from Others

Many times, those we count on for support end up being those who try to talk us out of being entrepreneurs. This is true for aspiring rockers, too. U2 singer Bono's father discouraged him from being a musician, even though that's all his dad wanted to be himself. This made Bono's burning desire for success even more intense. His father also told him not to have big dreams because Bono would only be disappointed; however, even though he lived in a dreary Dublin neighborhood, Bono did dream big. And when his father insisted his band wouldn't last five minutes–Bono made sure it did. In the end, it's best if you become your own biggest fan and strive to prove the naysayers wrong.

QUIZ: TRAGIC, BUT TRUE? (TRUE OR FALSE)

1. T/F – Eric Clapton lost a son when the toddler accidentally fell from a window.

2. T/F – Rush drummer Neil Peart lost his wife and only child in the same year.

3. T/F – Def Leppard drummer Rick Allen lost his left arm in an automobile accident.

4. T/F – Blink 182 drummer Travis Barker lost his mother when he was thirteen.

5. T/F – Grammy-winner Shelby Lynne lost both of her parents in one tragedy.

6. T/F – Lynyrd Skynyrd lost some of its original band members in a 1977 plane crash.

7. T/F – The Grateful Dead's Jerry Garcia lost his father and a finger in the same year.

8. T/F – Pink Floyd co-founder and original singer Roger "Syd" Barrett lost his head.

(See the end of this chapter for the answers and further details.)

THE BUSINESS BLUES: OVERCOMING DOUBTS AND FEARS

There are two types of entrepreneurs–those who have problems and . . . wait, there are only those with problems. But that's what businesses do–solve problems. They say the secret to business success is to find a problem and solve it. It's true. What saves the day is a business owner's belief that they can deal with whatever comes their way. Whether it's through innovative thinking, putting your nose to the grindstone, surrounding yourself with good people, or just luck–if there's a will, there's a way to overcome any obstacle on your path to fame and fortune.

Keith Richards put it perfectly: "If you don't know the blues, there's no point in picking up the guitar and playing rock and roll, or any other form of popular music." The makeup and mindset of an entrepreneur usually includes resiliency, resourcefulness, and a real need to succeed—no matter what. Here are some examples of what can go wrong in both business and music, and how to handle it.

Don't give up. Even the best of businesses will have a tough time or two. At the age of thirty-two, Brian Johnson seemed washed up. His '70s' glam rock band, Geordie, was over. His marriage was over. His career was essentially over, and—being broke—he earned a meager wage putting vinyl roofs on cars. If it weren't for the premature death of AC/DC frontman Bon Scott (from alcohol poisoning), this story might not have a happy ending—at least for Johnson. He auditioned for and easily won the role of the new lead singer for AC/DC on April 1, 1980. In July, the band released their album *Back in Black*, which has gone on to sell a record-holding forty-two million copies.

Bounce back. The Who lost their drummer (Keith Moon) but continued to record and tour—first with Kenny Jones and then with Ringo Starr's son on drums. Other groups have also lost a band mate but came back strong. If you lose an important employee, key client, or a valued supplier, you have to hold on until help or a replacement arrives.

Don't let a sales slump or slow start put you out of business. If you're suffering from slow sales, you are not alone. Many of rock's biggest bands and solo artists had sales numbers near the bottom of the barrel. Lindsey Buckingham and Stevie Nicks were struggling Los Angeles musicians, and their only album, *Buckingham Nicks*, was a poor seller. So they joined Fleetwood Mac in 1975 and the rest is (sales) history. Their 1977 *Rumours* album is a platinum-seller twenty times over. Billy Joel's first solo album, *Cold Spring Harbor*, was a disaster. It wasn't until his fifth album, *Stranger*, came out (over ten million sold) that he had huge sales and success.

Even Bruce Springsteen's and Bob Dylan's early albums didn't sell well. Reportedly, when Dylan's record label at the time (Columbia) learned he might be leaving for MGM (for a million-dollar deal), they showed his sluggish sales figures to MGM, which then reneged on their offer.

"It" happens. Turn lemons into lemonade—and sell it. Business problems can be both a blessing and a breakthrough. Paul Burlison was the guitarist for the Burnette Trio, and while he was recording *Train Kept A-Rollin'* in 1956, a tube dislodged in his amp and created a fuzzy sound–making him perhaps the first guitarist to "discover" distortion. A few years earlier, Chuck Berry was getting ready for a show in New York City when he discovered the dry cleaner had badly shrunk his suit. Not wanting to wear street clothes (not a good thing on stage in that era), the story goes that he had to walk in a funny way to keep his pants from splitting. And that funny walk evolved into a "duck walk" that became his signature for years to come.

A not-so-funny occurance was the 1971 burning of the Montreaux Casino on Lake Geneva in Switzerland, where Frank Zappa was performing. All his band's gear burned as Deep Purple watched from where they were recording across the lake. (Zappa's band and fans got out safely.) Ian Gillan, singer and songwriter for Deep Purple, turned the tragedy into the band's biggest hit when he wrote *Smoke on the Water*.

Similarly, Don McLean's 1971 hit *American Pie* is about "the day the music died," referring to the plane crash eleven years earlier that killed early rockers Buddy Holly, Richie Valens, and J. P. Richardson (a.k.a, The Big Bopper). Sometimes action is the antidote to despair. Think you're having a bad day at the office? Green Day resurrected punk music with *Dookie* in 1994. But their next few albums were never as popular until they released *American Idiot* a decade later, putting them back on top with a #1 album, a Grammy for Best Album, as well as other accolades. The "lemons" in this tale was the theft of the master tapes for the album. As a result, they had to rerecord them and, in the process, rethought their approach–with award-winning results. Whatever the circumstances, bounce back the best you can, because it may be the best thing that ever happened to you.

It doesn't matter where you start, it's where you finish that counts. James Blunt didn't take the typical path to rock stardom. He came from a middle-class family and was an officer in the Army (he served in Bosnia) before *Back to Bedlam* was released in 2004. When it came out, it didn't chart or even get good reviews. However, the single *You're Beautiful* became a mega-hit in 2005 with airplay on radios all across the U.S.

And how about this one. A young singer-songwriter was rejected by twenty-six record labels before finally getting a deal. Unfortunately, his debut album sold a less-than-impressive 324 copies, and his record company "lost" the tapes for his next release. Not to be deterred, the young man—Jimmy Buffett—continued performing until he'd built up enough of a following to get another record deal. Three decades later, he's one of the wealthiest and highest-earning rock stars.

Don't let bad reviews bog you down. The Beatles weren't an overnight sensation. The band was first turned down by Dick Rowe at Decca Records—as well as other record companies—despite a strong following in Liverpool. And many concert promoters didn't want to work with them. To make money, John Lennon and Paul McCartney wrote songs for others before their big break. (During this time, they offered a song called *Yesterday* to Billy J. Kramer, who turned it down. Ouch.)

Dealing with people's opinions are simply a part of being in business. Rolling Stones manager Eric Easton once said of Mick Jagger, "The singer will have to go." Of course, the band didn't sack Jagger—but they did put keyboardist Ian Stewart backstage to perform during concerts because he didn't have the right look.

Take rejection and poor reviews and turn them into the fuel that stokes your fire. That's what Stephen Stills did. He was a finalist in the tryouts for the comedy series *The Monkees*, but didn't make the cut because of his thinning hair and crooked teeth. So he went out and formed Buffalo Springfield with Peter Tork and Neil Young. Then he really proved himself with the success of Crosby, Stills, and Nash.

Don't let your employees' problems become yours. There are so many examples where band mates just didn't get along . . . or bad behavior and drug abuse by one member threatened to drag the group down . . . or personal politics created a fracture between members of the band . . . and these are from groups that *made it.* One story stands out because the implications from this "employee problem" were extraordinary. In 1962, Pete Best was dumped by the other three Beatles at the request of producer George Martin for reasons never revealed. For years, Best was bitter—until 1995's *Beatles Anthology* was released and netted the former Beatle over $17 million in royalties for songs he'd contributed to.

Don't let legal issues stop you. John Fogerty wanted out of his recording contract with Fantasy Records, with which his band Creedence Clearwater Revival (also referred to as CCR) had several hits. So, to win his release, he signed away the publishing rights to his CCR songs. Ironically, he was sued by his old record label ten years later when the songs on his solo album sounded too much like his old CCR music. (Fogerty won the suit.) Bad lawsuits happen to good people, but if you always do the right thing in business you'll have less to worry about— and fewer legal issues to deal with. No matter how much good karma you collect, make sure to protect your position, property (intellectual and otherwise), and any other assets you have by using any and all means available.

If you are not profitable and/or aren't earning a salary, cut costs. Mark Knopfler named his band Dire Straits because of the group's horrendous financial situation in their early years; however, they kept costs low enough to eventually succeed. Steve Winwood considered giving up after the dismal sales of his first solo album left him running out of cash. Searching for alternative ways to make money, he considered farming but felt he was more suited for working at a record company or producing other artists. He came to grips with the reality that he'd have to streamline his life and live on less. Once he realized he could, and would be okay, he went back to work on another record. Without the pressure of needing a hit, he wrote and recorded *Arch of a Diver*, a huge success.

The next example reads like a country music song, but it's the real deal. Rickie Lee Jones was flat broke before she wrote and recorded "Chuck E's in Love." During the day, she worked as a waitress, but was fired and her boyfriend left her. Unable to pay the rent, she became homeless and slept under the Hollywood sign at night. But she didn't give up, and she continued to write and perform around Los Angeles. Finally, one of the songs she wrote and recorded for her demo (ironically titled *Easy Money*) landed her a contract with A&M Records.

Another rock star who learned to live lean is Mark Slaughter of the '80s' glam-metal band Slaughter. He lived in a dingy apartment with nothing more in it than a bed and credits that experience for helping make him hungry for success.

The dreaded day job. Independent artist Cindy Lee Berryhill had quite a cult following (but never mainstream success) when she went to work for Neil Young's Vapor Records and its sister company Look Out Management to receive a steady paycheck. She still writes and performs but has the basics covered. It's not a bad idea to get a day job while working on your dream, so you're learning and earning at the same time.

In fact, Billy Joel was a piano player in a Los Angeles bar when he wrote "Piano Man," his signature song. Likewise, singer/songwriter Jesca Hoop was working as a nanny while recording her demos and her subsequent breakthrough CD, *Kismet*, which came out to strong sales and positive press. Of course, it helped that she was nannying for Tom Waits and Kathleen Brennan. And we wonder if that was a better gig than Chrissy Hynde of the Pretenders—her day job was cleaning Keith Richards' home.

It's business, not personal. When Tina Turner left her husband Ike (literally running away from him while on tour), she had thirty-six cents in her pocket. She had no money because he controlled all the finances, and she had to live with friends. Later, with two kids and big debts to the IRS and music promoters (because she'd broken contracts in leaving Ike), she survived on food stamps. But through it all, she never let her personal strife keep her down in business. She started her solo career, and despite the mountainous debt, became a huge star in her own right.

Even if you fail you will still find work. Steve Katz (of Blood, Sweat and Tears fame) became the East Coast Artists & Repertoir (A&R) Director at Mercury Records when the band broke up. Later, he became the vice president of the label. Dee Snider of Twisted Sister can still be heard on the radio—only now as a disc jockey. He hosts the syndicated '80s' metal show *The House of Hair*. Guitarist Lenny Kaye (Patti Smith Group) became a rock historian and taught a popular class on the subject at Rutgers University.

MUSIC BUSINESS 101

Historically, a singer-songwriter's chance of getting a record deal was (and is) less than 1 in 10,000. Not good odds. And of those who actually released a record, only a fraction ever got any radio airplay. Wait, it gets worse. Even if a song did miraculously make it to the airwaves, being able to find it at your local record store (remember those?) was hit or miss.

The problem was (and to some extent, still is) the way the business was set up. A band would build a buzz and then be "discovered" and brought to the attention of a record label. But the label held all the cards, because without the label most artists or bands could barely afford the cost of renting a recording studio (and forget making a video). And, without a label, they could also forget about getting anything on radio or MTV—it cost a small fortune to "land" a song on either one. Lastly, and maybe more importantly, the labels' relationships with manufacturers and distributors was so tight that independent artists couldn't get past the gatekeepers. However, when an artist was signed to a contract, the label miraculously opened doors and fronted money to record, manufacture, market, and promote the music—and get it distributed.

That was then, this is now. Today, a band can write and record their songs on a computer in a home studio. Then, they can start their own record label to promote their music online with minimal expense and sell it (via downloads) without the need to press, print, stock, and store CDs in a huge warehouse or on store shelves. With music now digitized and distributed electronically, the costs are a fraction of what they once were. Essentially, every musician now has every chance of landing a record deal—with their own label. So, the question is, what can you do to emulate this turn in the music business and take more control of your promotion, distribution, sales, and customer interaction?

CHECKLIST: Sound Success

Why do businesses (and bands) fail and how can you avoid the same fate? Check off any (or all?) of the challenges you face.

__ Money problems

It's not how much money you make, it's how much you get to keep that counts. You know, the profits. Many a business has run out of money when sales slowed OR increased too much too soon and they became overextended. A good rule of thumb: don't run out of money–it can take years to become steadily profitable–and don't spend what you don't have. See Chapter Eight, "From Rock to Riches," for more.

__ Lack of sales

Hopefully a sales slump is just that, a temporary slump and not a trend. Rush has sold more albums and concert tickets than almost any other rock band; yet they were almost dropped by their label after one of their early releases (*Caress of Steel*) failed to sell as well as hoped. The band bounced back–and never looked back. Slow album sales of his studio releases were Peter Frampton's reality until he did a live album, *Frampton Comes Alive*, which became a monster seller. Sales are the lifeblood of all for-profit enterprises because you need the revenue pumping into your business in order to survive. Being good at sales (or having people who are) is how you grow your business. Hey, hold your chin up. You can do this. Being good at sales is simply figuring out who benefits from what your business offers, then putting yourself in their path and educating them about what you offer. If you do this and the benefit is clear, the sales will occur. Selling isn't about you, it's about what you do for others.

__ Lack of promotion

The best bands you've never heard of might include Queens of the Stone Age, Wilco, Nickelback, 311, Tool, and Biting Toenails. (Okay, we made that last one up to see if you're paying attention.) Actually, the best bands you've never heard of are still toiling in obscurity–not because they lack talent, but because they lack promotion. Don't let this happen to you. When you struggle with promotion, it's probably the lack of one or more of these three things: time, money, or know-how. But all of these can be overcome with one thing: passion. When you believe so much in what you and your business are doing, you'll want to tell everyone and shout to the world, "Look at me!" Ask yourself, "Is there something I can change about my offer to raise my excitement level so it goes to 'eleven'?" (Think: *This Is Spinal Tap*.)

___ Lack of research and planning

In retail and real estate, location is everything. Many businesses fail because of this alone. A LOT of homework would have saved them from this fate. The same goes for doing due diligence when it comes to gauging market size, choosing a vendor, and running the numbers to back up your gut instincts. In 1990, newly formed Interscope Records signed No Doubt to a multi-record deal based on their live performances and popularity in Southern California. However, the band's sound was in sharp contrast to what was hot at the time (grunge) and their debut in 1992 only sold 30,000 copies. To make matters worse, the label refused to underwrite their tour and when the band did go out on the road, their CD was not available in the cities they were playing. Come on, now!

But by 1995 they got it right with *Tragic Kingdom*, which had sales in excess of sixteen million copies. Business people make better decisions when they are informed (have all the facts and use their head) and get a good feeling about something as well (their heart).

___ Bad business decisions

In baseball, spring training is the only time when every team can feel good about their chances of winning during the regular season because anything is possible. When entrepreneurs first start out, they're usually filled with the same sense of optimism—and make decisions based on that warm fuzzy feeling. This doesn't mean entrepreneurs don't make poor choices later in their businesses. That happens a lot as well. But to avoid these potential pitfalls, read as many business books as you can (like this one), take advantage of a mentor or a Service Corps of Retired Executives volunteer (www.score.org), and never lose sight of what matters most—the bottom line.

___ Bad publicity

"You stick your head above the crowd and attract attention and sometimes somebody will throw a rock at you. That's the territory. You buy the land, you get the Indians," quipped David Lee Roth about publicity in a rather politically incorrect way. Speaking of bad publicity, Indians, and being politically incorrect . . . British rocker Ozzy Osborne once urinated on the Alamo (a historic landmark) and was arrested. It's hard to spin that in a positive way. Biting the head off a dove during a business meeting with record executives, something else Ozzy did, was probably less offensive for some people. Good publicity or reviews, on the other hand, are like gold for your business. For more on publicity, we have a whole chapter dedicated to it–Chapter Six, "Rock the World."

__ Legal problems

Legal problems can bring a company to its knees in no time. Generally speaking, it's best to avoid litigation in every way possible. While it may feel good to get the justice you deserve (if you get it, that is), the process can completely drain you of the resources and energy needed to run your company, much less grow it. The band Boston arrived on the rock scene during the Bicentennial as if it had been shot out of a cannon. Their first album is the most successful debut of all time with seventeen million copies sold. In the late '70s, few bands were as big as Boston, which had another hugely successful album in 1978 with *Don't Look Back*. But the '80s brought the band to a virtual halt, due to numerous legal battles involving founder Tom Scholz. The lawsuits–involving band members, a former manager, and the record label–slowed the creative progress to the point that only one Boston album was released between 1978 and 1994 (*Third Stage* in 1986). And as the 1990s arrived, Boston had been reduced to a one-man band–Tom Scholz. Was all the litigation worth it? Were the settlements worth more than the band would've made had it been more prolific? It's hard to say. But it was clearly a costly process that most of us would be wise to avoid the likes of.

__ Not diversified enough and/or don't embrace change

Don't rock the boat can be a rallying cry when things are going great. However, a wave of change is just around the corner (we guarantee it) and can capsize any business that isn't prepared to change course. Failure to change with the times, which can include embracing innovation and technology, has led many businesses to their graves.

Bands that thrived then changed and thrived again include Jefferson Airplane (later Jefferson Starship), Moody Blues, Duran Duran, Santana (with the *Supernatural* album), ZZ Top (with their MTV videos), Yes (with Trevor Rabin in the '80s), Aerosmith (after their 1986 video with Run DMC), and KISS (from makeup and costumes to none back to makeup and costumes again). And some bands have been savvy enough to ride through the changes, adapting along the way, to maintain their longevity–the Rolling Stones, Rush, and U2, for example.

To stay on top, it takes flexibility, willingness to try new things, staying true to your overall mission, constant efforts to get new customers, not putting your eggs all in one basket, and doing something beneficial for the long term every day. Don't be like the record companies that are struggling to keep up with the digital revolution in music, hanging on to the old paradigm. Read Chapter Eleven, "Topping the Charts," for more.

__ Miss or don't take advantage of opportunities

"We were pullin' the same-sized crowds as Genesis, the same people were buying our records. They cracked it because they went commercial about two years earlier," laments John Weathers of Gentle Giant, one of the most critically acclaimed bands of the 1970s you probably never heard of. Don't be one of those frustrated people or entrepreneurs who didn't move fast enough when you needed to. Conversely, sometimes you need to take advantage of an opportunity others aren't seeing. The song "My Eyes Adored You" was rejected by a number of record labels for not being commercial enough. Frankie Valli bought the song for $4,000 and recorded it with a small label that just wanted his name on their roster. Released in late 1974, the song was a #1 hit a few months later.

__ Personnel problems

They call it "Human Resources" for a reason. As a business owner you will be dealing with (flawed) human beings who also are an invaluable resource when it comes to the growth and success of your enterprise. A bad employee or two can just as easily cost you your company. No Doubt lost their lead singer (John Spence committed suicide), their main songwriter (Eric Stefani left the band to become an animator on *The Simpsons*), experienced a major relationship break-up (after seven years between Gwen Stefani and Tony Kanal), and went through changes on guitar (Tom Dumont replaced Jerry McMahon), and drums (Adrian Young replaced Chris Webb)—and all *before* the band hit it big with their 1995 album, appropriately titled *Tragic Kingdom*. You have to find ways to make it through rocky personnel issues and create policies to proactively prevent or address them.

__ Don't service existing customers

Sly Stone (of the early-1970s' band Sly and Family Stone) became known as "the man who wasn't there" for his consistent lack of showing up for his concerts or playing a little bit and leaving. And although it was eventually dismissed, four concertgoers sued the band Creed in 2003, alleging that singer Scott Stapp was so intoxicated or medicated that he couldn't sing properly, thus ruining the performance.

Fred Durst of Limp Bizkit was also sued for "breach of contract" that year for not completing a show, although he left because fans were reportedly taunting, booing, and throwing things at him. Regardless of who did what, these stories remind us that our customers are always watching—and we need to deliver the goods or we'll lose them.

KISS could've easily fallen into 1970s' rock history when they alienated much of their fan base with their 1979 and 1980 pop-disco albums and their failed 1981 concept album, *The Elder*. However, they learned from that experience, returned with a hard rock album in 1982 and have stayed very in tune with their fans since. And thrash-metal Metallica neared career suicide by cutting their hair and wearing a little makeup in the mid-1990s, followed by their vocal (and to fans, hypocritical) involvement in the lawsuit against Napster over MP3-sharing.

Not only do you need to remain true to your fans and deliver on your brand promise (see Chapter Three, "The 'It' Factor"), but you have to ask yourself, is your competition doing what you are not? If you lose a big sale (or lots of little ones), find out why and what you can do differently. Don't underestimate your competition. Instead, see them as mentors and learn from them.

In some cases, it's even beneficial to team up with non-direct competitors, just as bands do when they collaborate on festivals such as Ozzfest, Lilith Fair, and Lollapalooza. If you don't make your customers say "Wow!" (in a good way) and give them more than they expect, someone else will. Remember, it's easier to maintain and please an existing customer than it is to constantly replace unhappy ones. So, keep 'em happy.

__ Let down by others who drop the ball

After willing himself to success through relentless touring in the Midwest, Bob Seger was about to break out—when his record label went bankrupt and his first single languished. Sometimes others let us down. And sometimes in a big way. Life's circumstances can shatter our expectations, leaving us to pick up the pieces. But just as Seger carried on and rose to even bigger success, we can persevere and not let anything or anyone stand in our way. Ultimately, we have only ourselves to rely on as our biggest supporter.

__ Start your business for the wrong reasons

People start businesses for all sorts of reasons, and they're not all good ones. Sometimes we lose track of what we want (or get bored) and take up an endeavor for the novelty. Maybe we just want to get away from what we're doing. And occasionally we're dazzled by the promises of a particular franchise or network-marketing opportunity.

Whatever the case—being true to ourselves is the biggest clue to starting a business for the *right* reasons. Stanford University studied 250,000 people and came to the conclusion that we are most successful when matched with activities we love to do. It seems hard work and enthusiasm—*in our field of choice*—were the leading indicators of success. An advanced degree, superior intelligence, or a family member in the industry are not the big indicators of success we'd like to think them to be. (They're often excuses for our own lack of effort.) Truth is, it's more about loving what we do and focusing on what we do well—and then working our butts off.

___   **Wait too long to start**

In business, success often comes more to those who are *first* than those who are better. Rock music is full of examples of bands or artists who weren't necessarily more musically talented or technically proficient than their contemporaries, but were more clever in starting something new and different: Elvis, Black Sabbath, KISS, the Cars, R.E.M., Metallica, Guns N' Roses, Soundgarden, and Korn, to name just a few.

___   **Overexpansion and hubris**

Sometimes we just get too big for our own good—at least in our minds. Rockers, who are often successful due to their big thinking and egos, have tripped up from time to time. Styx became one of the biggest acts of the 1970s and early 1980s, but due to founder Dennis DeYoung's vision for a bigger and more-theatrical Styx, which clashed with Tommy Shaw's vision of a harder rocking style, the band broke up. And while John Lennon's comment that the Beatles were "bigger than Jesus" didn't directly lead to their breakup, it was certainly an indication of their mindset at the time.

ARE YOU DOING ALL YOU CAN FOR YOUR BUSINESS?

While watching a VH-1 *Behind the Music* special about Madonna, we were inspired—not by her music, but by her story. When Madonna moved to New York, she didn't know a soul. She and her band lived (and practiced) in a dingy apartment in a crime-ridden neighborhood. (We found it interesting that Madonna was the drummer.) She actually ate food out of a trash can and slept on the floor. To earn enough money to record a demo (late at night when the rates were cheaper), Madonna posed for pictures (in the nude—no big surprise there).

Finally, a deal was made, which Madonna had the poor record executive sign in his hospital bed. Wow. That's a prime example of what it takes to make it in music and business. By the way, Madonna's current net worth is estimated at over $300 million dollars, earning her a spot in the *Guinness Book of World Records* as the "World's Most Successful Female Musician." But does Madonna belong in a book about rock stars? Well, since she is a newly honored member of the Rock and Roll Hall Of Fame, we guess the answer is yes.

ANSWERS TO "TRAGIC, BUT TRUE?"

From page 195.

Sadly, all of these are true (with a slight embellishment on #8). But they reveal that from tragedy can come recovery *and* success. In many cases, the musicians mentioned here used their tragedy to spur them on to new heights and passion. Whatever setbacks you encounter in life, big or small, you can do the same.

1. Eric Clapton's four-year-old son, Conor, accidentally fell from a fifty-third-story Manhattan window in 1991, inspiring Clapton to express his grief in his massive hit *Tears in Heaven*. It was only a few months earlier that Clapton had lost fellow guitarist and friend Stevie Ray Vaughn in a helicopter crash.

2. Neil Peart lost his nineteen-year-old daughter, Selena Taylor, in a 1997 car crash. His common-law wife of twenty-two years, Jacqueline Taylor, then died of cancer the following summer. Peart later said it was from a broken heart that she simply gave up the will to live.

3. Rick Allen lost his left arm in an automobile accident on New Year's Eve 1984. Following an extensive recuperation, Allen re-learned to play the drums with one arm on a specially designed kit. Recently, however, he returned to playing a standard kit.

4. Blink 182 drummer Travis Barker lost his mother the day before he began high school in 1989. She was a major inspiration in his life—her dream was for him to be a drummer in a rock band. Following her death, he took his drumming more seriously, joining his high school marching band and participating in competitions.

5. Shelby Lynne's father shot her mother and then turned the gun on himself. After their deaths, she pursued her music with renewed passion and vigor. After five CDs, with three different labels, Lynne finally landed the record deal that led to her success.

6. Three of the members of Lynyrd Skynyrd (Ronnie Van Zant, Steve Gaines, Cassie Gaines), as well as one of their road managers, died

in a 1977 plane crash that seriously injured the other members and crew. But after a long recovery, they eventually regrouped and carried on, and they're still touring over thirty years later.

7. At age five, Jerry Garcia watched from the shore as his father drowned in a fishing accident. Later that same year, his brother inadvertently cut off one of Jerry's fingers while chopping wood.

8. Syd Barrett didn't literally lose his head, but rather lost his mind from a combination of drug use and apparent (but undiagnosed) mental illness. This led to his outster from Pink Floyd in 1968 when the band simply didn't pick him up on the way to a gig (due to his unstable behavior) and officially fired him a few weeks later.

TOPPING THE CHARTS

Ways to Stay on Top in Times of Change

"Mostly, we're on the road working, because that's how we earn our
living, by playing."
–(THE LATE) JERRY GARCIA–

Sadly, many businesses and bands don't last. Most of the reasons
are preventable. This chapter contains eleven practices that led to
lasting success for bands—practices that can also keep your business
thriving for the long run. But knowing how to keep your business
going won't matter unless you embrace and enact these valuable
lessons. So for each of these tips, we'll include a simple action item
to help ramp up the success of your business and keep it on top of
the charts.

#1

**Bands and businesses that continue to fill a need—and solve
people's problems—remain relevant and attract a loyal following.**
Pink Floyd's masterpiece album *Dark Side of the Moon* stayed on the
U.S. charts for a record-setting 741 weeks (that's fourteen years three

ONE-HIT WONDERS

There are hundreds of one-hit wonders. Here are our favorites from each decade.

1960s

"Wipe Out" (The Surfaris)

1970s

"Kung-Fu Fighting" (Carl Douglas)

"My Sharona" (The Knack)

1980s

"Take on Me" (Aha)–The only U.S. hit from a Norwegian band

"99 Luft Balloons" (Nena)–One of only a few U.S. hits not sung in English

1990s

"Walking in Memphis" (Marc Cohn)

2000s

"Teenage Dirtbag" (Wheatus)

months) and has sold an estimated forty million copies worldwide. When it came out, and for years after, many people used it as a soundtrack to their lives. (Read: The music on *Dark Side of the Moon* went well with a number of different highs–or so we've heard.)

Bruce Springsteen, as well as anyone, captures the struggles of working-class Americans on *Born in the USA* and other albums. And he takes on other timely topics in his lyrics as well. This is why he's still "The Boss" and winning awards (nearly twenty Grammys and counting), recording relevant albums (that sell extremely well), and selling out stadiums on his tours.

Speaking of touring, Jimmy Buffett and the Dave Matthews Band provide fans with more than a stellar show–the parking lot parties are as much a part of the experience as the actual concert–and that's part of the reason they both topped the list of highest-grossing tour acts of 2007. Also on the list were the Police, Van Halen, Genesis, Roger Waters, and Rod Stewart, which shows that people pine for a little nostalgia–and will pay more than $100 a ticket to get it.

There is still a market for bands that make you proud to be from the south (Lynyrd Skynyrd), the east (Bon Jovi), the west (Red Hot Chili Peppers), and everywhere in between (the Eagles). And there are bands that have created such a strong brand they continue to sell well— AC/DC comes to mind with 150 million albums sold, many of them to a whole new generation of fans.

Of course, bands that make you dance, sing, and feel good will always have a place to play and a way to continue to sell their music. Many bands fit this bill, but one instantly comes to mind for us—War. With over fifty million records sold over five decades, they certainly qualify as successful and enduring. You may know (and love) their songs "Low Rider," "Water to Wine," and "Why Can't We Be Friends?"—and many of their hits have been covered or sampled by some of today's biggest acts (from Janet Jackson to Korn). If you've been lucky enough to see them in concert (they're still touring), you know why they're considered one of the best bands to see live. What we love about them (in addition to the way they fuse ten different styles of music into one) is the band's business acumen. If you go to their website, you'll see they sell their songs as downloads and ringtones. They sell themselves in concert and to corporations (such as playing at Harley-Davidson's anniversary in August 2008). They realize the importance of multiple streams of income for long-term success.

BUSINESS LESSON: Find a problem and solve it. Find a need and fill it.

#2

Be the best at what you do—and be a leader and innovator in your field.

Being the best at what you do is one way to stay on top. Another is to be the first (or one of the firsts) to do something. If you can combine the two, well, you really have a chance at lasting dominance. A good example is Tina Turner. Not only was she a trailblazer and influential figure in the history of rock, she's still got it going at the age of sixty-eight (as her performance at the 2008 Grammy Awards proved). Turner is known as "The Queen of Rock & Roll" and for good reason–she has sold more concert tickets than any other solo performer and has sold over 100 million records.

Speaking of millions of records sold, there are some lessons to be learned from some of the names on the "biggest selling" list. The Beatles and Elvis Presley are at the top with more than 500 million records sold each, because they were both the best at what they did and one of the first with their own style and sound. Although Elvis has left the building and the Beatles are no longer together, many of the longtime artists with tens of millions of records sold are still going strong: the Rolling Stones, AC/DC, Aerosmith, the Eagles, Metallica, KISS, and U2. Many of them are considered the best at what they do and have stuck with it. Others were innovators. A good example of being both is the Beastie Boys. This influential and accomplished band went from hardcore punk to rap (and created the fastest-selling CBS Records album ever with *Licensed to Ill*) to alternative-rock and funk, then back to rap and hip-hop–and are still enjoying commercial success and critical acclaim. As a matter of fact, they also have a little-known instrumental jazz album to their credit (1996's *The In Sound from Way Out!*).

Staying on top with leadership and innovation also means keeping an eye on technology and formats and experimenting. In October 2007, Radiohead released its seventh album, *In Rainbows*, as a digital download with customers paying a voluntary price of their own choosing. Because Radiohead wouldn't release sales figures for this release, questions arose as to its success. Those questions were quickly answered, however, when the CD was released at the beginning of 2008 and debuted at #1 on three prominent charts–the UK Album Chart, the United World Chart, *and* the U.S. Billboard Chart. Following on the heels of that success, the Nine Inch Nails' album *Ghosts I-IV* was released in March 2008 as a free download (for part of the album), a $5 download (for the whole album), a $10 two-CD set, a $75 deluxe edition, and a $300 limited edition (which quickly sold out all 2,500 copies).

BUSINESS LESSON: Look for ways to be the first or at the forefront of something with the potential to be big. Find innovative ways to stay ahead of the competition.

#3

Be passionate about your product, and stay true to your vision.
Donald Fagen and Walter Becker (Steely Dan) were famous for their attention to detail when working in the studio. They would have several guitarists come in to record a guitar solo–then not use any of them. There are songs where the drum parts are an amalgam of two or more different drummers. During the *Aja* sessions, Michael McDonald was brought in to sing backup vocals and recalls spending an entire day trying to get the phrasing of a single lyric just so. Guitarist Larry Carlton recalls rehearsing a song until it was perfect and then going past that point to make it sound natural. The point is, Fagen and Becker cared about the little things, and the result is music that still sounds great decades later.

The duo has also been rewarded for their efforts with solid sales (over thirty million records sold) and stellar reviews (they won their first of four Grammys in 2001 and were elected into the Rock and Roll Hall of Fame that same year.) For years, Steely Dan was solely a studio band because they couldn't find musicians to play their complex songs perfectly and consistently during concerts–but they started performing live again in 1993.

Likewise, some of the most complicated music to play live was composed by Frank Zappa. (His only Top-40 song was "Valley Girl" and is *not* a good representation of his body of work.) An underrated guitarist himself, he led a live band consisting of a rotating lineup of some of the very best musicians of all-time. Zappa prided himself on putting his band through the paces, and, as a result, people eagerly awaited his arrival to town each year.

When the Beach Boys' Brian Wilson was working on *Pet Sounds*, he poured ample amounts of sand under his piano to help him get the feel of the beach. Wilson, the primary songwriter for the band, was known as an extreme stickler in the studio, often upsetting the other band members with this quest for perfection. The results were timeless music that influenced an entire generation of musicians–including the Beatles–and an album considered one of the best of all time (*Pet Sounds*). Use your competition to push you to better yourself and try new things–like Brian Wilson and the Beatles did.

Boston's Tom Scholz–guitarist, songwriter, and producer–was obsessed with getting the right sound on record. He played most of the instruments on the demo he recorded in his own makeshift recording studio–located in his basement. Then, when he got a record deal, the label wanted him to re-record everything. However, most of the demo ended up on the debut. Scholz's reputed perfectionism would delay the follow-up release for two years. Unhappy with that album, *Don't Look Back*, he claimed it was released under pressure from the record company. He then declared he wouldn't be forced to release any more music unless he was completely satisfied with the final product. Consequently, Boston's third album, *Third Stage*, did not appear until 1986–and was a success, featuring the high-charting single, "Amanda."

BUSINESS LESSON: Do what you do best and stick with it. Quality never goes out of style.

#4

Be smart with your money so you can survive the slow times.

Many rockers haven't been smart with their earnings. However, there are plenty who were not only on top of their game musically, but also monetarily. To have long-term success in business, you need to get a handle on your finances; unlike drawing a salary from a 9-to-5 job, sales (and income) vary from year to year (and even from month to month).

Van Morrison is considered one of the most accomplished songwriters and performers of the past thirty years–*Rolling Stone* magazine ranked him 42nd on their list of *The Immortals: 100 Greatest Artists of All Time*. But he struggled financially at first and even considered quitting the music business more than once. Morrison has said, "When *Astral Weeks* came out, I was starving, *literally*." His daughter Shana Morrison (she is also a recording artist) recalls how when she was growing up she envied other kids whose parents didn't have to worry where their next paycheck was coming from. She says there were times in her youth when she and her father would live in a mansion and buy a new car and stereo system one year, and the next year they'd have to sell it all and move into an apartment. (And this is Van Morrison we're talking about!)

Much of Morrison's financial problems were the result of disputes with people in the music business and his record label. So he did something that would ensure his long-term financial success and help him gain control over his creations—he formed his own independent label, Exile Productions Ltd. Now, Morrison is able to record each album the way he wants, delivering a finished product to another recording label of his choice for marketing and distribution. He also signed a contract with Polydor Records in 2007 that gives him the licensing rights to his back catalog. When Van Morrison sings "Days Like This," he's now singing about the best of times.

Another musician with a long history of hits—and a track record of fiscal responsibility—is Ian Anderson of Jethro Tull. The band has sold millions of records (*Aqualung, Thick as a Brick, Living in the Past*) and toured successfully over the years. Not one to squander his earnings, Anderson became one of the biggest salmon farmers in the world, which has made him a millionaire in that business on top of his millions from music. It came out of his desire to use his music money to do something positive—that was socially redeeming and would create jobs in his community. He (and his wife) now operate several successful companies, and his royalties from Jethro Tull tunes add up to a tidy annual sum. Likewise, Rush has sold millions of records over the years, and has been wise with the proceeds, leaving all three members of the band set for life. Here's how bassist and singer Geddy Lee describes his retirement plans: "Some writing and production projects will be a great way to spend my elderly rock years."

BUSINESS LESSON: Almost every business will go through up and down cycles. Savvy entrepreneurs save something to survive the down times.

#5

Adapt and change to meet the market, and be diversified enough to make it through the slow times.

Steve Miller started out as a blues guitarist but adapted his sound over the years and had a string of hits in the '70s, including "The Joker," "Fly Like an Eagle," and "Jungle Love," as well as one in the '80s with "Abracadabra." His greatest hits album alone has sold over thirteen million copies in the U.S.—and he still tours today.

Ambrosia is best known for songs like "How Much I Feel" and "Biggest Part of Me," featuring rich vocal harmonies and a slick pop sound. It surprises people to learn the band began as a progressive rock group ("Mama Frog" and "Nice, Nice, Very Nice"). If you listen closely to their earlier (and less popular) work and their more mainstream (highly successful) songs, you'll notice the similarities. The same can't be said for Journey and Genesis, however. If you listen to the self-titled *Journey* (1975) or Genesis' *Trespass* (1970) and then listen to these bands' later work, they are decidedly different—almost unrecognizable.

One group has always been known for one of the best horn sections in rock (besides Tower of Power): Chicago. The band had one of the best runs in terms of charting singles during the 1970s. What makes this more impressive is how Chicago did it with such diverse sounding songs—from "Does Anybody Really Know What Time It Is?" and "Beginnings" (upbeat jazz-rock) to "Colour My World" and "Wishing You Were Here" (slower ballads). Later, they scored big with power ballads like "Will You Still Love Me" and "Look Away." Similarly, the Doobie Brothers had success with straight-ahead, guitar-based rock songs like "Listen to the Music" and later with pop-sounding, keyboard-based songs like "It Keeps You Running" (during the Michael McDonald era of the band).

While adapting and changing are key ingredients to topping the charts, the risk is trading your core audience or customers (a small, but loyal following) for a more mainstream crowd (a bigger, but fickle following). This happened to Queen when they recorded disco-oriented music in the 1970s and recorded "Under Pressure" with David Bowie. Fans weren't thrilled. However, after Freddie Mercury died, their catalog continued to sell and, soon after, when "Bohemian Rhapsody" was featured in *Wayne's World*, sales of their old albums soared.

Other bands dabbled in disco-rock to prolong careers, including the Rolling Stones ("Miss You"), Rod Stewart ("If You Think I'm Sexy"), the Kinks ("Superman"), the Grateful Dead ("Shakedown Street"), and KISS ("I Was Made for Loving You"). The good thing about being open to change and willing to meet the market is that you don't become obsolete when your brand (or band) falls out of favor. You just change and adapt.

Take Kid Rock for example. It would be hard to pigeonhole him in any one genre because he has had success in rock, rap, country—and a combination of all three—and that was his plan all along. He didn't want to get labeled as anything but a musician.

Speaking of planning, Bon Jovi said it best: "Map out your future, but do it in pencil." And Todd Rudgren probably didn't expect to become a sought-after producer when he was a successful act himself ("Hello, It's Me"), but he has produced records for Hall and Oates, Meat Loaf, and Cheap Trick.

Ric Ocasek of the Cars has produced the Killers, Weezer, and No Doubt. Another phenomenon among rock stars is a transition from albums and touring into scoring films—for added success. The list is long and includes Danny Elfman (Oingo Boingo), Trevor Rabin (Yes), and Phil Collins.

BUSINESS LESSON: Do what you do best, but be willing to adapt and change with the times—whether that means making the most of new technology or exploring new uses (and markets) for your products and service.

#6

Work harder than anyone else.

Think of a band. Any band. We'll bet the band you're thinking of has worked extremely hard to get where they are—or were. There simply aren't many shortcuts to success in the music business. Bands usually begin by building a buzz about their music on a local level—playing anywhere and everywhere they can. This is all while holding down a day job (or two) and serving as their own managers, promoters, and roadies.

The band must then rehearse and record a demo, followed by a long and difficult quest for a record deal. (If they don't get a record deal, they will most likely have to produce and promote a CD themselves.) Songs must be written and recorded (no easy task itself) while continuing to promote and play live. Once the album is done, the band will almost always begin a grueling tour that could include 300 dates in 300 different cities in a single year.

Oh, then there are promotion and publicity appearances. And this pattern continues even after a band has a hit. They will still have to tour, but they'll probably be playing bigger venues, have better buses, and have more people helping (managers, publicists, and roadies). Being in a successful band requires constant attention, as well as drive, determination, and dedication. It's the same way when you own and operate a business. If your business isn't where you want it to be—and whose is?—then you may want to look in the mirror and ask yourself, "Am I doing *everything* I can to build my business?" (By the way, the only honest answer to that question is almost always NO.)

Usually the difference between a thriving enterprise and one just striving to make ends meet is the level of commitment and hard work of the entrepreneur. Most bands that make it big live and breathe music. And most entrepreneurs who make it big also live and breathe their business.

There's no doubt this grueling schedule can burn someone out—the band Phish comes to mind. But to get to the point where you can cruise a little means you have to pay your dues first and collect the dividends later. Korn has sold over thirty million records and has had nine consecutive albums debut in the top ten of the Billboard 200. Is it luck that led to their success? Not really, when you consider their 2008 tour dates include stops in Mexico, Brazil, Argentina, Australia, Germany, Ireland, and the UK—just to name a few. Their success is the result of relentless touring and hard work.

BUSINESS LESSON: The best business leaders are able to dial it up a notch to out-hustle and outlast the competition. There is always something more you can do to give your business edge—do it, or your competition will.

#7

Take care of your customers, and have a loyal and dedicated following.

We have an entire chapter dedicated to the care and keeping of your customers (Chapter Seven, "Raving Fans") because building and maintaining a fan base is arguably the most important part of being a rock star—and an entrepreneur. Without fans, a band can call it quits (professionally). Without customers, a business is just a hobby—if that.

Throughout this book, we have mentioned the masters of maintaining a fan base: the Grateful Dead have their "Deadheads," Jimmy Buffett has his "Parrotheads," Phish fans refer to themselves as "Phishheads," and Dick Dale fans call themselves "Dickheads." Seriously.

It would be easy to write about any of these artists and feature them here. Instead, let's look at a lesser-known artist (the equivalent of a small business) to see how important fans are to keeping your career and business alive, especially when you aren't a big star or a big-box store. We'll use singer-songwriter Bob Schneider as our example, but there are literally thousands of musicians who aren't enjoying mainstream success and yet make a living doing what they love—writing, recording, and performing their songs for adoring fans.

You may have a hard time finding a Bob Schneider record in the bins at Borders, but he has several to his credit. His shows are often standing-room only (though, admittedly, he plays smaller venues that don't have assigned seating). Yet, year after year, he hits the road, leaving his home base of Austin, Texas, to tour. He has released several solo albums (two of which, *Lonelyland* and *I'm Good Now*, were major-label releases). His music and (introspective) lyrics can be compared to Tom Petty and Dave Matthews, and his concerts are reminiscent of Bruce Springsteen for the banter between songs and audience enthusiasm. Having seen him several times, purchased his CDs, and created a Bob Schneider radio station on Pandora, we get the impression he's on the verge of something big. For followers like us, we're just as happy to buy an independent release and see him with 500 of our fellow fans in an intimate setting. True fans are there for a band or a business no matter what.

BUSINESS LESSON: You are only as successful as your customers decide you will be. When you win them over, you get repeat business, referrals, and ongoing (and beneficial) relationships that pay the bills. Your goal is to do everything in your power to make people say, "Wow!" (in a good way) about you and your business.

#8

Keep key players together for consistency, but bring in new people for fresh ideas.

The band Golden Earring ("Radar Love") has been together since 1961, making them the longest-running intact band. ZZ Top still boasts the same lineup they did at their start in 1969. Other examples of bands that haven't changed their lineup (or much) and are still going include Aerosmith, Rush, and U2. Add to that the many long-standing bands with the same manager (U2 and Genesis), producer (ZZ Top until 2006), or road crew (Iron Maiden).

Neil Aspinall's career with the Beatles began before the Fab Four were stars. He hauled and set up their gear and was appointed road manager. He then became their personal assistant, doing a number of odd jobs, and played harmonica on "Being for the Benefit of Mr. Kite" and sang as one of the drunken chorus members on "Yellow Submarine." He also stood in for the band during sound checks. After becoming the band's driver, he studied accounting and the Beatles made him managing director of Apple Corp, their corporation and record company. He still holds that position.

Consistently sticking with what has worked doesn't, and shouldn't, stop a band from collaborating with new and interesting talent. The most obvious example of this is Aerosmith collaborating with Run DMC to rework "Walk This Way" and reinvigorate their career. Bassist Chris Squire and drummer Alan White (Yes) teamed up with Trevor Rabin (who was a solo artist without a record deal) and wrote and recorded as a band called Cinema. During this time, Rabin wrote "Owner of a Lonely Heart" and Chris Squire invited Jon Anderson to be a part of the project (now titled *90125*, Yes's Atlantic Records catalog number). Pretty soon, the Cinema project became a Yes record—and was their most commercially successful album to date. ("Owner of a Lonely Heart" was the band's first and only #1 hit.)

Yet another example of successful collaboration involves Leo Sayer. After a series of hits in the '70s, including "You Make Me Feel Like Dancing" (#1 in 1976) and "When I Need You" (#1 in 1977), Sayer disappeared from the scene. (He had moved to Australia.) Three decades later, in 2006, British DJ Craig DiMeck remixed and released on old Sayer song called "Thunder in Your Heart (Again)" and scored a hit.

Successful entrepreneurs aren't afraid to bring in outside consultants to help with specific projects or to provide fresh ideas to move their business forward faster. Many bands stay together because their members are able to experiment and explore (musically) on their own. Phil Collins joined Brand X when he felt stifled creatively as a drummer in Genesis and wanted to experiment with other forms of music. "Brand X was where I went to have fun," said Collins. "An analogy would be that it was a place I could go and take off all my clothes and live, to do things I couldn't do with Genesis." As a songwriter he explored songs of a more personal nature, and "In the Air Tonight" (on his solo album) became a big, big hit. Tina Wymouth (bass) and Chris Franz (drums) were one half of the Talking Heads when they had a side project as the Tom Tom Club. The couple hit #10 on the U.S. Modern Rock Chart with their 1989 "Suboceana," but is best known for their 1981 hit single "Genius of Love."

BUSINESS LESSON: Loyalty, consistency, and longstanding teamwork can be the not-so-secret key to success. A willingness to bring in outside consultants or form strategic partnerships could also be considered a "secret" to success.

#9

Do what you do best, and stay in the game until the tide turns.

Fans are fickle, and so are clients and customers. Chances are, you will see attrition with your customer base—you'll lose some and gain others, depending on a lot of factors. The trick is not to get too giddy when you have more than enough and not to get down when you don't have enough. For instance, when CDs replaced vinyl records, people flocked to their local record store to repurchase their favorite records on disc. Sales boomed. Now, there aren't many record stores left; CDs are being replaced by downloads, and you no longer *have* to buy an entire album just to get that ONE song you want.

So what's the good news? Business is cyclical, and if you can hang on long enough, times change and you'll see success. In our lifetimes, we've seen ZZ Top go from being one of the best bands of the time (*Fandango* was a mid-seventies classic) to being on hiatus and then to unprecedented heights with *Eliminator* in the early '80s (thanks to MTV videos).

The same is true of Carlos Santana. He was huge in the '70s, but by the early 1990s, his album sales were extremely slow, and he was without a recording contract for the first time in years. Late in the decade, however, he recorded *Supernatural* and collaborated with younger artists such as Rob Thomas of Matchbox 20. The result: *Supernatural* was a super seller (over fifteen million sold), and Santana was back on top.

So what do you do with the downtime when your business isn't doing as well as you'd like? Maybe you just need to take a break. If you're burned out on one aspect of your business, switch to another. Just stay visible in your customers' minds. Take Eric Clapton, for example. He was first in the Yardbirds, then left for John Mayall's Bluesbreakers, then formed Cream (with Ginger Baker and Jack Bruce), then went into Blind Faith (with Steve Winwood), then joined Delany & Bonnie and Friends, then released a self-titled solo album in 1970 (which included "After Midnight"), and then formed Derek and the Dominos and recorded one album that included his most famous song, "Layla." And this was all done in several years, long before his later solo success in the 1980s and 1990s.

After *Brothers in Arms* sold twenty million records, Mark Knopfler left Dire Straits and played guitar with Steely Dan (on their *Goucho* album), Van Morrison, Bryan Ferry, and Eric Clapton. Knopfler also produced an album for Bob Dylan and wrote "Private Dancer" for Tina Turner.

No matter what, you keep doing what's necessary to keep your business in the black. Many longtime bands are still actively touring–the Rolling Stones, Great White, Thin Lizzy, Van Halen (with Eddie Van Halen's son, Wolfgang, on bass), the Who (with Ringo Starr's son on drums), Asia, Santana, Bon Jovi, Queensryche, AC/DC, Rush, Iron Maiden, INXS, Alice Cooper, Aerosmith, Joan Jett, Black Sabbath, Queen (with Paul Rodgers, formerly of Bad Company), the Cult, the Beach Boys, Robin Trower, Tom Petty, Jethro Tull, Foghat, .38 Special, Loverboy, 10CC, and Jefferson Starship . . . to name a "few."

Sometimes timing is everything. Pearl Jam's *Ten* didn't sell a whole lot of copies until early 1992, after Nirvana turned the rock world upside down and made mainstream radio receptive to alternative rock acts. (Ironically, Pearl Jam outsold Nirvana with radio-friendly hits like "Jeremy," "Evenflow," and "Alive.") The timing was perfect because radio stations and MTV were looking for the next big thing–and Pearl Jam was it.

Drummer Cozy Powell is considered one of the best rock drummers of all time. Before his 1988 death in a car crash, Powell had played and recorded with everyone from Ritchie Blackmore and Robert Plant to Black Sabbath and Whitesnake. (Powell had been the drummer on over sixty albums.) Known for his precision, timing, and speed, Powell was the go-to guy in the studio–until drum machines came along. Facing the loss of his fat studio fees, he then became the go-to guy when you needed a live drummer, and he toured with some of the biggest bands.

BUSINESS LESSON: Believe in your potential–that success and big bucks are around the corner–and stay the course.

#10

Capitalize on opportunities, and maximize their success.
The late Bo Diddley lamented, "I opened the door for a lot of people, and they ran through and left me holding the knob." Bo Diddley is often credited with leading the transition from blues to rock and roll with his sound. He was also influential in creating a unique guitar sound

and rhythm structures within his songs, which have been used by everyone from Elvis Presley to the Rolling Stones to Guns N' Roses. And his own songs have been covered by the Who, Aerosmith, and Bob Seger.

In music and business, everything is in a constant state of flux, and this means new opportunities develop every day. In the late 1970s and early 1980s, technology changed everything, and synthesizer-based music opened the door for a lot of acts, such as Kraftwerk, Gary Numan, Depeche Mode, and Howard Jones. Also in the '80s, there was the trend of female-fronted bands (the Pretenders, Blondie, and the Eurythmics), as well all-female bands (the Bangles and the Go Go's). Similarly, in the 1990s, Tracy Chapman, Jewel, Joan Osborne, Shawn Colvin, Sheryl Crow, and others capitalized on the revival of female folk-rock.

Not all bands or businesses are able to spot a trend or take advantage when they do. One that did was Coldplay. When Radiohead released the less-than-celebrated *Kid-A* and Oasis experimented with psychedelic sounds, Coldplay positioned themselves perfectly with a sound that was right on the mark at the right time. The reward was multi-platinum record sales and a place on the charts for both their debut album and their follow-up.

The key is to be able to move fast and seize the moment, because in the music business and other businesses, things move fast. "The single most disorienting thing about success was that it happened so quickly," said Seal (Sealhenry Samuel). When singer-songwriter Jim Croce ("Time in a Bottle") was killed in a plane crash, his label at the time looked at their roster for a replacement. It so happened they had someone named Jimmy Buffett buried down the list, and they decided to move him to the top of artists to focus on.

We're not sure if Phil Collins knew Ken Kragen, a manager who handled several well-known stars, including Kenny Rogers, or ever read his book. But he sure proved that Kragen's "Power of 3" theory works. In a nutshell, the strategy is: when you're hot, turn one opportunity into three. When Phil Collins was at the peak of his popularity, he was producing records for Eric Clapton, Robert Plant, and Adam Ant; writing, recording, and touring with Genesis; and pursuing his successful solo career. As if that wasn't enough, he had small acting roles on TV and in movies, played drums on tour with Peter Gabriel, jammed with Brand X, and was married and divorced—twice.

Sometimes opportunity comes through "creating once and selling often." The 1980s' song "I Melt with You," by Modern English, has been licensed for use in numerous commercials, TV shows, and movies. It's probably no coincidence that the band has sold over three million records despite their brief run of popularity.

BUSINESS LESSON: Opportunties don't come every day, but they do come. Keep your eyes open for them and develop a talent for maximizing any success you have.

#11

Exit strategy: Getting out when the going's good.

Boz Scaggs ("Lowdown" and "Lido Shuffle") once said, "When you discover an instrument, a way of using your voice—whole worlds open up." Not only has Scaggs enjoyed a successful career behind the mic, he is also the owner of the San Francisco nightclub, Slim's. Although he still tours and records (he's very popular in Japan), he has been out of the limelight for a few years. "I know that I might be out of the mainstream, but I'm still exploring the music that I love," he said.

Being an entrepreneur is both a blessing and a curse. There is great satisfaction from building a business, and it is a labor of love for most—requiring long hours and a lot of sacrifice. But the bigger the business gets, the bigger a burden it can become. That's why many business owners look forward to the day when they can either cash out (sell off parts or all of a business) or pass the enterprise on to someone else, possibly one of their children. Knowing what your end game is can be good for the future—and the present.

When Jimmy Buffett received his first advance check, he asked for two checks—one he gave to his manager and the other he used to buy a sailboat. This might seem foolish, but from Buffett's perspective it made sense. He figured if his career went south, so would he (to the Caribbean), and he was guaranteed a place to live—on his boat. As another hedge against a career crash, Buffett started a small T-shirt shop on Duvall Street in Key West. That tiny Margaritaville store has grown into a wildly successful chain of restaurants and clubs. And in a cool twist of fate, the more successful his businesses have become, the more successful his music career has become, too.

The fact that Mike Nesmith (the Monkees) was the son of the woman who invented White Out (she sold the company for millions of dollars) didn't deter him from joining the band. Anticipating the shelf life of the band to be short, Nesmith started writing songs for other artists and founded Pacific Arts Video, a booking and multimedia agency in Northern California.

The lifespan of a business can be quite short, and so can a rock star's. The list of rockers who have passed away in their prime is quite lengthy, especially the list of legends who died at the age of twenty-seven. This includes Jim Morrison, Janis Joplin, Jimi Hendrix, and Kurt Cobain—as well as the less-famous Alan Wilson (of Canned Heat), Ron "Pidgeon" McKernan, (a founding member of the Grateful Dead), and Pete Ham (lead singer of Badfinger). That's why a few years ago we were interested to learn that a band based in San Diego named themselves Dead by 27.

BUSINESS LESSON: There will come a time when you'll want to, or need to, step away from your business. Start planning now for the future and how you will get out when the getting's good, or how you will leave the business to family or friends.

RECOMMENDED READING

While a ton of books went into the research of this one, we can't list them all here. In fact, we don't even remember some of them. But they were all fun to read. So we decided to narrow this list down to the ones we most recommend for one reason or another. As for the Internet, well, we went through a ton of resources there as well. And one website made the final cut below as an outstanding resource.

Billboard's American Rock 'n'Roll in Review, Jay Warner, Schirmer Books, 1997.

The New Rolling Stone Album Guide, Nathan Brackett and Christian Hoard, Fireside, 2004.

Uncle John's Bathroom Reader Plunges into Music, Bathroom Readers' Institute, Portable Press, 2008.

KISS and Sell, C.K. Lendt, Billboard Books, 1997.

Bang Your Head, David Konow, Three Rivers Press, 2002.

Wikipedia.org

Other significant resources can be found on our website: RockToRichesBook.com

ABOUT THE AUTHORS

Lee Silber is the author of thirteen books, including *Time Management for the Creative Person* and *Organizing from the Right Side of the Brain,* and has received seven awards for his books, including the Theodor S. Geisel Award for *Self-Promotion for the Creative Person.* He is the founder of five companies, including a chain of retail stores (Waves and Wheels Surfcenters) and a training company (Deep Impact Training). In his spare time, Lee is both a drummer and bassist playing in various bands in San Diego, California, where he lives with his wife and two sons. For more, go to www.leesilber.com.

A longtime drummer and serial entrepreneur, **Andrew Chapman** has worked in almost every aspect of independent publishing for over twenty years. He is an award-winning writer, author of seven books and three audio books, president of Publishers & Writers of San Diego, and a professional speaker with nearly 300 engagements to his credit throughout the U.S. and overseas. Andrew lives in the peaceful and rustic art town of Idyllwild, a mile high in the mountains of Southern California. His website is www.achapman.com.